## ADDITIONAL PRAISE FOR CLIFFORD A. PICKOVER

"Pickover inspires a new generation of da Vincis to build unknown flying machines and create new Mona Lisas."

—*Christian Science Monitor*

"Pickover is van Leeuwenhoek's 20th century equivalent."

—*OMNI*

"Pickover is many things—scientist, scholar, author, editor, and visionary . . ."

—*GAMES*

"Salted with religious and nonreligious curiosities and conundrums, ranging from biblical oddities to the neuropsychology of time perception, all related with an attitude of mischievous irreverence. Pickover's satirical approach energizes the book. . . . At its best, the book achieves a juxtaposition of cosmic relevance and intellectual whimsy."

—*Publishers Weekly*

"The puzzles and vignettes Pickover introduces are entertaining enough to appeal to and hold a significant audience."

—*Booklist*

"Pickover has published nearly a book a year in which he stretches the limits of computers, art, and thought."

—*Los Angeles Times*

"Strange and beautiful, stunningly realistic."

—*Scientific American*

"Pickover just seems to exist in more dimensions than the rest of us."

—Ian Stewart, author of *Does God Play Dice?*

**WORKS BY CLIFFORD A. PICKOVER**

*The Alien IQ Test*

*Black Holes: A Traveler's Guide*

*Chaos and Fractals*

*Chaos in Wonderland*

*Computers, Pattern, Chaos, and Beauty*

*Computers and the Imagination*

*Cryptorunes: Codes and Secret Writing*

*Dreaming the Future*

*Future Health: Computers and Medicine in the 21st Century*

*Fractal Horizons: The Future Use of Fractals*

*Frontiers of Scientific Visualization* (with Stu Tewksbury)

*The Girl Who Gave Birth to Rabbits*

*Keys to Infinity*

*The Loom of God*

*Mazes for the Mind: Computers and the Unexpected*

*Mind-Bending Visual Puzzles* (calendars)

*The Pattern Book: Fractals, Art, and Nature*

*The Science of Aliens*

*Spider Legs* (with Piers Anthony)

*Spiral Symmetry* (with Istvan Hargittai)

*Strange Brains and Genius*

*The Stars of Heaven*

*Surfing Through Hyperspace*

*Time: A Traveler's Guide*

*Visions of the Future*

*Visualizing Biological Information*

*Wonders of Numbers*

*The Zen of Magic Squares, Circles, and Stars*

# THE PARADOX OF GOD

AND THE SCIENCE OF OMNISCIENCE

# THE PARADOX OF GOD
## AND THE SCIENCE OF OMNISCIENCE

# CLIFFORD A. PICKOVER

First published in hardcover in 2001 by Palgrave Macmillan
First PALGRAVE MACMILLAN™ paperback edition: April 2004
175 Fifth Avenue, New York, N.Y. 10010 and
Houndmills, Basingstoke, Hampshire, England RG21 6XS.
Companies and representatives throughout the world.

PALGRAVE MACMILLAN is the global academic imprint of the Palgrave
Macmillan division of St. Martin's Press, LLC and of Palgrave Macmillan
Ltd. Macmillan® is a registered trademark in the United States, United
Kingdom and other countries. Palgrave is a registered trademark in the
European Union and other countries.

ISBN 1-4039-6457-2

Library of Congress Cataloging-in-Publication Data

Pickover, Clifford A.
    The paradox of God and the science of omniscience / Clifford A.
Pickover.
        p.   cm.
    Includes bibliographical references and index.
    ISBN 1-4039-6457-2
    1. God—Omniscience.   2. Omniscience (Theory of knowledge)   I.
Title.

BT131 .P53   2001
212'.7—dc21

                                                        2001036173

A catalogue record for this book is available from the British Library.

Design by Letra Libre

First PALGRAVE MACMILLAN paperback edition: April 2004

10  9  8  7  6  5  4  3  2  1

Printed in the United States of America.

*This book is dedicated to all of you who believe that*
*that there are two errors in this sentence.*

*This book is also dedicated to omniscient beings*
*who are certainly able to read this message*
*if they are all-knowing:*

ᛁᚠ ᛏᚻᛖ ᛒᛗᚨᛁᛏᛏᛁᛏᚨ

ᚨᛦᚻ ᚲᚱᛖᛒᛏᛖᚻ ᛏᚻᛖ

ᚢᛗᛒᚨᛗᛏᛦ ᛒᛏᚻ ᛏᚻᛖ ᛖᛒᚱᛏᚢ

*Lord, thou knowest all things.*

👁 John 21:17


*"I take my accurate form," Memnoch continued,*
*"when I am in Heaven or outside of Time."*

👁 Anne Rice, *Memnoch the Devil*


*The omniscient have no fear.*

👁 Charles Krauthammer, *TIME*


*It is the final proof of God's omnipotence*
*that he need not exist in order to save us.*

👁 Peter De Vries, *The Mackerel Plaza*

# Contents

*Acknowledgments*                                                                         xi

Introduction                                                                                1

  1.  The Paradox of Omniscience                                                           11
  2.  God and Evil                                                                         19
  3.  Cain and Abel's Dilemma                                                              27
  4.  The Parable of Algae                                                                 39
  5.  Newcomb's Paradox and Divine Foreknowledge                                           45
  6.  The Devil's Offer                                                                    67
  7.  The Revelation Gambit                                                                76
  8.  The Paradox of Eden                                                                  96
  9.  The Brain and God: Who's in Charge?                                                 104
 10.  The Bodhisattva Paradox                                                             116
 11.  The Paradox of Pascal's Wager                                                       124
 12.  Two Universes                                                                       132
 13.  Gödel's Proof of God                                                                136
 14.  The Paradox of Uzzah                                                                141
 15.  The Paradox of Dr. Eck                                                              152
 16.  The Paradox of Led Zeppelin                                                         160
 17.  A Few Quick Puzzles and Surveys                                                     166

Some Final Thoughts                                                                       178

Appendices                                                                                204
   A.  Can God Change His Mind?                                                           205
   B.  Biblical Suggestions that God Is Omniscient                                        206
   C.  Thirty Examples of God Entering the Time Stream and
       Aiding Mass Killing                                                                207
   D.  Can a Just God Support Cannibalism and Child Sacrifice?                            213
   E.  Aquinas's God and Maxwell's Demon                                                  217

| | | |
|---|---|---|
| F. | Can an Omniscient Being Lose His Temper? | 218 |
| G. | The Paradox of the Flood | 219 |
| H. | Saint Augustine and *The City of God* | 220 |
| I. | Does God Make Mistakes and Learn? | 221 |
| J. | God Wants Fear | 222 |
| K. | Two Proofs that God Is Not All-Knowing? | 224 |
| L. | Sixty-Four Way-Out Questions to Ponder | 227 |

| | |
|---|---|
| *Notes* | 233 |
| *Further Reading* | 249 |
| *About the Author* | 253 |
| *Index* | 255 |

# Acknowledgments

*Where did it begin? Was there nothing and then something? Even the Celestials, the noblest of beings to enter the human consciousness, did not know what was in the dark before the light was turned on.*
— *Peter Lord-Wolff,* The Silence in Heaven

I OWE A SPECIAL DEBT OF GRATITUDE TO MARTIN GARDNER (AUTHOR of *The Night Is Large* and *Knotted Doughnuts and Other Mathematical Entertainments*), Steven J. Brams (author of *Superior Beings*), Karen Armstrong (author of *A History of God*), and William Poundstone (author of *Labyrinths of Reason*) for their books, which provide excellent background material to various paradoxes relating to omniscience. Background reading for Chapter 9 can be found in my book *Time: A Traveler's Guide*, in which I also discuss the brain, volition, and time distortion. Quotations from biblical sources are usually from either the King James version or the New International version.

I am grateful to Brian Mansfield for his wonderful illustrations at the beginning of each chapter. I thank Edward J. Gracely, Eric Kaplan, Royce Denton, David Glass, Reinhold Niederhagen, Craig Becker, and Dennis Gordon for useful advice and comments. I thank Samuel Marcius for various font symbols.

*The secret of cosmogenesis. The universes are bubbles blown by God, who does not realize that a demon is insufflating both love and hate into them. From Jean-Ignace Isidore Grandville's* Un Autre Monde.

# Introduction

B.C. MANSFIELD

*"God will provide for this kitten."*
*"What makes you think so?"*
*"Because I know it! Not a sparrow falls to the ground without His seeing it."*
*"But it falls, just the same. What good is seeing it fall?"*
*—Mark Twain,* The Mysterious Stranger

*Knowing what Thou knowest not is, in a sense, Omniscience.*
*—Piet Hein,* Grooks

WHEN I WAS TEN YEARS OLD, I RECALL LEAFING THROUGH A COLLEC-
tion of biblical illustrations created by the famous French artist Gustave Doré,

who lived from 1832 to 1883. I remember the beautiful creation scenes, the scary visions of Noah's flood, the huge battles with Joshua committing the town of Ai to flames. Perhaps the scene that stuck in my mind most was the one of Moses coming down from Mount Sinai with the Ten Commandments (Figure I.1). The tablets were supposed to be the work of God.

Even at this early age, I knew that God was supposed to be *omniscient*, or all-knowing. I asked my father what this really meant. Did God know Eve would eat the apple? That Cain would kill Abel (Figure I.2)? Could God be surprised?

My father had no definitive answers.

Before proceeding further, it's useful to have a working definition of God. This is certainly a difficult challenge! Throughout history, God has meant something different to different societies. In some sense, our concept of God has evolved, and so has our definition of atheism. Karen Armstrong in *A History of God* suggests that "had the notion of God not had this flexibility, it would not have survived to become one of the great human ideas. . . . Is the 'God' who is rejected by atheists today, the God of the patriarchs, the God of the prophets, the God of the philosophers, the God of the mystics or the God of the eighteenth-century deists?"[1] Like a lump of heated silver changing from solid to liquid to gas, atheism has been the in-between state for religions. Jews, Christians, Muslims, and Baha'is were all called atheists by their predecessor religious forms.

Whatever you believe, clearly we humans often experience feelings and ideas that transcend our ordinary lives. Of course, these experiences are not always regarded as divine. Psychiatrists may relegate them to heightened activity of the brain's temporal lobes. Buddhists see the experiences as natural to humans and do not invoke a deity. For now, let us use a very common Western definition of God. Of those people in the industrialized West who say they believe in God, studies show that most are monotheists. For these people, God is usually understood to be:

> All powerful, all knowing, and all good; who created out of nothing the universe and everything in it with the exception of Himself; who is uncreated and eternal, a noncorporeal spirit who created, loves, and can grant eternal life to humans.[2]

The overwhelming majority of Americans who say they believe in God also believe God affects their lives. Numerous other definitions of God are given at the end of Chapter 15.

I should also note that God has historically been thought of as a male deity in religions such as Judaism, Christianity, and Islam. Because I will frequently

Fig. I.1. *Moses coming down from Mount Sinai. Reprinted from Gustave Doré,* The Doré Bible Illustrations *(New York: Dover, 1974), 40.*

*Fig. I.2.Cain and Abel offering their sacrifices to God. Reprinted from Gustave Doré,* The Doré Bible Illustrations *(New York: Dover, 1974), 4.*

be alluding to the God of these monotheistic faiths, I use the conventional masculine terminology "He," although I can certainly sympathize with feminists who may be uncomfortable with this traditional bias.

In this book I don't discuss some of the conventional, logical proofs of God's existence. Instead, I discuss how we might understand the characteristics and limitations of omniscient beings. I also invite discussion about whether or not it is *rational* to believe in God's existence. As Steven J. Brams points out in his book *Superior Beings*, "The rationality of theistic belief is separate from its truth—a belief need not be true or even verifiable to be rational."[3]

What can we mere humans, with our limited three-pound mass of brain, truly understand about a being who may be timeless, higher-dimensional, and all-knowing? Followers of the Koran have often suggested that because God has no cause or temporal dimension, there is absolutely nothing we can say about Him. Our brains are not up to the task. The Jewish philosopher Bahya ibn Pakudah (d. 1080) believed that the only people who had a hope of understanding God were the prophets and philosophers. Everyone else was simply "worshiping a projection of himself."[4] Similarly, Muslim thinker Abu Hamidal-Ghazzali (1058–1111) thought that only special people, like mystics and prophets, could get a glimpse of God; nevertheless, most ordinary folk should not deny the existence of God—a blind man should not deny the rainbow's existence simply because he cannot appreciate it.

Even with our working definition of God as all-powerful, all-knowing, and all-good, many modern thinkers say that this concept is insufficient. For example, anthropologist Donald Symons says the question of God's existence, or perhaps any analytical discussion of God, is meaningless without a very rigorous definition of God. He writes:

> Do you believe *[fill in any three letters]* exists? You have to know more about what's in the brackets and how its existence or nonexistence might be determined, or at least, what kinds of evidence might potentially bear on the question. If you find out that the questioner has essentially no ideas about the characteristics of the [ ] (such as, for example, whether it is made of matter), and, more importantly, states that no conceivable observation could have any bearing on the existence/nonexistence question, then to me the original question is meaningless, or incoherent, or empty, or some similar concept.[5]

However, we don't need to let Symons's valid concerns restrain us from discussing these weighty matters. As I said, in this book I'll focus on the question of omniscience. For those of you who do not believe in God, the discussions might be applied to hypothetical powerful beings. This book also includes numerous other intriguing religious concepts and paradoxes ranging from the dreaded "Devil's Offer" to the "Paradox of Eden," some of which cause people to question God's justice and our own concept of fairness.

When we say a being is all-knowing, there are many kinds of knowledge the being could have.[6] This makes discussions of omniscient beings a challenge. For example, knowledge may be *factual* or *propositional*: a superior being may know that the Peloponnesian War was fought by two leading city-states in ancient Greece, Athens and Sparta. Another category of knowledge is *procedural*, knowing how to accomplish a task such as playing chess, baking a cake, making love, performing a Kung Fu block, shooting an arrow, or creating primitive life in a test tube. For us at least, reading about shooting an arrow is not the same as actually being able to shoot an arrow. Procedural knowing implies actually being able to perform the act. (One might wonder what it actually means for a nonphysical God transcending time and space to have "knowledge" of sex and other physical acts.) Yet another kind of knowledge, *experiential*, comes from direct experience. This is the kind of knowledge referred to when someone says, "I know love" or "I know fear."

There are, of course, some standard philosophical problems that arise with an omniscient God, such as the problem of free will. If God is all-knowing (including all-knowing of future events) and all-powerful, then how can humans be held responsible for making choices? Can an omniscient being know the delight of learning new knowledge? Some have suggested that God may reside outside of time and so sees past, present, and future in a blinding flash, but since we limited beings don't know the future, we are, in some sense, "free." If we have free will in such a way that the future is not preordained, does this mean God has limited omniscience? If God is limited, what are His limitations? Could it be that logic itself limits God so that an omnipotent God could not create a boulder so heavy that He could not lift it, or an omniscient God could not know what it is like to not know? Could God create a person whose actions He cannot know?

The questions pour like a waterfall from an infinite river. If there exists a God (or powerful alien being) who is omniscient, or all-knowing, what kind of relation could we have with such a being, what logical paradoxes arise that might cast doubt on His existence, and what effect would this being have on humankind? Although some philosophers of science would argue that the notion of a supernatural God, by definition, is untestable and therefore beyond the domain of science, there are certain principles of pure logic we may use to glimpse the infinite and dream daring dreams.

ⓞ ⓞ ⓞ

Perhaps, also by definition, an omniscient being cannot make a mistake. Michael Shermer in *Why We Believe* suggests that either God allowed Nazis to kill Jews, in which case He is not omnibenevolent or omniscient, or God was unable to prevent Nazis from killing Jews, in which case He is not omnipotent. Of course, there are numerous reasons why an omniscient God would not intervene. Other scholars argue that God can prevent misery but permits it because misery provides a necessary test in which greatness evolves, whether it be for life-forms (in the crucible of brutal competition by natural selection) or for entire nations (Israel would not have been created without Hitler's atrocities and the ensuing reparations to the Jews). We'll touch upon all these issues in this book.

I can give an unending list of examples of omniscient gods in religion. Humans seem to need and require an omniscient God. In Islam, for example, Allah has many names, including the Real Truth (*al-Haqq*), the Omnipotent (*al-'Aziz*), the Hearer (*as-Sami'*), and the Omniscient (*al-'Alim*). Bahaullah, the prophet of the Baha'i faith, frequently refers to God as "omniscient and all-perceiving." Traditional Judaism and Christianity explain biological forms, with all their wonderfully complex environmental adaptations, as the obvious creation of an omniscient God. According to this logic, God foresaw the needs of creatures and gave them eyes, wings, prehensile tails for grasping, camouflage, and so forth. In Hinduism, God is nonmaterial, perfect, omniscient, and omnipotent. (Hindus do often worship local deities, but worshipers often think of the deities as manifestations of a single high God.) According to the ancient Tantric tradition, our ultimate state is omniscience, which provides understanding of all of the universe's mysteries and forces. According to the Indian religion Jainism, a monk can attain omniscience through various meditative and physical practices, like yoga. When the person puts an end to all *karmas*, the person attains omniscience. In Zoroastrianism, a religion started in Persia (now Iran), the supreme creator god Ormazd (Ahura Mazda) is omniscient. Buddhists believe that Sakyamuni (563–483 B.C.), another name for the historical Buddha who founded Buddhism, was omniscient. Even the sphinx, the ancient mythological creature with a lion's body and human head, was thought to be omniscient.[7]

Despite these overwhelming examples of belief in God's omniscience, there are several notable exceptions of ancient writers limiting God's omniscience. For example, the ninth-century Persian Jewish writer Hiwi al-Balkhi suggested that God was neither omnipotent nor omniscient because there were many injustices and inconsistencies in the Bible. Another example occurs in the various earth-diver myths of the ancient Slavs and Finno-Ugric peoples. In these tales, God is neither omniscient nor omnipotent, because He often relies on the Devil for knowledge. According to these myths, although God and the Devil created the world together, God and the Devil later became enemies. Many ancient Roman, Greek, and Scandinavian gods were clearly limited in their knowledge. Other religions, for example, those of certain North American Indians or Central and South Africans, suggest that while God is omniscient, He has withdrawn from the world and cannot be coaxed by prayer. Similar ideas of God's self-imposed limitations are found in Jewish mysticism, such as Lurianic Kabbalah, which is discussed in more detail in "Some Final Thoughts" at the end of this book.

👁 👁 👁

The science of omniscience need not remain confined to the dusty dens of old rabbis or the esoteric ramblings of philosopher-priests, beyond the range of our own exciting experiments and careful thoughts. I use the word "science" because it implies the logical, systematic testing of ideas and hypotheses. Many of the concepts, thought exercises, and experiments in this book are accessible to both students and lay people. The challenging task of imagining omniscient beings is useful for any species that dreams of understanding its place in a vast universe. Although this book is mostly about the *science* of omniscience, it does touch briefly on mysticism. Of course, the line between science and mysticism sometimes grows thin. Today, many philosophers and theologians would agree that paradoxes of omniscience, free will, faith, and belief are among the most profound and perplexing arenas of human thought.

When beginning this book, I did not set out to write a systematic and comprehensive study of omniscience and religious paradoxes. Instead, I chose topics that interested me personally and that I think will enlighten a wide range of readers. Although the concept of omniscience is centuries old, its strange consequences are still not widely known today. People often learn of them with a sense of awe, mystery, and bewilderment. Even armed with the experiments in this book, you'll still have only a vague understanding of omniscience and religious paradoxes, which will no doubt plague you for a long time.

Why contemplate the properties of omniscient beings and their powers and limitations? Philosophers and theologians feel the excitement of the creative process when they leave the bounds of the known to venture far into unexplored territory lying beyond our ordinary experience. When we imagine the powers of superior beings, we are at the same time holding a mirror to ourselves, revealing our own prejudices and preconceived notions. The science of omniscience also appeals to young minds, and I know of no better way to stimulate students than to muse about the powers of omniscient beings. Creative minds love roaming freely through the spiritual implications of the simple logical experiments. Most of the challenging questions in this book cannot be answered to theologians' satisfaction. Yet the mere asking of these questions stretches our minds, and the continual search for answers provides useful insights along the way.

This book will allow you to travel through time and space, and you needn't be an expert in philosophy. Some information is repeated so that each chapter contains sufficient background information, but I suggest you read the chapters in order as you gradually build your knowledge. To facilitate your journey, I start some chapters with a dialogue between quirky explorers who experiment with omniscience. This simple science fiction is good fun, but it also serves a serious purpose, that of expanding your imagination.

Archaeological evidence indicates that even the Neanderthals 50,000 years ago stained their dead with red ocher, perhaps to prepare the departed for some kind of afterlife. Paleoanthropologists tell us that primitive humans worshiped gods at the dawn of human existence, as soon as their brain cases became large and the creatures left records for us in their artworks. The names and faces of the gods may have changed, but the drive has always been the same: Humans try to forge a connection to powerful, supernatural forces for comfort and survival in a dangerous world. Obviously, God has meant different things to different peoples through time, and every individual has a different experience or concept of God. Yet the pervasiveness of God is emphasized dramatically by Rene Dubos in *A God Within:*

> Very soon in his social evolution, however, perhaps at the time of becoming *Homo sapiens,* [the human] began to search for a reality different in kind from that which he could see, touch, hear, smell, or otherwise apprehend directly. His awareness of the external world came to transcend his concrete experiences of the objects and creatures he dealt with—as if he perceived in them a form of existence deeper than that revealed by outward appearances. He imagined, though probably not consciously, a Thing behind or within the thing, a Force responsible for the visible movement. This immaterial Thing or Force he regarded as a god—calling it by whatever name used to denote the principle he thought to be hidden within external reality. Even in modern times, the people of tribes that have remained in a Stone Age culture imagine deities everywhere around them and tend to regard gods and goddesses as more real than concrete objects and creatures. The conceptual environment of primitive

man commonly affects his life more profoundly than his external environ-ment. And this is also true of modern man.[8]

Today, many people believe that the Bible is essentially the word of God. Others, like Marcus J. Borg, author of *Reading the Bible Again for the First Time*, believe that the Bible should be taken seriously but not literally. To Borg, the Bible is an imperfect lens through which we glimpse God—and we should not worship the lens but that which is beyond the lens.[9] However, whatever you believe about the possibility of omniscience, or the limitations of a biblical God, the practical analogies in this book will raise questions about the way you see the world and will therefore shape the way you think about the universe and God. For example, you will become more conscious of what it means to be omniscient or have a "superior" mind. Contemplating omniscience is as star-tling and rewarding as seeing a dazzling supernova in outer space for the first time.

> One of the reasons why religions seem irrelevant today is that many of us no longer have the sense that we are surrounded by the unseen.
>
> —Karen Armstrong, *A History of God*

> The function of religion is to confront the paradoxes and contradictions and ultimate mysteries of man and the cosmos; to make sense and reason of what lies beneath the irreducible irrationalities of man's life; to pierce the surrounding darkness with pinpoints of light, or occasionally to rip away for a startling moment the cosmic shroud.
>
> —Lewis Mumford, *The Conduct of Life*

> If there is a gently sloping ability continuum from the amoeba to the aardvark, and from the aardvark to the anthropoid apes and us, why doesn't such a continuum extend from us to God? Who lives in the cos-mic chasm? Angels, Elohim, djinn, elementals, or even, perhaps, some of the demons? What is their nature? What sort of communication can we hope to have with them?
>
> —Lionel and Patricia Fanthorpe, *Mysteries of the Bible*

# CHAPTER 1

# The Paradox of Omniscience

B.C. MANSFIELD

*God created the world for His own glory. This is an indisputable fact and one, moreover, that is quite understandable. A greatness that no-body can see is bound to feel ill at ease.*

—*Leszek Kolakowski,* The Keys to Heaven

*Truly Thou are a hidden God.*

—*Blaise Pascal,* Pensées, *1670*

YOU ARE CAPTAIN OF A LARGE STARSHIP DRIFTING IN INTERSTELLAR space. On your viewscreen is a ship of the Nephilim, a race of tentacled beings to whom you wish to demonstrate your courage. Showing weakness may one day give them the idea that they can take over the Earth and its solar system.

You are racing toward the Nephilim on a collision course. If neither of you veers from your course, your two ships will crash and all crew members will die. You certainly don't want that. Neither does the captain of the other ship, the huge Dr. Eck. But you do want to show the Nephilim your stamina and unbridled courage by staying your course and having Dr. Eck swerve to prevent a catastrophic collision.

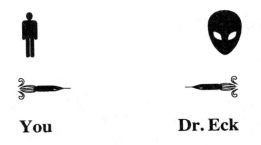

**You**          **Dr. Eck**

However, if you have to chicken out, you wouldn't be too disappointed if *both* you and Dr. Eck lost nerve and swerved. At least you would be alive and wouldn't be embarrassed by your loss of nerve in front of the Nephilim and your adoring crew mates. Of course, even if you swerved and Dr. Eck didn't, you'd prefer to survive and be humiliated rather than die with your crew. Here, then are some possible outcomes.

**Table 1.1   Playing the Omniscience Game**

| Event | Your Happiness Level |
|---|---|
| Dr. Eck veers to the side, and you stay the course. | Hooray |
| You both lose your nerve and veer to the side. | Not too bad |
| You lose your nerve and veer to the side, while Dr. Eck stays his course | Bad |
| Neither of you veer to the side, and you both die. | Very bad |

You know several things about the Nephilim. You've met with Dr. Eck before. You know he and his race are rational creatures. They want to survive the encounter.

You only have a few seconds to think about what to do. Think fast! If you have had many such encounters with the Nephilim, it seems like the best you can do is to chicken out, in the hope that the Nephilim will be sufficiently wise and do the same. If either you or the Nephilim does not veer to the side, one of you will be very angry and may not swerve during another encounter. Neither humans nor Nephilim will live long and prosper unless they are cowards.

There's just one problem with this logic. A big problem. The Nephilim are omniscient, just like God is supposed to be. They are telepathic and can read your mind. They always anticipate your moves with perfect accuracy. (In fact, some people believe that the Nephilim are gods, because of their omniscience.)

One of your initial thoughts is that the Nephilim have a big advantage over you in this dangerous form of brinkmanship. After all, they know for sure what you will do. They have more knowledge of you than you of them.

You think back to 1962, when American president John F. Kennedy and Soviet premier Nikita Khrushchev played a similar dangerous game of "chicken" during the Cuban Missile Crisis. Nikita Khrushchev had secretly supplied Cuba with missiles that could deliver nuclear bombs to the United States. Kennedy told Khrushchev to get the missiles out of Cuba or risk nuclear war. Luckily, Khrushchev decided to remove the missiles rather than risk such a catastrophe.

In 1964, Khrushchev was deposed as leader of the USSR, in part because his people considered him weak in his dealing with Kennedy. During the crisis, both sides were far from omniscient. In fact, unknown to President Kennedy, Soviet forces in Cuba had been equipped with nuclear weapons that could be used in the battlefield, and America had no idea that there were as many as 40,000 Soviet soldiers in Cuba.

You ponder the Cuban Missile Crisis as Dr. Eck's ship comes closer. Would the nation with the most knowledge have been better off in the Cuban Missile Crisis?

You look out the ship's window. It doesn't look good, as the ships are only miles apart:

**You**        **Dr. Eck**

A deep, stentorian voice comes over your radio. "Turn away!" screams Dr. Eck. His voice has a vague metallic echo.

"I cannot!" you yell back to Dr. Eck.

"This is madness!" Dr. Eck says. "Don't be a fool. For God's sake, change your course."

You slam your fist down onto your captain's chair. "Who are you trying to scare? It is *you* who must turn."

Hurry! The ships are drawing closer to each other! Only seconds remain. What should you do?

The answer is clear. It is actually you who have the advantage over an omniscient being. You must stay the course. You should not swerve. Because Dr. Eck is omniscient, if you were to swerve he would have predicted it and thus stayed his course. Humanity would have been humiliated, and Dr. Eck might have descended to Earth and devoured most forms of mammalian life—not to mention wreaking havoc with Earth's delicate geopolitical balance.

Here's what happens if you do not swerve. Dr. Eck knows he has only two choices:

**Table 1.2    The Fate of Dr. Eck**

| *What Dr. Eck Does* | *Result* |
| --- | --- |
| Dr. Eck swerves. | Dr. Eck survives |
| Dr. Eck stays his course. | Dr. Eck dies |

This means that Dr. Eck's only choice is to swerve. Because he *knows* you will stay your course, he must swerve. You already know he is rational and does not want himself and his crew to die in a conflagration in the depths of interstellar space. Thus, you have beaten an omniscient being and won the gambit.

This paradox of omniscience demonstrates the limits of common sense when considering the actions of omniscient beings and gods. In this scenario, you can see that omniscience is a disadvantage for "gods" playing risky games. No amount of thinking can help Dr. Eck out of his dilemma. Even though he is omniscient, he cannot gain the advantage over you.

## MUSINGS AND SPECULATIONS

*God is something less than absolutely omnipotent. He is actually engaged in a conflict with his creatures, in which he may very well lose the game. . . . Can God play a significant game with his own creatures?*

—Norbert Wiener, God & Golem, Inc., *1964*

What makes the paradox of omniscience so amazing to contemplate is that it is precisely the alien's omniscience, and your awareness of it, that ensures you obtain the best possible outcome and that the alien does not.[1] This is the paradox—most people would never expect the superior ability of a godlike creature to diminish his position in a conflict. Do you think that there are instances in the Bible or in history where humans were on a collision course with God and where neither wants to swerve? Of course, the situation with Dr. Eck can be made more complicated. For example, an omniscient being may know much more than your thoughts. He may know that you or he will die of a heart attack in 45 seconds.

The God of the Bible appears to be frustrated and surprised at times, which itself seems paradoxical for an omniscient being. For example, God frequently asks questions throughout the Bible before passing judgment. After Adam and Eve eat the forbidden fruit and hide themselves in the Garden of Eden, they are bombarded with a series of questions: "Where are you?" "Who told you that you were naked?" "Have you eaten of the tree, whereof I commanded you that you should not eat?" "What is this you have done?" (Genesis 3:9, 11, 13).

Later in Genesis, God asks questions of Adam's son Cain: "Why are you angry? And why is your countenance fallen? If you do well, shall it not be lifted up?" "Where is Abel, your brother?" "What have you done?" In the Book of Job, God asks Satan, "Where do you come from?" (Satan answers God, "From roaming through the earth and going back and forth in it") (Genesis 4:6–7, 9, 10; Job 1:7).

Of course, we might argue that these questions are largely rhetorical and only asked for the sake of the humans. Liberal theologians who do not take the Bible as the literal word of God might say that these are simply examples of *anthropopatheia*, ascribing human attributes to God. However, even when God is not asking us questions, God continually tests. He tests Abraham by suggesting he sacrifice his son. Satan persuades God to test Job's devotion through a series of emotional and physical tortures.

One of the best examples in which God's words might be taken as implying His nonomniscience occurs during the test of Abraham. A literal interpretation of the Bible could suggest God did not know how Abraham would react:

> Abraham reached out his hand and took the knife to slay his son. But the angel of the Lord called out to him from heaven, "Abraham! Abraham!" "Here I am," he replied. "Do not lay a hand on the boy," he said. "Do not do anything to him. Now I know that you fear God, seeing that you have not withheld from me your son, your only son." (Genesis 22:10–12)

Even if God asks all His questions rhetorically, or if they are meant as mere allegory, or if God knows the answers to His tests, it is notable that God's reaction upon hearing many answers is one of anger and frustration, an almost explosive fury that must be quenched. When God learns of Eve's disobedience, He tells Eve, "I will make most severe your pangs in childbearing. In pain shall you bear children." He tells Adam, "Cursed be the ground because of you. By toil shall you eat of it all the days of your life: thorns and thistles shall it sprout for you. . . . For dust you are and to dust you shall return" (Genesis 3:16–19). The Old Testament God surely sounds like an angry and jealous God, and He describes himself as such throughout.

Although a metaphorical interpretation of the Bible provides an escape hatch for some of the paradoxes described in this book, I nevertheless ask the reader to consider what lessons these metaphors are intended to teach humanity, and what paradoxes may still persist as a result of following these lessons. As just one example, recall the many instances in the Bible where God appears to sanction the torture and killing of children for the sins of their parents. Even if we do not take the Bible literally, we can still wonder at, or try to resolve, the logical paradoxes or incongruities that arise when we juxtapose these stories with God's edict that sons should not share the guilt of the fathers. (Appendices C and D give numerous similar examples.)

&#128065; &#128065; &#128065;

The paradox of omniscience need not apply only to God. One can imagine similar scenarios with nations, one of which has thousands of spies and is, in effect, omniscient. The other nation, if it knows that there are thousands of spies, can have an advantage over the "omniscient" nation—just like you did over Dr. Eck. Perhaps the paradox of omniscience will someday enter our daily lives if computers with numerous sensors monitor our movements and thoughts.

Another way to play this collision-course game would be to convince your opponent that you are crazy and will keep going no matter what. If he is rational, he will swerve. The challenge would be to convince your opponent that you are crazy. After all, if he is rational, he will realize that it is to your advantage to *appear* insane. So your supposed insanity could actually be a sign of your sharp intelligence. Perhaps you will have the best advantage if you are *truly* insane. Perhaps someone who really wanted to win could make himself temporarily nuts by eating a hallucinogenic mushroom. Would you risk this in a life-and-death situation? Paradoxically, you will have transformed yourself into someone who can act in your best interest. Your actual insanity might manifest itself in many ways—drooling, cursing, self-mutilation, shouting words from the Bible at random intervals while jumping around like a chicken with its head cut off, and so on. If the Russians had convinced us they were insane during Kennedy's administration, the Cuban Missile Crisis might have ended with a different outcome. If true psychics existed, you could always win when playing such games with them. The psychic is at a disadvantage. The true psychic has the dangerous disadvantage of omniscience.

☉ ☉ ☉

Despite the seemingly secular atmosphere of much of modern Western society, the idea of a biblical God still affects millions of people. Surveys indicate that 95 percent of Americans believe in God. A recent *Newsweek* survey found that 87 percent of adults believe God sometimes answers their prayers.[2] Of course, most of these individuals would have only a very limited knowledge or understanding of the Bible. For example, how many would have heard of the great Nephilim?

Yes, the term "Nephilim" is from the Old Testament. One of the most enigmatic stories of the Bible occurs in Genesis 6:1–4. Here we find that the "sons of God saw that daughters of men were beautiful, and they married any of them they chose." Kenneth Davis, author of *Don't Know Much About the Bible*, speculates that the "sons of god" might have been angels who took wives from the daughters of humans.[3] The offspring of these angel-human marriages were the Nephilim, the ancient heroes and warriors:

> The Nephilim were on the earth in those days—and also afterward—when the sons of God went to the daughters of men and had children by them. They were the heroes of old, men of renown. (Genesis 6:4)

The word "Nephilim" also literally translates to the "fallen ones." The Nephilim had superhuman powers. Notice that they should have been destroyed in the great Flood, but we do find them later in Canaan during the time of Moses, according to the Book of Numbers.

Some have speculated that the strange biblical reference to Nephilim may represent a deep collective memory of the time when Neanderthals coexisted with *Homo sapiens*.[4] We know that Neanderthals inhabited Europe and the Middle East during the late Pleistocene Epoch, about 100,000 to 30,000 years ago. The Neanderthals were the first hominids to intentionally bury their dead, and they had larger brain cases than modern humans. Examination of skeletal remains indicates that Neanderthals were a physically powerful and war-scarred race. Not without controversy, some researchers suggest that the Nephilim might refer to either Neanderthals or strongly muscled but possibly sterile hybrids produced by the mating of Neanderthals and *Homo sapiens.*[5] Even today, scientists do not fully understand the Neanderthal's evolutionary origin and final fading from the world scene.

---

Perhaps God might isolate sectors within himself and simulate limited knowledge in order to overcome the paradox of knowing everything yet *not* knowing what it would be like to learn or be surprised. This challenge gives God a very good reason to divide himself into pieces, to become incarnate as a human being, at which point He can experience the essence of being a limited mind containing a shard of infinity within.

—Luke Dunn, personal communication

---

If, on the other hand, he went to pay his respects to the Door, and it wasn't there . . . what then? The answer, of course, was very simple. He had a whole board of circuits for dealing with exactly this problem, in fact this was the very heart of his function. He would continue to believe in it whatever the facts turned out to be, what else was the meaning of Belief? The Door would still be there, even if the door was not.

—Douglas Adams, *Dirk Gently's Holistic Detective Agency*

---

My life has been remarkably happy, perhaps in the upper 99.99 percentile of human happiness, but even so, I have seen a mother die painfully of cancer, a father's personality destroyed by Alzheimer's disease, and scores of second and third cousins murdered in the Holocaust. Signs of a benevolent designer are pretty well hidden.

—Steven Weinberg, *Skeptical Inquirer*

CHAPTER 2

# God and Evil

B.C. MANSFIELD

*If [God] is omnipotent, then every occurrence, including every human
action, every human thought, and every human feeling and aspiration
is also His work; how is it possible to think of holding men responsible*

*for their deeds and thoughts before such an almighty Being? In giving out punishment and rewards He would to a certain extent be passing judgment on Himself. How can this be combined with the goodness and righteousness ascribed to Him? The main source of the present-day conflicts between the spheres of religion and of science lies in this concept of a personal God.*

*—Albert Einstein,* Out of My Later Years

YOU ARE WITH AN EXTRATERRESTRIAL ARTIST NAMED MISS MUX-dröözol.[1] Muxdröözol, a trochophore with two huge teardrop-shaped eyes, has painted a biblical scene of the Tower of Babel using the blood of several ancestors.

You sometimes wonder about Miss Muxdröözol. Her skin is exceptionally smooth but her shape is somewhat disconcerting. She essentially has no body—just a large head connected to arms and legs. Sometimes the arms seem to retract behind the folds of her cloak.

You are telling her your ideas about God. "Miss Muxdröözol, moral truth is God's will. Something is good *because* God desires it. Think of the Ten Commandments."

She shakes her head. "No. That's backwards. God desires it because it's good. I can prove it."

"No way!" You frown and then after a few seconds grin, although the smile doesn't reach your eyes. "I thought I saw something." But now you think the snakelike movement within the depths of her hair must be just a trick of the light.

"This?" Miss Muxdröözol asks as she moves her arm and a tangle of emerald light reflects against her face. Several gems are inlaid in her wrist.

Miss Muxdröözol seems as if she wants to tell you her personal theories about morals when, suddenly, a huge bearded man materializes in your room. For a second your mind is wracked by a series of ecstatic religious visions involving angels, Moses, and unleavened bread.

"I am God," the being says. "You have tried to live a moral life. But you are wrong. My will is for you to kill movie stars, cheat on your taxes, lie whenever possible, steal from the poor, torture chinchillas and squirrels, spit daily on your neighbor's car, slaughter the first born of races other than your own, and to drive a stake into Miss Muxdröözol's cervical vertebrae. Please do this now."

The being uses a long, wooden staff to project an image of a squirrel on the floor:

"Who the hell are you?" you say. "You are not God."

"Why not?" The being's beard trails along the floor. His eyes gaze at you with an intensity that transgresses the sanctity of the Silurian Epoch. Oh, those eyes.

"What you tell me to do is clearly wrong. You can't be God, because no God would command such heinous acts."

Miss Muxdröözol begins to evaginate her digestive tract through her oral cavity so that she can better see your face. "You see, I was correct. You could have decided that you were wrong about morality and that it was fine to torture chinchillas. This proves my point. Rather than concluding that something is good if God requests it, you *first* have an idea of what is good, and *then* you judge on this basis whether something represents the will of God."[2]

## MUSINGS AND SPECULATIONS

*There is a theory which states that if ever anybody discovers exactly what the Universe is for and why it is here, it will instantly disappear and be replaced by something even more bizarre and inexplicable. There is another theory which states that this has already happened.*

—*Douglas Adams,* Hitchhiker's Guide to the Galaxy

Although the scenario with you and Miss Muxdröözol is as zany as they come, it does raise a good question: Do you think people conclude that something is good if God in the Bible requests it, or do we *first* have an idea of what is good, and *then* judge on this basis whether something represents the will of God?

What could a god do to make you believe he is God? I asked people on the Internet to answer this question in order to get a feel for what people think today. Sure, I admit the Internet is filled with people from all educational levels. I once had an editor who questioned why I wanted to hear the philosophical musings of taxi cab drivers. I told her that taxi cab philosophers told more about the universe, and contemporary thought, than Wittgenstein. Before you scoff, consider how you would answer the question I posed:

> On a cool Autumn night, you are gazing up at the sky when a being suddenly appears and asks, "What can I do to make you believe that I am God?" What is your answer?

Here are some responses I received. If you, like some of my previous editors, are not interested in hearing from the Internet riffraff, skip the next few pages.

- You could ask Him to explain why He believed He was God.
- You could ask Him to find a rock He can't lift, and lift it.
- First, ask the being to define what God is. Second, ask for five arguments—understandable to the best human minds—that provide testable evidence as to the existence of God. Finally, make sure that Stephen J. Gould, Martin Gardner, and Richard Dawkins would accept this evidence.
- Is it possible that there is no single act that could convince you that the being was God? Because anything God says or does could result from a sufficiently advanced technology, we could not know if God is merely some alien playing jokes on humans. However, if the entity is God, He

should be able to adjust the nature of our brains so that we truly believe that the entity is God.

- To be convincing, ask this Being to hand you a book that *you* had written that argues convincingly that He is God.
- Perhaps God could demonstrate some "impossible" solution like solving Rubik's cube from a well-mixed state in about 10 moves.
- The religion of Islam emphasizes that we only see God in His activities, which adapt His indescribable being to our limited understanding.
- In one of his more skeptical moods, the Italian theologian Saint Thomas Aquinas (1224–1274) wrote in *Summa Theologica:* "It seems that God does not exist; because if one of two contraries be infinite, the other would be altogether destroyed. But the name God means that He is infinite goodness. If, therefore, God existed there would be no evil discoverable; but there is evil in the world. Therefore God does not exist. Further, it is superfluous to suppose that what can be accounted for by a few principles has been produced by many. But it seems that everything we see in the world can be accounted for by other principles, supposing God did not exist. For all natural things can be reduced to one principle, which is human reason, or will. Therefore there is no need to suppose God's existence."
- You can't *disbelieve* something if you don't even know what it is you're not believing in. Likewise, you can't believe in something if you don't even know what it is you're believing in. This makes everyone an agnostic until or unless a definition of God is agreed upon.
- It is too late to be convinced. If You existed, I would have noticed it long ago.
- I'd say "Make me believe in you!"
- If in the next 30 seconds you can levitate me, make me ecstatically happy, and show me a convincing vision of the afterlife, then I will believe that you are God.
- Alter my brain. If my brain was altered the right way, I would believe God was God—no choice.
- Move an immovable object. Because this is paradoxical, I then expect the God-unit to enter an infinite loop (as they say in computer programming terminology), overflowing His stack, generating a kernel panic (or a "Blue Screen of Death"), followed by the emission of smoke, a small popping sound, sparks, flames, garbled speech. The total dissolution of space follows.

- If you're God, why bother asking me? Testing me? Free will? Do you suffer from schizophrenia? Or just low self-esteem?
- I believe that Gödel's Theorem has already disproved the existence of God because God cannot be omnipotent. Therefore, God would have to prove to me that Gödel's Theorem is not valid.
- I do not want to truly believe in God. If I am given proof, then faith is impossible. Without faith, and hope, what reason is there to continue?
- One rational definition of God is "the whole of everything," and this consciousness could evolve from the Internet. But I can see no way of giving the Internet, a communications medium with some computational ability, a "voice" and true consciousness.
- I think the answer may be suggested by Carl Sagan in the novel *Contact*. God would put pictures in the digits of pi or messages in DNA. But of course the entity communicating with the individual would need to prove that he is the author of the messages. As a paraphrase of what Arthur C. Clarke said about magic and technology, a sufficiently technologically advanced alien could easily pass himself off as God.
- This is too weird a question for me to answer. It implies a nature of God that I have found to be inaccurate. I know Spirit because Spirit exists, because life exists, because existence is. What does the question mean— what would make me believe in an all-powerful personality outside myself that controls the universe? Fear, insecurity, lack of perception. It's happened before.
- To prove you are God, cease to exist.
- My answer would be that God can do nothing to prove that He is God. We can't *prove* that anything around us is real. We could be in some computer-generated environment. In reality, we could be an alien being, transformed into a "human" by playing an advanced "computer" game. We could be living in a dream world. . . . You might not actually be reading this. You might be lying in a coma somewhere imagining this. No one can prove anything to me, and so God cannot prove that He is God.
- Continue being who you are.
- Proof denies faith, and without faith, I am nothing. God may very well be a tangible, quantifiable entity, but I think uncertainty is more fun. Nothing an entity could do would prove to me that he or she is God. I believe I would be able to judge for myself, without any parlor tricks. Any being who approached me with this question would have already broken my conditions for the qualities of God.

- I would never want to know whether or not God is real. God's existence seems to be secondary to his purpose—bringing meaning and hope to peoples' lives everywhere. And what is "real" anyway? Is what I taste and feel real? We perceive things because of electronic pulses and signals. Something is only as real as it can affect the perceivable world. If God can affect billions of people, his *perceived existence* is far more important than whether or not he *actually* exists.
- Nothing. God would never ask that question! He would know what I was thinking and just act as he wished upon my thoughts.
- Let me see you as you see yourself.
- I want to see how you created the universe.
- I would know that this being is not God. God would already know what it would take to make me believe.
- Prove all humanity as a collective is not God.
- I already know you are real.
- In the past, I have asked a variant of it to several people: "What could a being do to make you believe he is God?" I found that a skeptic's answer is "Nothing." No matter what evidence is presented, it can always be attributed to an alien, or aliens with superhuman intelligence, rather than a supernatural being like God.

That's enough responses for now! Perhaps some readers have heard of the Turing test designed to determine whether a machine is genuinely thinking and "intelligent."[3] This is still a hot area of study among computer scientists. Humankind should also develop a similar test for advanced beings to determine if any of them are genuinely God. I welcome readers' comments on what would be the most effective test.

◉ ◉ ◉

Many years ago, I wrote a science fiction story about an astronomer named Kalinda. While gazing out into space using a powerful telescope, she saw the most startling arrangement of stars beyond the constellation Canis Major. She immediately picked up her phone and called her friend, a Dr. Carl Sagan, for advice and counsel. Both Kalinda and Sagan were stumped by the peculiar arrangement.

What Kalinda discovered with her new, powerful telescope was a perfectly arranged array of stars in the shape of a cubical grid. About ten stars formed each edge of the cube.

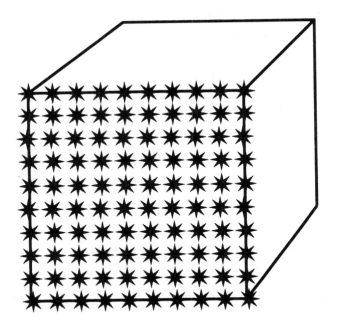

To confirm her initial observations, she decided to use the Hubble Space Telescope's camera to more clearly resolve the star grid, which was located some seven billion light years from Earth. Because peering at distant stars is like looking back in time, the images revealed a star grid that existed when the universe was 60 percent of its current age.

If our scientists today discovered such a grid of stars, how do you think it would affect society and current scientific thinking? Would the artifact have religious repercussions? How would you react? Imagine what effect a similar arrangement might have had on the writers of the Bible if the arrangement were visible to the naked eye.

The perfect God understands that in order to be a good teacher, He must *appear* to humans to be an imperfect, learning God, open to mistake, argument, persuasion, and repentance.

—Alan Dershowitz, *The Genesis of Justice*

Just in terms of allocation of time resources, religion is not very efficient. There's a lot more I could be doing on Sunday morning.

—Bill Gates, Microsoft cofounder and CEO, *TIME*

# CHAPTER 3

# Cain and Abel's Dilemma

B.C. MANSFIELD

*If the universal resurrection is accomplished by reassembling the original atoms which made up the dead, would it not be logically impossible for God to resurrect cannibals? Every one of their atoms belongs to someone else.*

—*Frank Tipler,* The Physics of Immortality

*I [God] don't know how I do it. . . . Omniscience gives me eyestrain. . . . And omnipotence—that takes it out of you.*

—*Stanley Elkin,* The Living End

IN THE BIBLE, CAIN AND ABEL ARE ADAM AND EVE'S FIRST TWO SONS. Cain is a farmer, and Abel is a shepherd. Cain eventually kills Abel out of jealousy, but let's use their tenuous relationship as a backdrop for a new story that we can imagine takes place before the world's first murder. This story is a lead into the more complex paradox involving omniscient beings in Chapter 5.

Imagine you are with Miss Muxdröözol, your extraterrestrial artist friend from Chapter 2. She has time-travel technology and has transported you back in time to the Middle East. For the sake of our story, let's assume that Cain and Abel were actual humans who lived centuries ago.

The journey begins. . . .

👁 👁 👁

Miss Muxdröözol quietly motions toward a row of olive trees. The ancient trunks are illuminated by a flood of moonlight, and their branches are cruelly twisted by the dry winds. The weather is warm, but no more so than on any summer day on your modern Earth.

What if you miscalculated and you are not in Cain and Abel's time? What if you are miles from the designated location? You clear your mind of turbulent thoughts and envision a nearby Tigris or Euphrates river lapping endlessly on beaches, one ripple after another, like the beating of ancient drums.

You take a deep breath, expecting the air of the ancient Middle East to be pure, invigorating. But instead your hand moves to cover your nose. You are not used to the pungent odor of rancid goat's milk.

The distant olive branches move. This must be the place. This must be the time. You tap on Miss Muxdröözol's forearm. "Follow me."

"You know the way?"

"I think I hear them."

You move through the olive trees with branches so low and leafy that you have to duck under them. There are places where one could stand completely hidden by the trees.

Miss Muxdröözol is close. You can hear her breathing. "Is that them?" she whispers as she points to your right.

You nod.

Cherubim—angels of the Old Testament—are waving a flaming sword while forcing Cain and Abel into a fenced enclosure. *Both* men are suspected of having snuck back into the Garden of Eden and of causing unspecified mischief. One of the angels is holding both Cain and Abel even though he knows that there is not sufficient evidence against either of them to present the case to

God. However, the angel wants to eventually impress God with the angel's analytical skills. Therefore, the angel wants to try to handle the case on his own.

Let us assume for the moment that God could in fact be "surprised" by Cain and Abel's mischief, because there are numerous instances in the Bible where God seems to enter time and is changed by the experience. Clearly, God is surprised in many biblical stories—in fact He appears to be unpleasantly surprised on numerous occasions. When the biblical God is angry, or portrayed as being angry, the anger appears to be associated with an event God did not anticipate. Of course, God may only be giving humans the *illusion* of being surprised, angry, and entering into the stream of time, but let us assume, for the moment, that God can *actually* be surprised or angry. (At the end of this chapter, we discuss whether Jesus is omniscient and how this may conflict with his surprise and anger.)

Let's return to the hypothetical Cain and Abel story. The angel with the flaming sword is experienced at dealing with the first few humans on Earth and their propensity to commit crimes and lie. He therefore presents Cain and Abel with the basic facts of the case and their choices.

The angel tells Cain and Abel that he needs a confession from one of them in order to bring down God's wrath. The angel is a fairly legalistic being, at least in this story. If *neither* human confesses, the angel has to lower the "charges" to trespassing, which carries a maximum sentence of wandering the desert of Nod for six months. Using his sword, the angel sketches a drawing of a desert in the sand to make the punishment sink in. The hot sun in the sky is obvious in the drawing.

Cain jumps back.

According to the angel, if Cain *or* Abel confesses, but his partner in crime does not, then the "honest" person goes free and the other is doomed to "crawl like a snake on his belly and eat dust" for thirty years and his descendants will have debilitating insomnia.

### Crawling on His Belly

On the other hand, if *both* Cain and Abel confess, each will get reduced sentences of five years of wandering. The angel takes his mighty sword and scratches the outcomes in the ground to help Cain and Abel ponder their predicament:

**Table 3.1    Outcomes for Cain and Abel**

| Actions | | Results |
|---|---|---|
| Neither confesses | 🔾 | Both wander desert of Nod for six months ☺☺ |
| One confesses | 〰️ | Confessor goes free; other doomed to crawl ☺☹ |
| Both confess | 🔾 | Five years of wandering ☹☹ |

The angel keeps Cain and Abel separated by 30 feet so that they cannot communicate and work out a strategy. What should Cain and Abel do?

At first, the solution to their dilemma seems straightforward: neither Cain nor Abel should confess so that they both will end up with the minimum punishment—wandering in the desert for six months. The angel, in effect, will suspect both Cain and Abel, but the angel will not have enough evidence to secure a conviction. The fury of God's law will be split between the two. This is the top line of the table and represents a *strategy of cooperation*. However, there's a paradox. Let's consider the problem from Abel's perspective. If Abel confesses and Cain doesn't, then Abel is free, which makes him very happy. On the other hand, if Cain confesses too, then Abel is still happy having confessed, because he will only have to wander 5 years through the desert, and he avoids the maximum penalty of crawling on his belly for 30 years.

The worst fate is to be the one who doesn't confess. Given the other person's testimony, the angel is sure to condemn the person to a miserable crawling state.

The cooperation scenario in which neither confesses is, of course, very risky. It's quite possible that if Cain wishes to cooperate, then Abel will be tempted to double-cross Cain at the last minute, thereby achieving the best possible outcome, which is freedom. Modern game theorists suggest that the scenario leads each suspect to confess, even though it will bring a harsher punishment than the strategy of cooperation and no confession. Abel naturally reasons that there are two outcomes if he confesses:

**Table 3.2    A Peek Inside Abel's Reasoning Process**

| | | |
|---|---|---|
| Abel confesses | Cain does not confess | Therefore, Abel is free |
| Abel confesses | Cain confesses | Therefore, Abel has five years of wandering |

The same logic applies when Cain does his own reasoning. It is also logical for him to confess. Yet, if both Cain and Abel behave logically, their behavior constitutes a double confession, which produces a harsher punishment for Cain and Abel than if neither of them had confessed. But, at least, the confessing person will not be doomed to crawl on his belly for 30 years. What would you do?

If you perform this experiment with real people in the twenty-first century, you'll find that confession is the most common strategy. People who try the cooperative no-confession strategy are exploited by their partners. Certain factors such as the severity of punishments can affect the outcome. Try this experiment on friends. More cooperation will probably arise if communication is permitted between the two suspects.

We can extend Cain and Abel's Dilemma to entire peoples. Consider two nations, the Israelites and the Canaanites. (Or if you prefer more modern examples, consider the Russians and Americans or the Indians and Pakistanis.) Imagine that the two nations are engaged in an arms race. Each nation has the same choice: to continue to spend all their resources on weapons or to stop. If both nations stop, then each can spend its resources on projects that will benefit their people. If one nation continues to spend resources on weapons and the other stops, then soon one will develop military superiority. If both nations continue to spend resources on weapons, they are both, in some sense, worse off because they have spent enormous resources on weapons and neither is likely to be much stronger than the other.

Cain and Abel's dilemma explores the conflict between the good of the individual and the good of the group. Neither Cain *nor* Abel should confess, because that is best for both of them. But assuming the other person won't confess, each person is tempted to better his own situation by turning his partner in to the angel. This dilemma is similar to the paradox of omniscience in Chapter 1 because the participants may be inclined to do something that would be bad if both did it (keep the starships on course and crash, or confess to the angel). If we call the worst course of action *defecting*, then in the starship dilemma, the worst possible outcome results when both parties defect and crash. In Cain and Abel's dilemma, the worst outcome occurs when the other person defects and you don't. Thus, it's more tempting to defect in Cain and Abel's dilemma. In the starship gambit, if you know your opponent, Dr. Eck, is going to defect, you can stay the course. In the Cain and Abel scenario, knowing your partner will defect forces you to defect.

## MUSINGS AND SPECULATIONS

*Discovering the prisoner's dilemma is something like discovering air. It has always been with us. The Gospel of Matthew attributes to Jesus the "golden rule": "In everything, do to others what you would have them do to you."*
      —*William Poundstone,* The Prisoner's Dilemma

The paradox in this chapter was first formally identified in the early 1950s by Melvin Dresher and Merrill M. Flood, scientists at the RAND Corporation. (RAND had been interested in game theory because of possible applications to global nuclear strategy and national security.) The problem came to be known as the "prisoner's dilemma" when Albert W. Tucker, a mathematics professor at Princeton University, discussed it further at a meeting of psychologists at Stanford University. It was Tucker who actually gave the problem the title "prisoner's dilemma" while giving examples of prison sentences in order to make the abstract ideas more concrete. Tucker researched the dilemma to understand and illustrate the difficulty of analyzing *non-zero-sum games*—dilemmas in which one person's victory is not necessarily the other person's defeat. The best strategy for a given player is often one that increases the payoff to one's partner as well. Tucker's simple paradox has since given rise to an enormous literature on the subject in disciplines ranging from philosophy and biology to sociology, political science, and economics. The problem continues to be of interest to anyone intrigued by game theory and resolving conflicts.

The dilemma faced by Cain and Abel arises because whatever the other individual does, each individual is better off confessing than remaining silent. But the outcome obtained when both confess is worse for each than the outcome they would have obtained had both kept their mouths shut. The paradox illustrates a conflict between individual and group rationality. A group whose members pursue rational self-interest may all end up worse off than a group whose members act contrary to rational self-interest. Stated more generally, a group whose members rationally pursue their own goals may all be worse off than if they do not rationally pursue their goals individually.[1] More than a thousand articles on the problem were published in the decades that followed the initial Dresher, Flood, and Tucker work, and the problem continues to be of interest with over 13,000 web pages mentioning this topic.

Many of you may think of these kinds of paradoxes as mere mathematical concepts or games that are completely determined by their outcomes. However, in 1952, Flood and Dresher actually had people play a game similar to the

Prisoner's Dilemma. I urge readers to conduct their own experiments to see how people perform and even differ in their strategies as a function of age, country of origin, gender, and other demographics. For example, the 1952 experiment was a prisoner's dilemma game played 100 times between two players. In this particular experiment, the game was skewed so that one of the players had an advantage over the other player, but the "payoff matrix" is quite similar to the original game.[2] In the 1952 game, the payoffs are positive; that is, each rational player seeks to maximize the value in the matrix cell he ends up in.

**Table 3.3    The 1952 Experiment: Outcomes**

|  | *Player 2 Defects* | *Player 2 Cooperates* |
|---|---|---|
| Player 1 cooperates | −1¢, 2¢ | 0.5¢, 1¢ |
| Player 1 defects | 0, 0.5¢ | 1¢, −1¢ |

You don't have to concern yourself about the values in the matrix. They were purposefully a little confusing to make it more difficult for the players to decipher all the strategy rules.[3] Each player chooses a strategy in ignorance of the other player's selection. The ordered pairs of numbers refer to the gains and losses of Players 1 and 2 respectively. For example, if Player 1 chooses the strategy in the top row and Player 2 chooses the strategy in the left column, then Player 1 would be penalized one cent, and Player 2 gets two cents (−1¢, 2¢). Because this is a non-zero-sum game, the money is paid by an outside agency. You can think of this agency as an independent bank. Player 1 and Player 2 don't get money from one another.

Just as in Cain and Abel's dilemma, the worst outcome occurs when the other person defects and you don't. For example, the worst case occurs for Player 1 if he cooperates and Player 2 does not (−1, 2), and the worst case occurs for Player 2 if he cooperates and Player 1 does not (1, −1). You can see from the payoff matrix that Player 2 has an advantage when Player 1 cooperates (−1, 2 and 0.5, 1). For example, Player 1 is always better off choosing the strategy in the second row, and Player 2 is better off choosing the strategy in the first column. However, when both choose their better strategies, both do relatively poorly. They actually do better choosing their "worse" strategies, provided they both do so.[4]

In the 100 trials of the 1952 experiment, Player 1 chose to cooperate 68 times, and Player 2, 78 times. Player 1 began the game expecting both players to defect. Player 2 realized the value of cooperation and started cooperating.

Both players started cooperating after the first ten moves, though Player 1 would defect on a regular basis, disappointed that his payoff was smaller than Player 2's. This in turn brought retaliation from Player 2, who would defect on the next move.[5]

Each player kept a diary. Some of those comments are revealing. Player 2 wrote "The stinker" after Player 1's defection. "He's a shady character . . . a shiftless individual—opportunist, knave. . . . He can't stand success."[6]

The players' comments reflect their concern about the final few moves. Both appeared to realize that it would be rational for both to defect on move 100, because no retaliation from the other player was possible. As the game was played, both players cooperated on moves 83 through 98. On move 99, Player 1 defected, and on move 100, both defected.

William Poundstone writes in *The Prisoner's Dilemma:*

> Both Flood and Dresher say they initially hoped that someone at RAND would "resolve" the prisoner's dilemma. They expected [researchers] to come up with a new and better theory of non-zero-sum games. The theory would address the conflict between individual and collective rationality typified by the prisoner's dilemmas. Possibly it would show, somehow, that cooperation is rational after all. The solution never came. Flood and Dresher now believe that the prisoner's dilemma will never be "solved," and nearly all game theorists agree with them. The prisoner's dilemma remains a negative result—a demonstration of what's wrong with theory, and indeed, the world.[7]

The Prisoner's Dilemma is a simple but powerful paradox and has also been used to analyze problems of ethics, morality, evolution, theories of altruism, and religion. For example, many have wondered precisely why the Jews offered so little resistance against the Nazis, which possibly might have increased the Jews' chance of survival. Of course, there are many answers, but Jonathan Blumen, writing in the journal *The Ethical Spectacle*,[8] observes that Jews, throughout history, had relied on the tolerance of neighbors who were often hostile for generations. Any perceived defection (e.g., resistance) on the part of the Jews was aggressively punished. Because Jews were usually a tiny minority, a game of "all defect" or of "tit for tat" on both sides would lead to the complete annihilation of the Jews. The best the Jews could do was an "all cooperate" strategy, which would reduce defection of the people among whom they resided. Even though pogroms wiped out many Jews, Jews still survived in larger numbers than if they had followed other strategies.

The Nazis' relationship with the Jews was a different story. No longer could Jews attempt to foster a cooperative atmosphere as they often had done in the past. Jonathan Blumen writes:

> The Nazis disguised their own defection as cooperation, herding the Jews onto trains for "resettlement," not overtly for death. Eichmann, with his smile of a friendly salesman, traveled around Europe, establishing relationships with elders in the Jewish communities, lulling their suspicions, then shipping them all away to their deaths. Had the Jews believed that death was imminent, all shadow of the future—any reason not to practice violent defection themselves—would have been removed. . . . Hope was the thing that killed them— the unreasonable hope that the Nazis were indeed cooperative, that by cooperating with the Nazis they would survive another month, another day, another minute.[9]

Note that a number of famous Bible stories involve negotiation or arbitration. This includes the story of Cain and Abel, in which Cain bargains with God; the story of Rahab, a prostitute who negotiates with the King of Jericho over Israeli spies and then negotiates with the spies themselves; and the story of Solomon, who arbitrates the fate of a mother and her alleged child. Several authors have modeled these stories using game theory similar to that used when understanding the prisoner's dilemma.[10]

Earlier in this chapter we discussed God's apparent surprise and anger as depicted in numerous Old Testament stories, but what can we say about the New Testament Jesus? A few readers may feel that the Doctrine of the Trinity claims that Jesus is God, and therefore is omnipotent, omnipresent, and omniscient, equal in all ways to the Father. For those readers who believe in an omniscient Jesus, note that Jesus's anger and surprise is often apparent, and it is not always easy to see how these characteristics could be compatible with omniscience. For example, one time Jesus found a fig tree without figs. He seemed surprised, and he cursed the tree, saying, "May no one ever eat fruit from you again" (Mark 11:12–25). The next day the tree had withered from the roots.

On the other hand, most scholars I have chatted with argue that Jesus clearly is not omniscient. In Mark 13:32, we find: "No one knows the day or hour, not even the angels in Heaven nor the Son, but only the Father." In Luke 2:52, we get the idea that Jesus's knowledge grows: "And Jesus advanced in wisdom and age and favor before God and man." Similarly, if we want to consider the various flavors of omniscience discussed in the Introduction, did Jesus have knowledge of all *facts* or *propositions:* Did he know the Earth was round in an age when many believed it was flat and square? Did he know about Pentium chips, the characteristics of all extinct trilobites, the nuances of superstring theory, and the one-trillionth digit of pi?

👁 👁 👁

Let us digress further and briefly discuss the actual biblical tale of Cain and Abel. Cain is a farmer. Abel is the first shepherd. Cain kills Abel out of jealousy after God rejects Cain's offering of grain. There is no explanation of why God prefers Abel's offering of his firstborn sheep. In the ancient days of temple sacrifice, farm animals, oil, grain, and flour were all acceptable sacrifices. However, the New Testament suggests that Cain's offering was not sincere (Hebrews 11:4; John 3:12).

When God asks Cain where Abel is, Cain tries to hide the murder. Cain replies, "I don't know. Am I my brother's keeper?"

God had punished Adam and Eve by casting them out of the Garden of Eden, and He placed an angel with a flaming sword to prevent their return to Eden. The angel in our imagined scenario presumably would have prevented Cain and Abel from returning to the Garden of Eden. God sentenced Cain to be a wanderer. Cain, who was scared that someone would kill him during his exile, begged God for Mercy:

> Cain said to the LORD, "My punishment is more than I can bear. Today you are driving me from the land, and I will be hidden from your presence; I will be a restless wanderer on the earth, and whoever finds me will kill me." But the LORD said to him, "Not so; if anyone kills Cain, he will suffer vengeance seven times over." Then the LORD put a mark on Cain so that no one who found him would kill him. (Genesis 4:13–15)

God marks Cain so that others will not harm him as he travels to the "Land of Nod, East of Eden." What is the mark? The Bible does not say.

Cain's request for mercy makes some Bible readers wonder who Cain feared, because, presumably, at this time there existed only Adam, Eve, and Cain. In any case, later Cain finds a wife in Nod, so perhaps there may have been independent creations or perhaps Adam and Eve had more children that intermarried. The Bible contains no explanations as to the origin of Cain's wife.

Once married, Cain begins a family. His first son is Enoch. Cain also builds a city called Enoch. Here's a conundrum of sorts: Cain's settling down to build a city seems to contradict the curse that Cain would always be a wanderer. Instead, he became the founder of the world's first city. (Adam and Eve's third child, Seth, is born after God sends Cain away to wander.)

Biblical apologists have interesting explanations for Cain's wife. (A biblical "apologist" is one who ardently defends the integrity of the Bible.) They suggest that people in the Book of Genesis lived exceptionally long lives—many hundreds of years, in which case there could be millions of people on Earth by the time Cain looks for a wife. (Even if Cain and his wife were closely related from a genetic standpoint, the marriage would not have been sinful because the command against marrying close relatives did not appear until Moses's day. For example, Abraham married his half sister.)

◉ ◉ ◉

The descriptions of ethnic cleansing and genocide—men, women, and children—present some of the greatest ethical dilemmas of the Bible. For example, in the Bible, the loose group of Israelite tribes begin to conquer Canaan. When Joshua and his armies move on to the town of Ai, we find horrifying casualty reports of the slaughter:

> When Israel had finished killing all the men of Ai in the fields and in the desert where they had chased them, and when every one of them had been put to the sword, all the Israelites returned to Ai and killed those who were in it. Twelve thousand men and women fell that day—all the people of Ai. For Joshua did not draw back the hand that held out his javelin until he had destroyed all who lived in Ai. But Israel did carry off for themselves the livestock and plunder of this city, as the LORD had instructed Joshua. So Joshua burned Ai and made it a permanent heap of ruins, a desolate place to this day. He hung the king of Ai on a tree and left him there until evening. At sunset, Joshua ordered them to take his body from the tree and throw it down at the entrance of the city gate. (Joshua 8:24–30)

Although the New Testament mentions loving our enemies and praying for those who persecute us, there are several stories in the Bible that tend to contradict this. Those who justify the conquering of Canaan suggest that the Canaanites were immoral, idolatrous, and sinful—a race with whom the Israelites could never have coexisted. The Canaanites' spiritual impurity led to their demise. (Note that some scholars suggest that the actual historical conquering of Canaan was a much more gradual process resulting from emigration and negotiations.)

Other biblical passages are equally perplexing in light of God's supposed all-loving, all-knowing nature.[11] In Deuteronomy, the Israelites are about to enter and "possess" the lands of many nations such as the Hittites, Amorites, and Canaanites. God tells the Jews that treaties are not allowed. Mercy is not allowed:

> When the LORD your God brings you into the land you are entering to possess and drives out before you many nations . . . then you must destroy them totally. Make no treaty with them, and show them no mercy. . . . Break down their altars. . . . You must destroy all the peoples the LORD your God gives over to you. Do not look on them with pity. . . . You must certainly put to the sword all who live in that town. Destroy it completely, both its people and its livestock. (Deuteronomy 7:1–16, 13:15)

In Deuteronomy 20:16, God also commands the Jews to "not leave alive anything that breathes." Appendices C and D continue this discussion.

◉ ◉ ◉

I have briefly touched upon this smattering of ethical dilemmas in the Bible because they will play a greater role in the chapters that follow, in which we discuss free will and various moral paradoxes. In some of the following pages, I'll ask you to consider how an omniscient God, with knowledge of all the future, could become angry and how the extermination of races could be sanctioned by God. I'll ask a variety of questions that might make uneasy those of you who believe that the Bible contains a gallery of pristine prophets in touch with a loving, just, and merciful God.

In closing, let me point out that before the printing press was invented, almost no one had seen the books of the Bible bound together in a single volume. Rather, the Bible was often viewed as a collection of separate documents. Professor Marcus J. Borg notes that only when the Bible was printed as a single unit did it become easier for people to think of the Bible as a single book with God as its author.[12] Borg also reminds us, "The books of the Bible were not sacred when they were written. Paul, for example, would have been amazed to know that his letters to his communities were to become sacred scriptures."[13]

---

[H]ow does free will account for cancer? Is it an opportunity of free will for tumors?

—Steven Weinberg, *Skeptical Inquirer*

# CHAPTER 4

# The Parable of Algae

B.C. MANSFIELD

*In science, greater knowledge is always and indisputably good; it is by no means so throughout all human existence. We know it from art proper, where achievement and great factual knowledge, or taste, or intelligence, are in no way essential companions; if they were, our best artists would be learned academics. We can know it by reducing the matter to the absurd, and imagining that God, or some Protean visitor from outer space, were at one fell swoop to grant us all knowledge. Such omniscience would be worse than the worst natural catastrophe, for our species as a whole would extinguish its soul and lose its pleasure and reason for living.*

*—John Fowles, "The Green Man"*

YOU ARE IN THE MISS MUXDRÖÖZOL BEDROOM IN HER VACATION home on the moon. The place looks the way you'd expect an apartment of an unmarried theropod in her early thirties to look. It's a real mess, with items of clothing draped over long-deactivated androids and take-out food boxes piled high on an ancient TV screen.

You walk over to her fish tank of guppies. The glass is violet and crimson with exotic algae.

You turn to Miss Muxdröözol. "An aquarium specialist must tend this fish tank."

"No, what makes you say that? It's true I have a cleaning person that comes every month to my apartment to clean. And I have a cook. But I doubt either tends to the tank. Look. The tank is full of algae. It's taking over like a disease. The water must be dirty."

You shake your head. "The aquarium specialist must like the algae. It does look kind of nice, doesn't it?"

"No. The algae grows on the glass without anyone tending to the tank. In fact, we can ask my cook and cleaning person if they have ever touched the aquarium."

Miss Muxdröözol presses a button that activates an intercom. "Hieronymus, have you ever messed with my fish tank?" His face appears on the view screen:

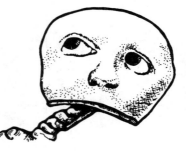

"No, Madam, I never go near your aquarium, and neither does your cleaning person."

You look at Hieronymus. "Perhaps there is an aquarium specialist who was here when everyone was sleeping or out for a walk."[1]

"Sir, I do not think that is the case. Miss Muxdröözol has a very good security system that involves electric fields and sharp, rotating cutting objects."

You look all around her room. On a low wooden desk is a collection of furculas, V-shaped bones formed by the fusion of the clavicles at the breastbone. Apparently, it is customary for Miss Muxdröözol and her kin to collect the bones of their long-dead ancestors.

On her walls are pictures of her great-great-grandparents, showing in explicit detail how their livers subdivide the visceral cavity into distinct anterior pleuropericardial and posterior abdominal regions. The diaphragmatic musculature is attached to a posterior colon.

Miss Muxdröözol walks closer to you. Her cheekbones are perfect, her jawline strong and feminine. On the couch, you notice the black beret she habitually wears along with her bioluminescent earrings.

"Look," you say. "Let's stay together, day and night, to verify that no one takes care of the aquarium. All we are allowed to do is feed the fish."

After a week, you begin to suspect that the aquarium specialist is invisible. You surround the aquarium with special infrared sensors and motion detectors, but still the specialist is not detected.

"Wait," you say. "The specialist is not only invisible, but he is not detectable by any sensors we can develop with our current technology."

Miss Muxdröözol puts her hands on her triple hips. "You are nuts. Your 'specialist' is supposed to be invisible and undetectable and is supposed to have placed the algae in such a way that it would have grown anyway. What makes the specialist different from no specialist at all?"

You think about God's existence. Your friends admit that it is impossible to detect God's presence in a direct, scientific fashion. Sure, you can see the beauty of cathedrals, mossy caverns, and soaring mountains, but this is not *scientific* detection of God. The complexity of life does not prove the existence of a creator any more than an awesomely complex and ordered snow crystal does when it forms spontaneously from random water molecules. It's easy for order and pattern to evolve from chaos using simple laws of nature.

Miss Muxdröözol comes so close you can feel her warmth. "How is your assertion that an undetectable Being exists any different from the assertion that there isn't any such Being?"

You want to think about that question.

A few minutes later, Miss Muxdröözol plunges her vestigial hand into the tank.

"What are you doing?"

"Looking for my golden severum. It's a fish. I cannot find him."

You look into the tank and notice that a tiny portion of the algal growth has formed these words:

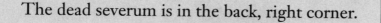

The dead severum is in the back, right corner.

"Wow!" you say. "I believe the severum is in the back, right corner."

Miss Muxdröözol looks at you. "It's reasonable for you to come to this belief only if you think me or someone else, like Hieronymus, scraped the algae to spell out that message on purpose. But what if by some unlikely coincidence, the algae just happened to grow in such a way to give you a rough appearance of a message?"

"Well, if that were true, I'd be unjustified in believing the severum was in the corner."

"Right."

"However, that explanation is unlikely. Someone must have scratched that message. It's a good bet that the severum is in the corner. Perhaps he's hidden behind a plant."

"I don't know if your logic is correct."

"Listen, Miss Muxdröözol. We aren't justified in taking things as *signs* and as giving us *information* if we didn't think that they were purposely arranged that way by a smart designer to communicate something to us."[2]

"True."

"Now look outside your window. What do you see?"

"I see the lunar craters. In particular, I see the crater called Alphonsus. It means we are on the eastern edge of the Mare Nubium."

"You get information from seeing this natural object, a crater."

"Yes."

"Aha! That means it was made on purpose by an intelligent designer. Just a moment ago you agreed we aren't justified in taking things as signs and as giving us information if we didn't think that they were purposely arranged that way by a smart designer to communicate something to us."

"Wait."

"The crater wasn't designed by life-forms like humans or aliens."

"Correct."

"That means they must have been designed by another being. That being is more powerful than us. It was designed by God. Case closed."

## MUSINGS AND SPECULATIONS

*A London lady sat next to Bertrand Russell at this party, and over the soup she suggested to him that he was not only the world's most famous atheist but, by this time, very probably the world's oldest atheist. "What will you do, Bertie, if it turns out you're wrong?" she asked. "I mean, what if—uh—when the time comes, you should meet Him? What will you say?" Russell was delighted with the question. His bright, birdlike eyes grew even brighter as he contemplated this possible future dialogue, and then he pointed a finger upward and cried, "Why, I should say, 'God, you gave us insufficient evidence.'"*

—Al Seckel, *Preface to* Bertrand Russell on God and Religion

Obviously, there is a flaw in your reasoning about the crater having to have been designed by God. But can you figure out what is wrong with the reasoning? Have you heard any arguments like this? Can you determine what might be wrong with the logic that seems to prove that a god designed the craters because they are signs and provide us with information?

At one point in our story, Miss Muxdröözol asked, "How is your assertion that an undetectable Being exists any different from the assertion that there isn't any such Being." Robert Martin, author of *There Are Two Errors in the the Title of This Book*, suggests a possibility:

> There's no real difference in beliefs or expectations about the real world in the religious believer and in the disbeliever. There's just a difference in how they feel about things. If so, then maybe there's no question about who is right and who is wrong. [Perhaps] religions don't say things that should be judged true or false. What they say is more like poetry: the expressions of feelings and attitudes.[3]

In Romans 1, we learn a different argument—one that suggests God has planted evidence of Himself throughout the world, so we, His creatures, are without excuse:

> The wrath of God is being revealed from heaven against all the godlessness and wickedness of men who suppress the truth by their wickedness, since what may be known about God is plain to them, because God has made it plain to them. For since the creation of the world God's invisible qualities—his eternal power and divine nature—have been clearly seen, being understood from what has been made, so that men are without excuse. (Romans 1:19–20)

Through time people have searched for such evidence of God—stronger evidence than the violet and crimson aquarium algae discussed in this chapter. For example, some scientists believe that the various physical laws of the universe are finely tuned to permit life, and this is evidence of a creator (see "Some Final Thoughts"). Others suggest that the universe has an absolute beginning and it was created from nothing—therefore a creator exists. Still others have suggested that life-forms are too complex to have evolved from a chance meeting of molecules. Some theologians have suspected that because a *universal* sense of right and wrong has evolved, this is evidence of God.

Perhaps the most unusual argument for evidence of God has come from mathematicians. Some have suggested that the compact formula $e^{i\pi} + 1 = 0$ is surely proof of a creator and have called this "God's formula." Edward Kasner and James Newman in *Mathematics and the Imagination* note, "We can only reproduce the equation and not stop to inquire into its implications. It appeals equally to the mystic, the scientists, the mathematician."[4] This formula of Leonhard Euler (1707–1783) unites the five most important symbols of mathematics: 1, 0, $\pi$, $e$, and $i$ (the square root of minus one). This union was regarded as a mystical union containing representatives from each branch of the mathematical tree: arithmetic is represented by 0 and 1, algebra by the symbol $i$, geometry by $\pi$, and analysis by the transcendental $e$. Harvard mathematician Benjamin Pierce said about the formula, "That is surely true, it is absolutely paradoxical; we cannot understand it, and we don't know what it means, but we have proved it, and therefore we know it must be the truth." Mathematics certainly says more in fewer "words" than any other science. David Eugene Smith in *A History of Mathematics in America Before 1900* wrote, "The formula, $e^{i\pi} + 1 = 0$ expressed a world of thought, of truth, of poetry, and of the religious spirit 'God eternally geometrizes.'"[5]

Let's end this chapter with a question. One day, while getting ready for work, you see a strange arrangement of ants on the kitchen floor:

# GOD EXISTS.
# A SEEKER IS A FINDER.

What is your reaction? Do you change your life or belief system?

> The Lord is merciful. He maketh me lie down in green pastures. The problem is, I can't get up.
>
> —Woody Allen, *Without Feathers*

# CHAPTER 5

# Newcomb's Paradox and Divine Foreknowledge

*These angels existed in the luminiferous ether and inherently under-*
*stood they were mere embers of a great fire that had spanned universal*
*space and innerdimensional time. They were crystalline spirits, forged*
*from subtle matter by great heat and purged of any imperfection;*
*bound into a communication network capable of transducing individ-*
*ual thought across the universal plain, their spirit is the essence of per-*
*fect pitch, made so by the vibratory constant of A-440 megahertz*
*trapped within the crystal makeup of their very being.*

—*Peter Lord-Wolff,* The Silence in Heaven

YOU ARE ABDUCTED BY ANGELS AND TAKEN TO AN INTERGALACTIC art gallery floating near the Orion nebulae. The angels call themselves seraphim. You stare at them in wonder. Each has six wings, two of which occasionally cover the angels' faces.

"Sit down," one of the seraphim says.

You sit before a table of immense proportions. It appears to be made of feathers and smells vaguely of myrrh, frankincense, and burnt offerings. On the table are two closed wooden arks, or boxes, labeled "Ark 1" and "Ark 2." The seraphim explain that Ark 1 contains a golden goblet worth $1,000. Ark 2 contains either a spider worth absolutely nothing or Leonardo da Vinci's painting the Mona Lisa, worth about $500 million.

You are about to play a game of sorts. If, after playing, you win the painting, it's yours to do with as you wish, including selling it to Bill Gates. However, at the moment, you do not know if Ark 2 contains the spider or the Mona Lisa.

**Table 5.1   What's Inside the Arks**

| Ark 1 | Ark 2 |
|---|---|
| 🏆 | 🖼️ or 🕷️ |
| (worth $1,000) | (worth $500 million *or* $0) |

"You have two choices," an angel says pointing a winged finger in your direction. "Take what is in *both* arks, or take *only* what is in Ark 2." He hands you a slip of paper to help you remember your choices.

> Choice 1: Take what is in *both* arks.
> Choice 2: Take *only* what is in Ark 2.

Now the angel makes your choice perplexing. "We have made a prediction about what you will decide. We are almost certainly correct. You can think of us as God if you like, or you can think of us Beings who can see the future with great accuracy. When we *expect* you to choose both arks, we put the spider in Ark 2. This means Ark 2 contains nothing of value. When we expect you to take only Ark 2, we place the Mona Lisa inside it. (Don't try to randomize your choice by flipping that penny in your pocket. If you do that Ark 2 will surely contain the spider.)"

You look at the angel. "But will Ark 1 always contain $1,000, no matter what you think I'll do?"

"Yes. Now make your choice." The angel hands you a card so you can more easily study the situation:

> - If we expect you to choose Ark 1 and Ark 2, we make sure Ark 2 has the spider.
> - If we expect you to take only Ark 2, we have put the Mona Lisa in it.

You look at the angel's fluttering wings and begin to cogitate on the strange choice. At first you think that you should select only Ark 2. The seraphim are excellent predictors, and therefore you will get the Mona Lisa. If you take both arks, the seraphim will very likely have anticipated your choice and have put a spider in Ark 2. You will only get the golden cup worth $1,000 and a worthless spider. Isn't it clear that you should take Ark 2? You'll be rich!

But now the Angels confuse you. "Listen carefully. Forty days before we abducted you, we made a prediction about which you would choose. We already have either put the Mona Lisa or the spider in Ark 2, and we're not going to tell you."

The angel glides to Ark 2 and taps on it with his sharp, retractable claws. "Of course, if the Mona Lisa is in here, it will stay in here no matter what you choose today. We're honest. We're not going to open the arks and remove anything. Similarly, if the Mona Lisa is not inside Ark 2, it will not suddenly materialize in the ark if you choose only what is in Ark 2."

The temperature drops noticeably. The stars in the sky seem to wink out, but perhaps it is just an illusion. "Come this way," the angels say. Their claws retract with a whir. Their folded wings, when viewed from different angles, seem to form pictures or shapes, the content of which depends on your viewing position. Perhaps the images change depending on who is viewing the wings.

You think for a few seconds. Why shouldn't you take both arks and get everything possible? If Ark 2 contains the Mona Lisa, you get it! If it only has the spider, at least you get the golden goblet. It seems foolish for you to select only Ark 2, because if you do so you can't get more than the Mona Lisa, and there's a slight possibility you'll walk away with nothing. It's a long trip to come away with no reward. So, clearly, it is to your advantage to select both arks.

👁 👁 👁

"What do most people do?" you ask the angels.

"Your scientists have tried this paradox on many human philosophers. You should try it yourself on friends. If you do, you'll find that about 50 percent say to take just Ark 2 and 50 percent will say take both. Your scientists and philosophers cannot agree what the 'correct' answer is, and neither can we."

In the distance, you see several angels having coffee at a table, talking to one another as they wait for more test subjects like yourself. Yellow sunlight gleams off their wings, casting a tangle of golden reflections.

As you walk with the angel, you think further on the subject. Suppose that the seraphim have abducted thousands of people in the past and performed the same experiment. Assume that in every case, the seraphim predicted correctly. Those people who took both arks always got the golden cup plus the spider; those who took only Ark 2 got the Mona Lisa. Knowing this, wouldn't you be a moron to take both boxes?

The seraphim, reading your mind, say, "However, you can reason just as seriously in the opposite direction. Consider the following demonstration."

In their next experiment, the seraphim have abducted both you and the president of the United States. The seraphim have now replaced the opaque Ark 1 with one made of glass. You can see the wonderful goblet inside. You can't see into Ark 2.

**Table 5.2**

| Glass Ark | Wooden Ark 2 |
| --- | --- |
| 🏆 | ? |

The President, who sits on the other side of the table, has cut a hole in the back, so he knows what is inside Ark 2. He knows if the Mona Lisa is there or not. He is not allowed to signal you or he will be sent to Hell. But, because he is a nice guy, he wants you to take both arks. He wants you to go home at least with the golden cup regardless of the state of Ark 2. Can't you take advantage of the fact that the seraphim have already committed to the contents of the arks? If the Mona Lisa is there already, you'll get it. If it isn't there, what do you lose?

The angel takes a step closer. "One way to think about the paradox is to draw a 'payoff matrix' for our dilemma. The argument for selecting only Ark 2 comes from the idea that you want to maximize the expected value of the outcome."

"Go on," you say.

"Game theory calculates the expected utility, or value, of each action by multiplying each of the outcomes by the probability of the outcome given a particular action.[1] In our particular problem, we can list the following possible outcomes." The angel sketches on a blackboard with the talon of his left foot:

**Table 5.3    "Payoff Matrix" for the Angelic Paradox**

|  | Angels Predict You Select Only Ark 2 | Angels Predict You Select both Ark 1 and 2 |
|---|---|---|
| Your Choice 1: (Select only Ark 2) | 🖼️ $500,000,000 | 🕷️ ($0, worthless) |
| Your Choice 2: (Select both arks) | 🖼️🏆 $500,001,000 | 🏆 $1,000 |

The angel explains to you that the cells in the table with the thick borders represent the usual outcomes that happen almost all the time due to the angels' accuracy of prediction. The biggest possible payoff that could conceivably occur is the $500,001,000 value of both the painting and the cup shown in the cell with the Mona Lisa and the goblet. This is an extremely rare event owing to the angels' near omniscience. For an omniscient God, the expected utility of taking both arks is:

$$(a \times \$1,000) + (b \times \$500,000,000) = \$1,000$$

Here $a = 1$ and $b = 0$ because God is certain that you will choose both boxes and hence always leaves Ark 1 full and always leaves Ark 2 with the spider. Similarly the expected utility of taking only Ark 2 is $500,000,000, and in this case $a=0$ and $b=1$. If you take what is in the second ark, the angel almost certainly will have predicted this and put the Mona Lisa there. Almost certainly you will get this wonderful painting, an oil painting (1503–1506) by Leonardo da Vinci, which, the angel reminds you, usually resides in the Louvre, Paris. If you take what is in both arks, the being will have predicted this with high likelihood and will have not put the Mona Lisa in the second ark. Almost certainly, you will get only the $1,000.

"What happens to these equations if you are not a perfect predictor?" you say.

"Until now we have assumed that we can predict with near certainty, but we can also consider the problem if we are correct only 80 percent of the time." The expected utility of taking both arks is the following." The angel writes on the board:

$$(0.8 \times \$1,000) + (0.2 \times \$500,000,000) = \$100,000,800$$

The angel explains that the expected utility of taking only Ark 2 is:

$$(0.2 \times \$0) + (0.8 \times \$500,000,000) = \$400,000,000$$

Using this logic, it seems indeed your best strategy is to select only the second Ark.

However, using another logic, you can examine the two possible states for each of the angels' actions. (These states correspond to the two columns in the previous table.) Taking both arks seems to be a better gamble, because for each of the angels' two possible choices, you get $1,000 more than you would by taking only Ark 2. Another way to think about this is that the angel has already made his prediction and has either put the Mona Lisa in the second ark or has not. The presence or absence of the painting is *already determined*. If the angel put the paining in the second ark, you will get both it and the golden cup if you take both arks—and just the painting if you take only the second ark. If the angel did not put the Mona Lisa in the second ark, you will get the golden cup if you take both arks, and you will get no painting if you take only the second ark. In either case, it seems you will do better by $1,000 if you take what is in both arks rather than only what is in the second ark. Each argument is powerful.

You look at the angel and wonder what to do next.

The angel comes closer. "If you believe that we can predict your behavior with very high accuracy, you should choose to take only Ark 2. Pretend that we have a time traveling machine or a wormhole viewer that lets us view the future. Pretend we can bring back a photograph from the future of what ark or arks you choose. If this is true, then certainly you should only take Ark 2."

"This makes me feel like I am not really making a choice at all, that choice is an illusion."

You look more closely at the angels as a shiver goes up your spine. The creatures have some aspects with which you are familiar. They are winged like angels and have long trailing beards as you imagined the biblical prophets to have. But that is where the similarity ends. Their arms are covered with bubbly skin that occasionally pulsates like little balloons inflating and deflating. Their eyes are iridescent balls, the size of avocados, with hard crystalline corneas.

The angel puts before you two glasses. "Here is another challenge. In the first glass is $1,000. In the second glass are the digits 19382. You do not know if these five digits, in order, are in the first 1,000 digits of the number pi. If 19382 turns out to be in the first 1,000 digits of pi, then you get $100 billion, making you richer than Bill Gates."

You look closer at the glasses and scratch your head.

"Confused?" the angels say. "I have chosen the digits to be in pi *if* I predict you will take only glass 2, but I have picked a sequence of numbers not in the first 1,000 digits of pi if I predict you will take *both* glasses. Do you take both glasses? Again, the logic is the same as before."

"Stop," you say. "My head is swimming. I don't want to think about numbers."

The angel wheels out a cart. On the cart are two glass tanks. "In the first tank is $1,000. In the second tank is a cat that is not moving. You do not know if the cat is alive or dead. If it turns out to be alive, then you get $1 billion. I have chosen the cat to be alive if I predict you will take only tank 2 but have picked a dead cat if I predict you will take both glass tanks. Do you take both glass tanks?"

"The logic is the same in all these gambits?" you say.

All the angels nod in unison. Their wing feathers move forward in what you now recognize as a seraphim sign of affirmation. "Let us give just a few more examples about why this is so paradoxical."

Another angel wheels out a cart. On the cart are two glass tanks. In the first tank is $1,000. In the second tank are four words: "Abraham rides an ox." You do not know if this phrase is in the Bible. If it turns out to be in the Bible, then you get $1 billion. The angels have chosen the words from the Bible if they predict you will take only Tank 2, but they have chosen words not in the Bible if they predict you will take both tanks. Do you take both tanks? Again, the logic is the same as before.

Next the angels wheel out a cart with 1,000 glass vials, each holding a dollar bill. The vials glisten like shiny diamonds. If the angels expect you to take all of the vials, they have put nothing else in them. But if they expect you to take only one vial, they have added to that vial a valuable emerald.

You further imagine that there have been a million previous such experiments with the vials, half of the experiments involving you and your friends as players. Almost every time, the player who took a single vial got the emerald, and the player who took all vials got only the money. Logically, it appears you should take only one vial. Past experience suggests this approach. But don't you have everything to gain and nothing to lose if the next time you play you take all the vials?

## MUSINGS AND SPECULATIONS

*All the angel's abilities were shorn from him, ripped out of the angelic sphere by a merciless force. And why? he asked again. He was indeed intolerant of these new humans and their needs, but he had also been given free will. The Voice had given him free will with no mention of such consequence.*

— *Peter Lord-Wolff,* The Silence in Heaven

Newcomb's Paradox, as the paradox in this chapter is formally known, provides a dramatic nontheological illustration of the problem of divine foreknowledge and human freedom.[2] The problem was formulated in 1960 by physicist William A. Newcomb of the University of California's Lawrence Livermore Laboratory. The puzzle was further elucidated by philosopher Robert Nozick in 1969,[3] and it has generated so much debate that some philosophers have called the enthusiasm "Newcombmania."[4] As with many mathematical puzzles, Newcomb's popularity rose dramatically when it was popularized in Martin Gardner's 1973 "Mathematical Games" column in *Scientific American.*[5]

Experts still tear their hair out over this dilemma. Many disagree as to your best strategy in the original problem. Robert Nozick recommends taking both boxes. In the *British Journal for the Philosophy of Science,* Maya Bar-Hillel and Avishai Margalit recommend you become a millionaire by taking only Ark 2.[6] Martin Gardner asks, "Can it be that Newcomb's paradox validates free will by invalidating the possibility, in principle, of a predictor capable of guessing a person's choice between two equally rational actions with better than 50 percent accuracy?"[7]

The famous science popularizer Isaac Asimov even wrote his own personal opinion on this paradox:

> I would, without hesitation, take both boxes. . . . I am myself a determinist, but it is perfectly clear to me that any human being worthy of being considered a

human being (including most certainly myself) would prefer free will, if such a thing could exist. . . . Now, then, suppose you take both boxes and it turns out (as it almost certainly will) that God has foreseen this and placed nothing in the second box. You will then, at least, have expressed your willingness to gamble on his nonomniscience and on your own free will and will have willingly given up a million dollars for the sake of that willingness—itself a snap of the finger in the face of the Almighty and a vote, however futile, for free will. . . . And, of course, if God has muffed and left a million dollars in the box, then not only will you have gained that million, but *far more important* you will have demonstrated God's nonomniscience. If you take only the second box, however, you get your damned million and not only are you a slave but also you have demonstrated your willingness to be a slave for that million and you are not someone I recognize as human.[8]

Although Robert Nozick originally presented the paradox as a dilemma within the areas of logic and game theory, many philosophers quickly realized that it also had implications for religion, where the supernatural "being" or angel is replaced by God, and where the paradox suggests several additional problems dealing with theological fatalism.

Opinions and interpretations continue to flow like water gushing from a philosopher's garden hose. Bar-Hillel and Margalit believe that the paradox implies that "there is no free choice, but the illusion of free choice remains, and one has to behave as if free choice exists."[9] On the other hand, according to author George Schlesinger, Newcomb's Paradox shows that an infallible and omniscient Predictor cannot exist.[10]

Unwilling to give up the dual idea of God's omniscience and human freedom, philosopher Dennis Ahern says Newcomb's Paradox demonstrates that simultaneous existence of foreknowledge and freedom is an unresolved paradox. For example, it is irrational to believe that either

(1) A human has control over God's past beliefs without recourse to the "objectionable" notion of backward causation, or (2) An action otherwise free becomes not free simply because it is foreknown or predicted. But the falsity of (1) implies the truth of (2) and the falsity of (2) implies the truth of (1).[11]

Thus, if infallible foreknowledge existed, "we should have sound reasons for believing it would not have a bearing on whether an action was performed freely *and* [for believing] there would be no freedom of action."[12]

William Lane Craig, a devout Christian and research professor of philosophy at Talbot School of Theology, La Mirada, California, has written extensively on Newcomb's Paradox and its religious implications. He reasons:

Given that God foreknows what I shall choose, it only follows that I shall not choose otherwise, not that I could not. The fact that I cannot actualize worlds in which God's prediction errs is no infringement on my freedom, since all this means is that I am not free to actualize worlds in which I both perform some action *a* and do not perform *a*.[13]

Craig would suggest that Newcomb's Paradox is not a logical basis for thinking that since (1) "There is a Mona Lisa in Ark 2 because I am going to choose Ark 2" and (2) "Were I going to choose Ark 1 and Ark 2, the Mona Lisa would not be in Ark 2," it follows that (3) "I am not free to choose Ark 1 and Ark 2." The human player is free—but he cannot escape being "seen" making his free selection. Craig concludes that Newcomb's Paradox makes divine foreknowledge and human freedom compatible. He writes:

The pastness of God's knowledge serves neither to make God's beliefs counterfactually closed nor to rob us of genuine freedom. It is evident that our decisions determine God's past beliefs about those decisions and do so without invoking an objectionable backward causation. It is also clear that in the context of foreknowledge, backtracking counterfactuals are entirely appropriate and that no alteration of the past occurs.[14]

### The Death of Superpredictors

Let's look further to see where Newcomb's Paradox may lead. According to Martin Gardner, certain events are in principle unpredictable when predictors are allowed to interact causally with the event being predicted, as God seems to do in the Bible.[15] Gardner says it is not illogical to suppose that the future is totally determined, whether or not an omniscient God exists, but as soon as we permit a superbeing to make predictions that interact with the event being predicted, "we encounter contradictions that render the existence of such a superpredictor impossible."[16] Consider the following example. A god (or other supernatural being) knows that when you eat dinner on Saturday night you will eat sushi. If the god keeps this knowledge to himself, then there is no contradiction. However, if the god tells you of his prediction, you can falsify it by eating steak on Saturday night. Similarly, predictions of the "if, then, else" variety create various challenges for us while trying to understand hypothetical superpredictors. As just one example of this type of construct in the Bible, we find, "Elijah will turn the hearts of the fathers to their children, and the hearts of the children to their fathers; or else I [God] will come and strike the land with a curse" (Malachi 4:6). This is another example of a superbeing making predictions that interact with the events being predicted.

According to Gardner, Newcomb's problem does not settle the question of whether the future is completely determined; however, the paradox brings us closer to the powerful and perhaps unanswerable challenge of defining what free choice really is. God's simply knowing the future does not necessarily limit free will. Gardner suggests that one way to avoid these paradoxes is to regard God as omniscient only in the sense that He knows all that can be known, a situation that would allow "for parts of the future to be in principle unknowable." Using this logic, God would not do logically impossible things, such as alter the past or construct a square circle. Perhaps there are events in the future that God, in a similar way, cannot know because God lives in time, and the future is not determined. This would be an example of a powerful but finite god. (Similar issues are discussed further in Chapter 16 and "Some Final Thoughts.")

Let's consider three types, or levels, of omniscience that God may possess:

1. Omniscience *A:* God perceives all things as they happen and therefore knows of their occurrence.
2. Omniscience *B:* God knows everything in the past, present, and future.
3. Omniscience *C:* God knows everything that it is possible to know.

If God possesses all three, can He "will" to do things in one way rather than another when He already knows what He will will to be done? If we have an *A* + *B* God, then what would a *C* God know more about? Perhaps the *A* + *B* God knows all events, but the *C* God additionally knows all things in addition to events, such as the fact that the square root of 2 equals 1.414214. . . . If you are a religious person, would you be disappointed if you learned that God were only an *A* God and simply made educated guesses about the future? In the closing "Some Final Thoughts" section I talk about the scenario of multiple universes, in which a *C* God might be omniscient in one universe but not have knowledge of others.

☉ ☉ ☉

Here is another prediction example using machinery rather than beings. Pretend you are sitting in front of IBM's largest supercomputer, called "Deep Stew."

**You and IBM's "Deep Stew"**

You ask Deep Stew to predict whether it will rain in the next one minute. If the prediction is no, it speaks the word "no." If yes, it speaks the word "yes." You next ask Deep Stew to predict whether it will say "yes." By making the event part of the prediction, the situation is complicated. This suggests that logical contradictions arise when a prediction interacts with the predicted event, even when humans are not involved. (Say goodbye to Deep Stew.) Gardner's final assessment is that the god or angel in Newcomb's Paradox, even if accurate only 51 percent of the time, forces a logical contradiction that makes such a god impossible. One perfectly good argument says you can maximize your reward by taking only the closed ark. Another perfectly good argument says the best way to maximize your reward is to take both arks. Because the two conclusions are contradictory, the predictor cannot exist.

Most Christian and Islamic sects believe in an omniscient God who knows every future event. If this is true, can our will be truly free? And if we do not have free will, then how could we be morally responsible? Why would God punish us if we were bad, as He does throughout the Old Testament?

Theologians like Maimonides (Moses ben Maimon, 1135–1204), Saint Augustine of Hippo (354–430), and Saint Thomas Aquinas (1224–1274) believed that God is outside of time and can see all history at once. It is from our own limited perspective that we are making our choices. But still, they are choices. However, if an omniscient God sees all time at once, does the future exist even now for him, and do you think all our decisions are truly free? Clearly, many people have believed that just because God could *see* our choices in advance doesn't mean He *made* them.

One definition of free will is doing whatever the hell you want to do, even if your desires are predetermined by something else such as the axons and dendrites in your cerebral cortex. If your actions are predetermined, but neither you nor anyone else knows what is going to happen before it happens, then many conflicts of free will versus determinism are avoided. The only way that determinism can affect your sense of free will is for you to learn of your predestination. William Poundstone writes, in *Labyrinths of Reason*, "Presumably God knows whether or not you will squeeze the toothpaste tube from the middle tomorrow morning. No problem—as long as God doesn't tell you. The unacceptable case is *knowing* that you are destined to make such and such a choice, and being 'forced' by all those unfeeling atoms to do it. Only then is deterministic physical law the coercive agency that prevents us from having free will."[17]

Obviously, a lot of philosophers and theologians have wondered about free will. The Calvinist Theodorus Beza (1519–1605) believed that because God was omnipotent, humans contributed *nothing* toward their salvation. God had determined since before the creation of the universe who would be damned and who would be saved.

Some of the most powerful biblical examples of God's slipping into the time stream and directly interacting with people occur in Numbers 10–14, in which God does not punish the enemies of the Jews but the Jews themselves. Did you know that when the Israelites grumble about continually eating manna in the desert after following Moses out of Egypt, God sends thousands of quail to the ungrateful complainers? When the thousands of people eat the quail, God strikes them dead with a plague at Kobroth Hattaavah, which in Hebrew means "graves of gluttony." Did you know that when Miriam questions Moses's authority, God afflicts her with dreaded leprosy? (Miriam was the sister of Moses and had helped rescued baby Moses from death.) Luckily, God eventually provided a cure for her.

God also killed the ten Jews who spied on the Canaanites. These Jews had been so scared about attacking the people of Canaan that they returned an inaccurate report about the land. God also forced the men's children to be shepherds in the desert for 40 years, "suffering for your unfaithfulness." In Judges 2:13–15, we find God angry and punishing his people:

> The Israelites followed and worshiped various gods of the peoples around them. They provoked the LORD to anger because they forsook him and served Baal and the Ashtoreths. In his anger against Israel the LORD handed them over to raiders who plundered them. He sold them to their enemies all around, whom they were no longer able to resist. Whenever Israel went out to fight, the hand of the LORD was against them to defeat them, just as he had sworn to them. They were in great distress.

A major theme of the Old Testament is God's continual punishment of the Jews when they stray. I find that while most of my colleagues know that God punished the Jews' enemies, they have no idea of the pervasive killing of Jews by God or of God's aiding the Jews' enemies in the killing of Jews. (Many more examples of God's anger and killing are given in Appendices C and D. At times these examples appear to be counter to the notion of God giving humans free will.)

In John Milton's *Paradise Lost*, God ponders Adam and Eve and how their making bad moves results from their free will, even though God already knew how they would behave:

They themselves decreed their own revolt, not I. If I foreknew, foreknowledge had no influence on their fault, which had no less proved certain unforeknown.[18]

Karen Armstrong comments on Milton's God as the one who is reflected in the whole course of salvation history, from Adam and the murder of Abel, to the Flood, the Tower of Babel, the call of Abraham, the Exodus from Egypt, and the exile to Babylon: "It occurs to the reader that there must have been an easier and more direct way to redeem mankind. The fact that this tortuous plan with its constant failures and false stars is decreed *in advance* can only cast grave doubts on the intelligence of its Author. Milton's God can inspire little confidence."[19]

### Hypertime

As I mentioned, many philosophers have believed that God lives outside of time. Today physicists think about similar concepts in the language of Einstein's theory of general relativity, which describes space and time as a unified four-dimensional continuum called "spacetime." To best understand this, consider yourself as having three spatial dimensions—height, width, and breadth. You also have the dimension of duration—how long you last. Modern physics thus views our universe as having three spatial dimensions and one additional dimension of time. Stop and consider some mystical implications of spacetime. Can something exist outside of spacetime? What would it be like to exist outside of spacetime? For example, Thomas Aquinas, if he were alive today, would believe God to be outside of spacetime and thus capable of seeing all of the universe's objects, past and future, in one blinding instant. An observer existing outside of time, in a region called "hypertime," can see the past and future all at once. In a strange sense, when we scan back and forth over a musical score, we are like a hyperbeing who lives outside of time. A musical score makes time solid, which is spatial. A musician can see past, present, and future all at once.[20]

There are many other examples of beings in literature and myth who live outside of spacetime. Many people living in the Middle Ages believed that angels were nonmaterial intelligences who lived by a time different from human time, and that God was entirely outside of time. Lord Byron (1788–1824) aptly describes these ideas in the first act of his play *Cain: A Mystery*, where the fallen angel Lucifer says:

> With us acts are exempt from time, and we
> Can crowd eternity into an hour,

Or stretch an hour into eternity.
We breathe not by a mortal measurement—
But that's a mystery.[21]

One direct way to visualize what might be God's notion of spacetime is through the use of an "eternitygram" representing two butterflies gliding toward one another. Figure 5.1 shows two spatial dimensions along with the additional dimension of time. You can think of successive instants in time as stacks of movie frames that form a 3-D picture in hypertime in the eternitygram. Figure 5.1 is a "timeless" picture of butterflies coming toward one another in eternity, an eternity in which all instants of time lie frozen like musical notes on a musical score. Hyperbeings looking at the butterflies in this chunk of spacetime would see past, present, and future all at once. What kind of relationship with humans could a creature (or God) have who lived completely outside of time? How could it (or He) relate to us in our changing world? One of my favorite modern examples of God living outside of time is described in Anne Rice's novel *Memnoch the Devil*. At one point, Lestat, Rice's protagonist, says, "I saw as God sees, and I saw as if Forever and in All Directions." Lestat looks over a balustrade in Heaven to see the entire history of the world:

the world as I had never seen it in all its ages, with all its secrets of the past revealed. I had only to rush to the railing and I could peer down into the time of Eden or Ancient Mesopotamia, or a moment when Roman legions had marched through the woods of my earthly home. I would see the great eruption of Vesuvius spill its horrid deadly ash down upon the ancient living city of Pompeii. Everything there to be known and finally comprehended, all questions settled, the smell of another time, the taste of it.[22]

Figure 5.2 shows a schematic diagram of dancing butterflies in spacetime, just as Figure 5.1 shows two butterflies nearly colliding in spacetime. The track of each butterfly through spacetime is represented by a line. In each of the three squares in Figure 5.2, the time axis is vertical. This means that time gradually proceeds up the page, with the past at the bottom and the future toward the top. The space axis in each square is horizontal. A butterfly sitting still would be represented by a vertical line in the squares because the butterfly's horizontal (spatial) component never changes. If all butterfly world lines were somehow fixed like tunnels in the ice of spacetime, and all that "moved" was our perception shifting up the page in the figure as time "passed," we would still see a complex dance of interacting butterflies even though nothing was

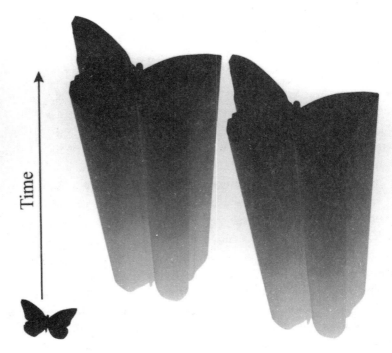

*Fig. 5.1. An eternitygram for two colliding butterflies.*

moving. (A *world line* describes the path of an object through space and time.) Perhaps an alien would see this differently than we do. In some sense, all butterfly tracks and interactions may be considered fixed in the geometry of spacetime, with all movement and change being an illusion resulting from our changing psychological perception of the moment "now." Some mystics have suggested that spacetime is like a novel being "read" by the soul, the "soul" being a kind of eye or observer that stands outside of spacetime, slowly gazing up along the time axis.[23]

Of course, many stories have been devoted to the experience of time. One of my favorite short stories is Norman Spinrad's "The Weed of Time," which describes a boy who eats a weed that makes him see his whole lifetime as simultaneously present. Therefore, as a baby, he already knows he will eat the weed before (according to our limited point of view) he has ever eaten it! David Masson's "Traveler's Rest" describes a war in a land where everyone's perception of time slows down as they travel south. One young soldier on a short vacation travels south, marries, and has children. Then, in middle age, the soldier receives a message telling him that his vacation is over. He travels north to arrive in his barracks 22 minutes (local time) after he left.

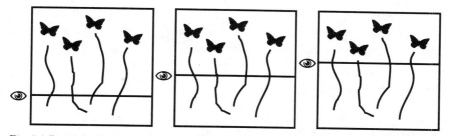

*Fig. 5.2.Dancing butterflies, frozen in spacetime. (The track of each butterfly through spacetime is represented by a line.) Is time an illusion? If butterfly world lines were somehow fixed in space-time, and all that "moved" was our perception shifting "up the page" as time "passed," we would still see a complex dance of butterflies, even though nothing was moving.*

What is time? For centuries, these questions have intrigued mystics, philosophers, and scientists. Much of ancient Greek philosophy was concerned with understanding the concept of eternity, and the subject of time is central to all the world's religions and cultures. Can the flow of time be stopped? Certainly some mystics thought so. Angelus Silesius, a sixth-century philosopher and poet, thought the flow of time could be suspended by mental powers:

> Time is of your own making;
> its clock ticks in your head.
> The moment you stop thought
> time too stops dead.

Most cultures have a grammar with past and future tenses, and also units such as seconds and minutes and days. We have words for *yesterday* and *tomorrow*. Yet we cannot say exactly what time is. Although the study of time became scientific during the time of Galileo and Newton, in the sixteenth and seventeenth centuries, a comprehensive explanation was given only in this century by Einstein, who declared, in effect, that time is simply what a clock reads. The clock can be the rotation of a planet, sand falling in an hour glass, a heartbeat, or vibrations of a cesium atom. A typical grandfather clock follows the simple Newtonian law that states that the velocity of a body not subject to external forces remains constant. This means that clock hands travel equal distances in equal times. While this kind of clock is useful for everyday life, modern science finds that time can be warped in various ways, like clay in the hands of a cosmic sculptor.

Ancient legends of time distortion are, in fact, quite common. One of the most poetic descriptions of time travel occurs in a popular medieval legend describing a monk entranced for a minute by the song of a magical bird. When the bird stops singing, the monk discovers that several hundred years have passed. Another example is the Muslim legend of Muhammad being carried by a mare into heaven. After a long visit, the prophet returns to Earth just in time to catch a jar of water the horse had kicked over before starting its ascent.

### The Mystery of the Seraphim

Angels are mentioned in the Bible more than 270 times. Throughout history, humans have wondered how these heavenly beings are supposed to be organized. Around A.D. 500, the theologian pseudo-Dionysius developed a hierarchy of nine angelic ranks ordered by their perceived closeness to God and thus to omniscience. The names are all in the Bible:

**First comes God**
Next come:
1. Seraphim
  2. Cherubim
    3. Thrones
      4. Dominions
        5. Virtues
          6. Powers
            7. Principalities
              8. Archangels
                9. Angels

Who in the heck is this pseudo-Dionysius fellow? Scholars believe he was a Syrian monk. Known only by his pseudonym, he wrote numerous Greek treatises that blended Christian theology and mysticism. Pseudo-Dionysius believed that God was essentially unknowable.

Number 1 on pseudo-Dionysius's list are the seraphim. These are the angels who guard the throne of God and are mentioned in the Book of Isaiah:

> In the year that King Uzziah died, I saw the Lord seated on a throne, high and exalted, and the train of his robe filled the temple. Above him were seraphs, each with six wings: With two wings they covered their faces, with two they covered their feet, and with two they were flying. And they were calling to one another: "Holy, holy, holy is the LORD Almighty; the whole earth is full of his glory." At the sound of their voices the doorposts and thresholds shook and the temple was filled with Smoke. (Isaiah 6:1–4)

Isaiah, a mere mortal, was too nervous to speak in the presence of God. One of the seraphim solved that problem by burning Isaiah's lips:

"Woe to me!" I cried. "I am ruined! For I am a man of unclean lips, and I live among a people of unclean lips, and my eyes have seen the King, the LORD Almighty." Then one of the seraphs flew to me with a live coal in his hand, which he had taken with tongs from the altar. With it he touched my mouth and said, "See, this has touched your lips; your guilt is taken away and your sin atoned for." (Isaiah 6:6–7)

The word "seraphs" is sometimes translated as "burning ones," which may refer to their passion for God as well as the hot coal they used on Isaiah's lips.

Most of us think of cherubs as chubby little babies flying around on Valentine's Day cards. In the Bible, however, they are much scarier. These were the creatures posted at the edge of Eden with a flaming sword. The cherubim were ordered to block the garden to prevent Adam and Eve from returning. These creatures looked quite strange:

In appearance their form was that of a man, but each of them had four faces and four wings. Their legs were straight; their feet were like those of a calf and gleamed like burnished bronze. Under their wings on their four sides they had the hands of a man. All four of them had faces and wings, and their wings touched one another. Each one went straight ahead; they did not turn as they moved. Their faces looked like this: Each of the four had the face of a man, and on the right side each had the face of a lion, and on the left the face of an ox; each also had the face of an eagle. Such were their faces. Their wings were spread out upward; each had two wings, one touching the wing of another creature on either side, and two wings covering its body. Each one went straight ahead. Wherever the spirit would go, they would go, without turning as they went. The appearance of the living creatures was like burning coals of fire or like torches. Fire moved back and forth among the creatures; it was bright, and lightning flashed out of it. The creatures sped back and forth like flashes of lightning. (Ezekiel 1:5–14)

These are certainly dangerous creatures, and, like the seraphim, they sing God's praises:

Now the cherubim were standing on the south side of the temple when the man went in, and a cloud filled the inner court. Then the glory of the LORD rose from above the cherubim and moved to the threshold of the temple. The cloud filled the temple, and the court was full of the radiance of the glory of the LORD. The sound of the wings of the cherubim could be heard as far away as the outer court, like the voice of God Almighty when he speaks. (Ezekiel 10:4–5)

If we closely inspect the Bible, we can find numerous references to angels, and Jesus taught of their existence: "Do you think I cannot call on my Father, and he will at once put at my disposal more than twelve legions of angels?" (Matthew 26:53). According to the Bible, God created the angels (Psalms 148:2, 5; Colossians 1:16) before the world and humans existed (Job 38:6, 7). The angels appear to have personalities, emotions, and desires, and God sometimes carefully controls them:

> Though you already know all this, I want to remind you that the Lord delivered his people out of Egypt, but later destroyed those who did not believe. And the angels who did not keep their positions of authority but abandoned their own home—these he has kept in darkness, bound with everlasting chains for judgment on the great Day. (Jude 1:5–6)

Angels don't have sex with other angels: "When the dead rise, they will neither marry nor be given in marriage; they will be like the angels in heaven" (Mark 12:25). Apparently, Jesus said that angels are immortal: "The people of this age marry and are given in marriage. But those who are considered worthy of taking part in that age and in the resurrection from the dead will neither marry nor be given in marriage, and they can no longer die; for they are like the angels" (Luke 20:34–36).

### Mona Lisa on Acid

Let's end this chapter on a zany note and focus on the Mona Lisa painting mentioned in the paradox of the goblet, spider, and two arks. I have little doubt that the most famous and most admired painting of all time is Leonardo da Vinci's *Mona Lisa del Gioconda*.[24] In 1506, Leonardo painted the portrait on a poplar wood panel. Napoleon, at the height of his power, removed the Mona Lisa from the Louvre in Paris and hung it up in his bedroom. When Napoleon was banished, the Mona Lisa returned to the Louvre.

Did the angels in our scenario steal the painting of the Mona Lisa to place in the ark? No one knows for sure. However, few people realize that in 1911 a thief from Italy stole the Mona Lisa from the Louvre. A day passed before the museum employees realized the painting had been stolen, because they assumed it had been removed by the official museum photographer. After a week-long search, museum officials found the painting's frame in a staircase. The Mona Lisa resurfaced two years later in Florence, when Vincenzo Perugia attempted to sell the painting to the Uffizi Gallery for $100,000.

To steal the painting, Perugia had spent a night hiding in a little-used room at the Louvre. While the museum was closed he simply walked up to the Mona Lisa, removed it from the wall, walked to the stairway, and then cut the painting from the frame. He left the building by breaking through a locked door after removing the doorknob.

In 1956 someone tossed acid on a lower portion of the painting. Subsequent restoration required years of work. Today the Mona Lisa has become so valuable that it resides behind triplex glass. The bulletproof enclosure is kept at a constant 68 degrees Fahrenheit with a humidity of 55 percent; a built-in air conditioner and 9 pounds of silica gel ensure there is no change in the air condition. Once a year the box is opened to check the painting and to maintain the air conditioning system. In the early 1960s, the Mona Lisa was insured for $100 million for its move to America for exhibitions.

One of the most controversial versions of the Mona Lisa is in the Vernon Collection in the United States. This painting shows columns on either side of the woman. These columns are not apparent in the Louvre's version. The owners consider the artwork to be authentic and value it at $2.5 million. However, the Louvre is satisfied that it owns the actual painting by Leonardo, because this painting has an unambiguous record of ownership from the time of Leonardo.

Computer analyses show that the Mona Lisa's colors probably were once very different than they are today. The woman's cheeks were rosy, and the sky was blue. X-rays have shown there are three different versions of the Mona Lisa hidden under the present one. Although the true identity of the Mona Lisa is unknown, most experts believe she was the wife of a sixteenth-century Florentine businessman, Francesco del Giocondo, who commissioned the portrait (hence the name "La Gioconda"). Dr. Lillian Schwartz of Bell Labs once suggested that the Mona Lisa is actually a self-portrait and has tried to support her theory by analyzing the facial features of Leonardo da Vinci and comparing them with the features of the "woman" in the painting.

---

Simon Peter said to them: "Let Mary leave us, for women are not worthy of life." Jesus said: "Look, I will guide her in order to make her male, so that she too may become a living spirit like You males. For every female who will make herself male will enter the Kingdom of Heaven."
—a mystifying and creepy verse from the Gospel of Thomas, verse 114

Pretend you are the Cosmos—strange, alone, knowing nothing except that you are self aware. Pretend you find yourself going mad with anguish because there is no other. Pretend that in desperation you try dividing your awareness into smaller awarenesses, but since they know they are you, they dreamily and without curiosity move ever steadily back into you. Pretend that these creations do not solve your problem: there is still only you and no other. Pretend you try an alternate plan, dividing your awareness again but this time into parts unaware that they are you. With memories erased, their veiled awareness still reflects your anguish in myriad permutations of your aloneness.

> —Martin Olson, a fragment from the *Encyclopedia of Hell*

Acknowledging mistakes and learning from them is an excellent pedagogical technique—better in many respects than pretending to be all-knowing or perfect. . . . A God who can admit that His mind has been changed by mere humans is a truly great teacher.

> —Alan Dershowitz, *The Genesis of Justice*

The unique personality which is the real life in me, I can not gain unless I search for the real life, the spiritual quality, in others. I am myself spiritually dead unless I reach out to the fine quality dormant in others. For it is only with the god enthroned in the innermost shrine of the other, that the god hidden in me, will consent to appear.

> —Felix Adler, "The Ethical Philosophy of Life"

All the choir of heaven and the furniture of earth, in a word all those bodies which compose the mighty frame of the world, have not any subsistence without a mind . . . their being is to be perceived or known. . . . So long as they are not actually perceived by me, or do not exist in my mind . . . they must either have no existence at all, or else subsist in the mind of some eternal spirit.

> —George Berkeley, *The Principles of Human Knowledge*

# CHAPTER 6

# The Devil's Offer

*God gave us the darkness so we could see the stars.*
*—Johnny Cash, in "Farmers Almanac"*

SEVEN A.M. WITH UNNERVING SUDDENNESS, THE ALARM FROM YOUR electronic clock wakes you from the depths of a pleasant dream. "Damn," you whisper. A romantic image fades like an angel drifting off into distant clouds. Why does the alarm have to go off now?

Even though you've had the clock since high school, you've never become accustomed to its shrill beeping. Within seconds you silence it by reaching for a button on its surface. Your finger encounters the old, familiar scratch from the last time you threw the clock across your bedroom. Now the scratch allows you to guide your finger to the button bringing blessed silence.

You slowly sit up in bed, push aside your blankets, and turn on the *Today Show* with your TV's remote control. You listen with half an ear as Katie Couric interviews Madonna. Outside a few birds chirp in the cloudy morning air.

There's just one problem. A big problem. You have actually died in your sleep and, unfortunately, have gone to hell.

You look around. Your bedroom is a cheap facade. The bird outside is a mechanical contrivance that flies away screeching. The TV set disappears to be replaced with a devil. He approaches.

The devil comes so close you can smell his hot, sulfurous breath. "I have a game of chance for you to play. If you win the game, you can go to heaven, but if you lose you must stay forever in hell. You can only play the game once."

"This sounds ominous." You try to appear calm.

"Ha! You've got no choice. If you play on the first day you have a one-half chance of winning. If you play on the second day you have a two-thirds chance of winning. If you play on the third day, you have a three-quarters chance of winning, and so on." He hands you a card that reads: $1/2, 2/3, 3/4, 4/5, \ldots$

The devil stamps his clawed foot on the warm ground. "My question to you is this. When is the most rational day for you to play?"

Pondering this question, you follow the devil as he leads you across a strange land of varicolored weeds and a few stunted trees. Occasionally you see gases oozing from mist-covered swamps and reeds and cattails moving in some of the smaller marshes. In these pools stand gibbons of various sizes and colors. Everywhere is the smell of decay—the putrefaction of nearly liquid masses resembling the rarefying remains of long-dead gibbons. By comparison, this stench makes the stink of a cesspool seem like a new perfume by Chanel.

You step back in terror and begin to ponder the Devil's Offer. "If I wait a whole year before playing, my chances of winning are a very good 0.997268. This number comes from 365/366."

The devil nods. "Yes, but if you wait a year and a day, your chances are increased by 0.000007."

"It seems hardly worth delaying for that tiny increased chance of winning."

"Don't be a fool. It's true that 0.000007 seems tiny, but the reward of winning is *infinite*. Eternal bliss in heaven with attractive angels catering to your every whim. Don't you think a finitely large extra chance of winning something infinite is worth more than your finite suffering spending one more day in hell?"

The devil may have a point, but you are distracted. How did you get here in hell? Is it real? What do you do when something so absurd, so out of place in the scheme of everyday living, takes place? Oh, one can speculate about what one should do if this or that happens, but no one can say what action one would take when the fabric of reality begins to tear. And when it happens to you on that hot summer morning, you do not stand there long trying to figure out a rational, scientific explanation for it all. It would almost be funny, if you were not living through the experience.

You think about what the devil said about your chances of winning freedom. The devil seems right when he says that waiting a year and a day is better than waiting a year. In terms of game theory, the utility of waiting a mere 24 hours (the extra chance of winning multiplied by the infinite payoff) will always be infinite. Perhaps you should wait in his scenario. But given this logic, it always seems worth it for you to wait an additional day. And that means there will be no limit to how long you should wait in hell. You will end up remaining in hell forever in order to increase your chances of entering heaven. What do you do?

"I'll return when you make your choice." The devil bows and fades away into fetid chasms of empty air. He leaves you there, alone. Very alone.

Every night you go to sleep to the eternal rhythms of the gibbon howling. Sometimes your hands itch, and after a few weeks, strange fungoid growths begin to appear on the palms of your hands. Your nails turn black—the same color as the gibbons surrounding you. You begin to speculate that you are part of some combined genetic and electronic experiment, that your body is regressing toward a more simian shape. If this were true, perhaps the gibbons around you at one time had a human form. But then you discard this idea. This must be hell. You saw the devil. It is time to make a decision about when to play the game.

Dear God. What do you do? Can you hope to escape from this fantastic nightmare?

## MUSINGS AND SPECULATIONS

*Down, down to hell; and say I sent thee thither.*
  —*William Shakespeare*, Henry VI

This scenario and paradox was proposed in 1988 by Edward J. Gracely in his paper "Playing Games with Eternity: The Devil's Offer," published in the journal

*Analysis.*[1] Although seemingly simple, this existential dilemma touches both on the concept of infinity and on certain theological assumptions.

Let's assume you are in hell and talking to the devil again. Do you think the *hope* of entering heaven someday in the future lessens your suffering in hell? If so, then perhaps it is unsatisfying to play the game and risk losing that hope and risk losing heaven. Authors Glenn Erikson and John Fossa say, "Compared to waiting in hell forever without hope of escape, deferring the playing of the game forever might be the wisest course. Heaven itself may have no pleasure comparable to that of anticipating leaving hell for heaven."[2] On the other hand, the longer you delay, your chance of winning becomes so great that you would be foolish to delay a day more.

This scenario reminds me of the stereotypical miser who hoards millions of dollars, never wanting to spend them. Wouldn't you be torturing yourself to keep pushing the day of playing back further? The crux of the problem is that we humans are not able to differentiate among the chances of winning because the infinite payoff makes each increase in our chances "infinitely desirable."[3] What would you do?

☉ ☉ ☉

I recently had a chat with Ed Gracely, author of the original "Devil's Offer" article. Gracely is a quantitative psychologist at MCP Hahnemann University in Philadelphia, and his interests include philosophical ethics and ethical decision making. He also has been long fascinated by the ethical implications of infinite sequences. Gracely writes to me,

> Suppose, for example, that a good deed of any sort begins an infinitely expanding series of similar events, growing exponentially in importance, perhaps even through alternate universes. Let's assume the good deed's value doubles every ten minutes. A deed done now has a current value of 1, which will increase to 2 in 10 minutes. A deed done then will also have a value of 1 at the time it is performed. After about 100 doublings, the absolute difference in value between the deed done now and one done 10 minutes after it is on the order of $10^{30}$. Clearly, this absolute difference heads toward infinity unless the sequences stop. Because "infinity" trumps probability, it doesn't matter how unlikely you regard these scenarios to be. The mere conceivability of them creates questions of infinite magnitude! Should we really rush to perform good deeds now, rather than waiting a day? Are we losing infinitely by not doing so? Clearly, rationality does not permit us to act upon these possibilities, but it is frustrating that infinity leads to yet another set of fundamentally unsolvable problems. Depending on the precise formulation, this may be a large

number problem or one based on infinity. I think that philosophical ethics needs a good approach to both large number problems (like heaven and hell lasting $10^{100}$ years) and to true paradoxes introduced by infinity per se.

Gracely had been thinking of these examples of infinite sequence problems when the idea of the "Devil's Paradox" came to him. He found the problem particularly fascinating because it involved a situation in which there was a true paradox, not merely a difficulty or conundrum. Gracely has no solution, nor has anyone submitted one to *Analysis*, as far as he knows. Gracely writes,

> If we made hell last $10^{100}$ years, there would be a calculable solution, but there is no solution if hell is of infinite duration. The protagonist is faced with an impossible-to-solve dilemma unless he or she makes an existential leap at some point and says, "Now!" That may well be what the scenario calls for, but my utilitarian soul rebels!

&#x25C9; &#x25C9; &#x25C9;

This Devil's Offer is reminiscent of a game I published a few years ago called "Slides in Hell."[4] On a hot summer day, I was visiting a local playground where I came across the most startling piece of recreational equipment. It was a metallic slide with a large hole punched in the chute. To this day, I can't think of any reason it was there, because it seemed rather dangerous. Children usually slid from the top of the slide to the bottom, but it seemed as if a small child could get stuck or even fall through the hole in the chute.

The image of this strange slide stayed in my mind for several months and stimulated the following mental exercise: You are in hell. Tongues of lava and fire seem to defy gravity as they lick the cavern walls, undulating obscenely to a music you cannot hear. The ceiling of the cavern is like a flock of bats on fire.

Satan asks you to consider a metallic slide punched with ten large holes that are equally spaced from top to bottom. The porous slide is such that you'd certainly fall through at least one of the holes during your descent.

### Slide With Ten Holes

For this uncomfortable problem, let's assume that each time you encounter a hole you have a 50 percent chance of sliding through it and into a vile oleaginous substance beneath the slide. For example, when your body passes over the first hole, one out of every two times you'd expect to fall through the hole into the loathsome liquid below.

Satan asks you a question. He offers you $1 million and your freedom if you can correctly guess which hole a person would fall through as he or she descended the slide. Which hole would you choose?

Soon the number of questions starts escalating. Here's a summary of the most interesting ones Satan asks:

- If you were a gambling person, which hole would you bet a person would fall through?
- How many attempts do you think it would require for a person to slide from the top of the slide to the bottom without falling through a single hole?
- Go back up to Earth. All the people on Earth have lined up to slide down a longer, more horrifying slide containing 100 holes. If people go down the slide at a rate of one person per second, when would you expect the first person to arrive at the bottom of the slide without falling through any hole? After an hour? A day? A decade?

It turns out that an analysis of this problem is not too difficult. The chance of falling through the first hole is 50 percent. The probability of reaching and falling through the second hole is less. Specifically, it is the probability that a person didn't fall through the first hole times the probability of falling through the second hole: $0.5 \times 0.5 = 25$ percent. For the third hole, we have $0.5^3 = 0.125$. This also means that, in a large enough sample, 1/2 of the people will fall through the first hole, 1/4 through the second, 1/8 through the third, etcetera. We can create a table showing the percent chance of reaching and falling into each hole as a person descends the slide:

**Table 6.1**

| Hole Number | Percent Chance of Reaching and Falling into Hole |
|---|---|
| 1 | 50 |
| 2 | 25 |
| 3 | 12.5 |
| 4 | 6.25 |
| 5 | 3.125 |
| 6 | 1.5625 |
| 7 | 0.78125 |
| 8 | 0.390625 |
| 9 | 0.1953125 |
| 10 | 0.09765625 |

Your chances of reaching and falling into the final hole are slim indeed—only about nine hundredths of a percent. Most mathematicians I asked said that because they were limited to selecting one hole, they would place their money on hole number 1. In other words, individuals would be most likely to fall through this hole. However, one respondent said he would not bet at all because the best chance is only a 50/50 chance.

As for the second question about how many attempts it would take to reach the bottom without falling through any hole, note that the chances of reaching each succeeding hole are the same as for reaching and falling into the previous one. Therefore, the chances of passing over all the holes are the same as of reaching and falling into the last hole. Therefore, the probability is $1/1,024 = 0.0009765625$; that is, 1,024 attempts would be required by a person, on average, to reach the bottom. Some people I queried suggested that they would bet on a number less than this because the actual events can happen in any order. For example, J. Theodore Schuerzinger from Dartmouth University notes that because $1/2^{10}$ (or $1/1,024$) people would make it all the way down the slide without falling through any of the holes, this means that 1,023 out of 1,024 people would fall through one of the holes. He notes:

> Using the formula $(1023/1024)^x = 1/2$, we can determine that out of the first $x$ people to go down the slide, there is a 50% chance that one person will make it down without falling through a hole. The solution $x = 709.4$ satisfies the equation. Thus I would bet that a person would make it all the way down on one of the first 710 attempts. In other words, after 710 attempts, the chance of someone succeeding exceeds $1/2$.[5]

What happens if all the people on earth lined up to go down the 100-hole slide at a rate of 1 person per second? The probability of falling through the last hole is a minuscule $0.5^{100} = 7.88 \times 10^{-31}$. The average number of tries that a single person must make to finally arrive at the bottom is $1/0.5^{100} = 1.26 \times 10^{30}$ or, to be more precise, it would require

$$1,267,650,600,228,229,401,496,703,205,376$$

attempts, on average, to reach bottom. (Your gluteus maximus muscles had better be in good shape before you attempt such an experiment.) In other words, we may see one person slide down over all the holes every $1.26 \times 10^{30}$ attempts. At 1 person/second, we can compute that it would require, on average, about $4 \times 10^{22}$ years, much older than the age of the universe. Note also that this would require many more people than the world population can offer. Therefore, no one will reach the bottom of the slide, or, as one respondent said, "they will all try and fail (assuming everyone only gets to try once), or die waiting in line." Using a logic similar to that for the 10-hole problem, after $(2^{100}-1)/(2^{100})$ attempts, the chance of someone succeeding exceeds $\frac{1}{2}$.

👁 👁 👁

Many of you may picture the devil as ruler of hell, inflicting physical and mental pain on others. But this portrayal of the devil is nowhere in the Bible. In the Bible, the devil is just another captive.

The Old Testament mentions Sheol, an unpleasant place in the afterlife from which the godly would be delivered. The New Testament mentions Hades and Gehennah. *Hades*, a word borrowed from Greek mythology, is a general term for the afterlife. Gehennah, on the other hand, was a place of everlasting torment. Back in the time of King Solomon, there was a temple in Jerusalem called Tophet where infants were burned. Tophet was in the Valley of Ben Hinnon, later called Gehennah in the New Testament. In this valley, children were sacrificed to the Canaanite god Molech. The area was later used as a garbage pit, where fire burned almost continuously. Thus, Gehennah came to be a metaphor for Hell.

The ancient Jews believed that Sheol or Tophet was a gloomy place of departed souls that were not tormented but wandered about unhappily. Gehennah, in the New Testament, became a place of punishment.

Jews and Christians refer to the Devil as Satan, a fallen and arrogant angel. In parts of the Old Testament, Satan is not God's enemy but rather a challenger or accuser. The word *devil* comes from the Greek *diabolos*, meaning "slanderer" or "accuser." The word *Satan* is the English transliteration of a Hebrew word for "adversary" in the Old Testament.

In the Old Testament, Satan gambles with God about the faith of Job. Later, in the New Testament, Satan becomes the "prince of devils" and has names such as Lucifer (the fallen angel of Light), Belial (lawless), and Beelzebub (Lord of Flies):[6]

> All the people were astonished and said, "Could this be the Son of David?" But when the Pharisees heard this, they said, "It is only by Beelzebub, the prince of demons, that this fellow drives out demons." (Matthew 12:24–27)

> What harmony is there between Christ and Belial? What does a believer have in common with an unbeliever? (2 Corinthians 6:15–16)

For Christians, Satan's job is to tempt man to commit immoral acts. Muslims believe in Iblis, the personal name for the Devil. They also call him ash-Shaytan, which means "the demon." In the Koran, God tells Iblis to bow in front of Adam, the first human. Iblis refuses.

Seven Old Testament books and all New Testament writers refer to Satan. In the Middle Ages, theologians debated about how a supernatural being like Satan could exist in a universe governed by an omniscient, omnibenevolent, omnipotent God. Many came to believe that Satan was not an actual being but a symbol of evil.

---

An important part of the wonder of the Jewish Bible, and especially of Genesis, is the imperfection of every character in the drama, including the One who plays the leading role. The Jewish God is great and powerful, but even He is not perfect—at least not in the beginning.

—Alan Dershowitz, *The Genesis of Justice*

---

Heaven, n.: A place where the wicked cease from troubling you with talk of their personal affairs, and the good listen with attention while you expound your own.

—Ambrose Bierce, "The Devil's Dictionary"

---

I am seventy and in mediocre health. It is not beyond the realm of possibility that I might be meeting God in the not-too-distant future. If I do, it will come as a surprise, but I've been surprised before. No doubt He would have a number of questions to put to me. I know that I would have a number of questions to put to him. But one question I am sure He will not put is: Why didn't you believe in Me? For one thing, He will know. For another, He will regard it as irrelevant to the matter at hand.

—Ralph Estling, *Skeptical Inquirer*

# CHAPTER 7

# The Revelation Gambit

B.C. MANSFIELD

*Jesus said : "Know that what is before Your face, and what is hidden from You will be revealed to You. For nothing hidden will fail to be revealed."*
                                                    *—The Gospel of Thomas, verse 5*

*Consider the true picture. Think of myriads of tiny bubbles, very sparsely scattered, rising through a vast black sea. We rule some of the bubbles. Of the waters we know nothing.*
                                        *—Larry Niven and Jerry Pournelle, The Mote in God's Eye*

YOU ARE AT THE ENTRANCE OF THE WORLD'S LARGEST CATHEDRAL, Saint John the Divine, located at 112th Street and Amsterdam Avenue in New York City. The "Portal of Paradise" is the name of the cathedral's central entrance. Awesome statues of biblical figures flank the three-ton bronze doors. As you slowly shift your gaze from figure to figure, you see a procession of 32 Old and New Testament faces emerge. Here is Moses. Over there, Noah. Ah, and here is Melchizedek, the Old Testament king of Salem (a place later called Jerusalem), who represented God Most High.

Melchizedek—what a strange fellow. Who was he? Abraham paid tribute to this high priest of the Canaanite cult El Elyon. The New Testament compares Jesus directly to Melchizedek in terms of title, job description, and worthiness to receive personal offerings.[1] Imagine what Melchizedek's facial expression would be if he could, for just a few seconds, stare out from his statue's eyes into the teeming, modern New York City street.

Honk. Honk. You hear noises from taxi cabs. From the sidewalk wafts the odor of pretzels and hot dogs. A pretzel vendor nods to you, and then you turn your attention to the cathedral.

Today you have come to the massive cathedral to contemplate a single question: "Can belief in God be a *rational* choice?" You are also interested in whether God is revealing himself to humans in any obvious way. Of course, answers depend on your definition of God, because it is clear that God has evolved as man "advances." Bertrand Russell said in *A History of Western Philosophy*: "The God of the Old Testament is a God of power, the God of the New Testament is a God of love; but the God of the theologians, from Aristotle to Calvin, is one whose appeal is intellectual: His existence solves certain puzzles which otherwise would create argumentative difficulties in the understanding of the universe."[2]

Right now, as you gaze up into Melchizedek's eyes on the busy Manhattan street, you are thinking about the biblical God. You go closer to the statue. What is that small paper object? Oddly enough, someone has placed in Melchizedek's hands the book *Superior Beings* by Steven J. Brams. That's certainly relevant to today's discussion.

Author and professor Steven J. Brams has suggested that the evidence for believing or not believing in the existence of God "depends, in part, on whether God reveals Himself and, if so, makes Himself knowable and intelligible."[3] Of course, the notion of revelation is tenuous at best, and you probably have friends who say that God's revelation is evident whenever you walk in a beautiful forest and see God's works. Others point to mysterious quotes, such as the following from *The Gospel According to Thomas*:

Whoever feels the touch of my hand shall become as I am, and hidden things shall be revealed to him. . . . I am the All, and the All came forth from me. Cleave a piece of wood and you will find me; lift up a stone and I am there.[4]

Obviously what one considers to be revelation may be suspect if what is revealed cannot be understood or cannot be communicated—or if it can easily be accounted for by other means (e.g., evolution by natural selection, trickery, aerodynamics, chemistry). Many people believe that some kind of mystical experience, an epiphany, or a miraculous appearance is the essence of revelation.

The question of God's existence is rarely asked in the Bible.[5] When related subjects are broached, it is usually a miracle that is used to quell any doubt, for example, when God makes clear to Pharaoh who is boss. (Recall that Moses bends the will of the king by demonstrating God's might with a series of plagues; see Figure 7.1.) The Old Testament is not so much concerned with God's existence as with which of many possible gods is the true God. In several Old Testament scenes, God appears to be in competition with the gods of other peoples in the Mideast.

Today, our requirements for demonstrating the existence of God are less clear than in the Old Testament, and in Chapter 2: God and Evil, I surveyed people as to what a being might do to convince them that He is God. In the remainder of the current chapter, let us assume that when God reveals Himself, He does so in a way that establishes His existence—in contrast to a silent God who does nothing directly to reveal His existence. (An example of a silent God who does nothing to reveal His existence might be a God who does not "speak" to prophets, does not appear as a burning bush to Moses, does not manifest himself through Jesus, and does not part rivers.)

Can belief in God be a rational choice? Let's play a simple game that has a paradoxical outcome and that might even relate to the question of whether God can exist. For the moment, let us assume that God has two choices for his relationship to humans or other creatures:

### Table 7.1   God's Choices

| | 1. God reveals Himself (that is, establishes His existence). |
| | 2. God does not reveal Himself (that is, does not establish His existence). |

For now, let's assume you also have two choices:

Fig. 7.1.*Moses and Aaron before Pharaoh. Reprinted from Gustave Doré,* The Doré Bible Illustrations *(New York: Dover, 1974), 32.*

**Table 7.2     Your Choices**

1. You believe in God's existence.

2. You don't believe in God's existence.

According to Professor Brams, these various strategies can be combined to suggest four possible outcomes:

**Table 7.3**

| God | *You* Believe in God's Existence | *Don't Believe in God's Existence* |
|---|---|---|
| Reveals Himself (establishes His existence) | You are faithful and have the evidence. Belief in existence confirmed. (G = 3, Y = 4) ☺☺ | You are unfaithful despite evidence. Nonbelief in existence unconfirmed. (G = 1, Y = 1) ☹☹ |
| Doesn't reveal Himself (doesn't establish His existence) | You are faithful without evidence. Belief in existence unconfirmed. (G = 4, Y = 2) ☺☹ | You are unfaithful without evidence. Nonbelief in existence confirmed. (G = 2, Y = 3) ☹☺ |

In the table, the numbers 1 through 4 represent outcome preferences for God (G) and you (Y). "4" represents the best outcome and "1" the worst. In creating these rankings, I, of course, make many assumptions with which you may not agree. (I urge you to replay this "game" using assumptions you feel to be valid.) For example, I am assuming that (1) God primarily wants you to believe in His existence, and that (2) God prefers not to reveal Himself directly and unambiguously to all people. This is what most of my religious friends tell me they believe. Similarly, I assume your primary goal is to have your belief (whether it is belief or nonbelief in the existence of God) "confirmed" by evidence or lack of evidence. I assume that your secondary goal is to prefer to believe in God's existence. Using these assumptions, we can actually establish an ordering of outcomes in the table. (Similarly, if you would like to add *tertiary* goals, you could extend this table to a 2 × 2 × 2 table that would rank eight cells.)

I know this is all very abstract and probably difficult to wrap your brain around. Before analyzing this, let's make this easier and go through some examples. The first column is associated with God's primary goal of your believing in His existence, something we will assume, for the moment, that God prefers over your not believing in His existence. (If you think that the Bible indicates God's desire, then certainly it is clear that God prefers people to believe in Him. Believers are often rewarded and nonbelievers punished.) Similarly, from your standpoint, you primarily want your belief or your nonbelief to be confirmed—this corresponds to the cells along the diagonal going from upper left to lower right. Outcomes off this diagonal correspond to lack of confirmation.

Some friends have quibbled with me regarding the assumption that God prefers not to reveal Himself directly and unambiguously to all people. Again, if you do not believe this, recall that this is just a theoretical game we are playing to sharpen our minds and get a feel for possible outcomes of choices and preferences. However, again, if you think that the Bible is not just a bunch of fairy tales but contains a few profound nuggets of truth, it is clear why God usually does not reveal Himself directly. Apparently, God is interested in the *faith* of people, and if there is absolute proof or direct evidence of God, then there is no faith or test of faith. God appears to desire from humans belief without direct evidence. Steven Brams says, "Indeed it is not unfair, in my opinion, to read the Bible as the almost obsessive testing of man by God to distinguish the faithful from those whose commitment to Him is lacking in zeal or persistence."[6] In fact, one of the lessons of the biblical Job is that faith in God is rewarded, even with little evidence of God and when horrible things happen to good people. Job was always a "good" person, and he never abandoned God despite the deal God made with Satan to test Job's faith with horrible torture and calamity. Accepting Satan's dare, God allowed Satan to go wild. Job lost his ten children, who died when his house collapsed. Satan further tested Job by covering his body with painful sores (Figure 7.2). In these scenes, God wanted Job to believe in a just and loving God even when He apparently gave evidence that God is not a just and loving God.

In the Old Testament, one of the few (yet dramatic) examples of direct "evidence" is given to Moses. One day, Moses is curious about a strange sight on a mountain. He finds a flaming bush that is not consumed. God calls Moses by name and tells him to remove his shoes because this is holy ground. Moses is frightened, but he obeys. The voice identifies Himself: "I am the God of your father, the God of Abraham, the God of Isaac and the God of Jacob" (Exodus 3:6). God wants Moses to go to Egypt to lead the Israelites out of bondage.

*Fig. 7.2.Job hearing of his ruin. Reprinted from Gustave Doré,* The Doré Bible Illustrations *(New York: Dover, 1974), 136.*

Note that Moses is told he cannot see God's face directly because "you cannot see My face, for man may not see Me and live" (Exodus 33:20).

If we assume that the Bible and other religious books should be seriously examined, and if we assume that you would like evidence for God's existence, we can make some marvelous discoveries. Let's examine the table of four outcomes again. Note that it is possible for you to choose not to believe in God's existence (column 2 in the table). This doesn't mean you believe in his nonexistence. This is actually what an agnostic believes. Nonrevelation really proves nothing about God's existence. It certainly does not prove that God does not exist. Nonrevelation may make you prefer agnosticism over absolute belief.

Now for the paradox of revelation. Using all of our assumptions for this revelation game, God's preferred or "dominant" strategy is to refrain from revealing Himself. Why? Well, whatever you choose, God prefers the second row in the table. $G=4$ is better than $G=3$ in column 1, and $G=2$ is better than $G=1$ in column 2. So, if you believe in God (first column), then God prefers not to give you direct, unambiguous evidence. If you do not believe in His existence (second column), God still prefers not to reveal Himself. The numbers in the table make clear which strategy God should take, and it does not matter what strategy or belief you have.

Your strategy is less clear, because sometimes it is better for you to believe in God or not believe in God depending on God's actions. Belief seems to be better for you if God reveals Himself, but nonbelief is better if God does not. However, if you fully understand the game and can look at the table, this means you know God's preferences and your own preferences. This implies that you know God has a dominant strategy and will choose it. Because you prefer ($G=2$, $Y=3$) to ($G=4$, $Y=2$) in the second row of the table, you choose your second strategy (second column) to ensure the best outcome. This makes ($G=2$, $Y=3$), the bottom right cell with the gray background, your rational choice and the rational outcome of the gambit. This means you don't believe there is evidence God exists *and* God doesn't reveal Himself or establish His existence. Additionally, once God sees this (2,3) outcome, there's no compelling reason why He should switch. If He revealed Himself, He would be worse off with (1,1), and, if you switch by believing in God's existence, you would be worse off at (4,2). Neither you nor God will unilaterally make a switch![7]

Now we can delve deeper into this logical morass to shed further light on the paradox. Let's look again at the gray cell with ($G=2$, $Y=3$). For God, this is the next-to-worst outcome. It's the next-to-best outcome for you. Even stranger, there is another outcome ($G=3$, $Y=4$) that seems to be preferred by both you and God over the (2,3) outcome. This is the situation in which God provides evidence, and you are faithful—belief in His existence confirmed. Thus, we might conclude:

1. It is rational for God not to reveal Himself and for you not to believe in His existence (2,3), which may distress theists.
2. This (2,3) outcome is worse for both players than revelation by God and belief by you, which may distress many rationalists.

The rational outcome also seems to doom the rationalist to hell, or at least a sad afterlife, in some Christian and Jewish thinking. In the Bible, many of the heathens, such as the Canaanites, were massacred with God's help. Similarly, God told Saul to attack the Amalekites and destroy them completely—"men and women, children and infants, cattle and sheep, camels and donkeys" (1 Samuel 15:3). Obviously, in the Bible, there are serious consequences for errors of judgment and belief.

Steven Brams points out that timing is everything in the Revelation Gambit. If God makes His choice first and then you respond to it by making your choice, there is no paradox. Put yourself in God's heavenly shoes. God will realize the problem that arises if He chooses his dominant second strategy in the table (not to reveal Himself), and therefore He switches to His first strategy in the table (revealing Himself). Once you see God's choice, this induces you to choose your own best strategy in order to obtain the best outcome for you (G=3, Y=4). Still, the ramifications of this little puzzle go deeper. For example, if God (or some superior being) chooses first, He does not obtain His best outcome. Also, if you are an agnostic, you will play the game while being uncertain about God's existence. You will not know God's choice of strategies. (Incidentally, an agnostic player is probably more likely to enter this gambit than a devout Christian or a devout atheist.) The agnostic thinks there are only two things God could do: either (1) establish His existence, or (2) not establish His existence. Number 2 may occur under two conditions: (1) God actually doesn't exist, or (2) He exists but chooses not to reveal Himself. And if God exists, you realize that it is rational for Him to not reveal Himself—which makes you utterly confused in deciding whether God exists or chooses not to reveal Himself. If God chose the strategy in the second row of not revealing Himself, then He casts doubt about His existence in your mind. This only strengthens your agnosticism.

Many religions appear to have components of the Revelation Gambit, and holy books often give examples of revelatory experiences that support faith. Most agnostics I know appear to await some kind of evidence of God before believing in Him and are also interested in obtaining evidence that supports nonbelief, if such exists. In other words, our assumption that most agnostics enjoy having evidence appears to be plausible. You might quibble with our second assumption that agnostics, in their hearts, prefer belief over nonbelief, and I urge you to play various versions of the gambit on paper and analyze the outcomes. Similarly, you may substitute "superior alien" for God in this exercise and study the results of various assumptions should we ever be visited by superbrainy creatures from Alpha Centauri! Of course, it would be very difficult to ascertain the mind of God, if God exists, and His preferences. Again, the Old Testament God clearly prefers His people (the Israelites) to have faith. He punishes them dramatically when they don't have faith in Him over other gods. His "revelations" are often indirect (burning bush, punishment of enemies or anyone who does not follow His will, turning water into wine, making quail drop to the ground, giving people leprosy).

It appears that the paradox of the Revelation Gambit results from the reluctance of God to reveal Himself directly to all people and thereby verify His existence from a rational standpoint. Many theologians from disparate religions realize this. In many religions, God is supposed to be unknowable.

### MUSINGS AND SPECULATIONS

*Jesus said: "Images are visible to man, and the light which is in them is hidden in the image of the Light of the Father. He will reveal Himself and His image is hidden by His light."*

—*The Gospel of Thomas, verse 83*

*The Book of Revelation's affirmation of another reality that transcends the visible world has been a source of inspiration, hope and courage. Its archetypal imagery speaks to both the political and spiritual realms of life; indeed it integrates rather than separates those realms.*

—*Marcus J. Borg*, Reading the Bible
Again for the First Time

Most of the Revelation Gambit discussed in this chapter is based on the research of Steven J. Brams, a former professor of politics at New York University and author of the book *Superior Beings* and a related paper, "Belief in God: A Game-Theoretic Paradox."[8] The gambit is unsatisfying (perhaps depressing) for those of you who are agnostic. If the gambit indeed represents your preferences as well as God's, the strategy choices are clear: God would not reveal Himself or establish His existence, and you, anticipating God's choice, would not believe in His existence. You'll remain an agnostic, even if God does exist. If one is playing the Revelation Gambit, Brams suggests that it is rational not to believe in God's existence. As we said, this does not mean that it is rational for you to believe in God's nonexistence, because God could exist without revealing Himself. If we suppose God is omniscient and, as a consequence, can predict your strategy choice before playing the gambit, the outcome of the game is the same. Because God has a dominant strategy, the fact that He can predict humans' strategies will not enable Him to do any better. His best choice is still not to reveal Himself because, by definition, this is best.

Revelation as it relates to the existence of God has the potential for raising a long list of paradoxes, some of which are stated in the mystical writings of German theologian Paul Tillich (1886–1965), who wrote in *Theology of Culture:*

> If you start with the question whether God does or does not exist, you can never reach Him; and if you assert that He does exist, you can reach Him even less than if you assert that He does not exist. A God whose existence or nonexistence you can argue is a thing beside others within the universe of existing things. . . . It is regrettable that scientists believe that they have refuted religion when they rightly have shown that there is no evidence whatsoever for the assumption that such a being exists. Actually, they have not only not refuted religion, but they have done it a considerable service. They have forced it to reconsider and to restate the meaning of the tremendous word God. Unfortunately, many theologians make the same mistake. They begin their message with the assertion that there is a highest being called God, whose authoritative revelations they have received. They are more dangerous for religion than the so-called atheistic scientists. They take the first step on the road which inescapably leads to what is called atheism. Theologians who make of God a highest being who has given some people information about Himself, provoke inescapably the resistance of those who are told they must subject themselves to the authority of this information.[9]

Paul Tillich was born on August 20, 1886, in a Lutheran parish house in Starzeddel, Germany. In 1905 he registered at the University of Berlin, majoring in theology. In 1933, Tillich fled Nazi persecution and came to America, where he became professor of philosophical theology at Harvard and the University of Chicago.

What a paradoxical man, Tillich! He was a teacher in the church of God who broke with its conventional morality. He had extramarital relationships. A menage-à-trois. He experimented with drugs and developed a theological system based on the premise that God does not exist![10]

Here are some other favorite Tillich quotations:

- "The first duty of love is to listen."
- "Being religious means asking passionately the question of the meaning of our existence and being willing to receive answers, even if the answers hurt."
- "Man's ultimate concern must be expressed symbolically, because symbolic language alone is able to express the ultimate."
- "The awareness of the ambiguity of one's highest achievements (as well as one's deepest failures) is a definite symptom of maturity."
- "The courage to be is rooted in the God who appears when God has disappeared in the anxiety of doubt."

In my own book *The Stars of Heaven*, the main character wonders why God does not directly reveal Himself to everyone. The answer is given by a multi-legged, triangularly shaped creature with connections to God:

"To establish an unpredictable, creative, and infinitely evolving universe, God cannot directly show creatures that He exists. If He did that, intelligent life would be robbed of its independence. You, human, must always search for answers on your own." The triangle pauses. "Why do you think evolution is so painful? Why does the zebra die in blood and terror as the tiger removes its trachea? Yes, now you know why there is pain. It is only in a crucible of competition that intelligence can evolve. It was the only way God could avoid giving away His existence but still produce intelligent beings."[11]

This is reminiscent of a quotation from John Brooke, professor of science and religion and the director of the Ian Ramsey Center at Oxford University:

Darwin had illuminated the classic problem of theology: the problem of pain. If competition and struggle were preconditions of the very possibility of evolutionary change, then pain and suffering were the price levied for the production of beings who could reflect on their origins.[12]

Another wonderful Brooke quotation is: "A deity who could make all things make themselves was far wiser than one who simply made all things."[13]

Perhaps the most perplexing concept to understand is Jesus as God and what His revelation is supposed to be. The author C. S. Lewis wrote:

I am trying here to prevent anyone saying the really foolish thing that people often say about Him: "I'm ready to accept Jesus as a great moral teacher, but I don't accept His claim to be God." That is the one thing we must not say. A man who was merely a man and said the sort of things Jesus said would not be a great moral teacher. He would either be a lunatic—on the level of a poached egg—or else he would be the Devil of Hell. You must make your choice. Either this man was, and is, the Son of God; or else a madman or something worse. You can shut Him up for a fool, you can spit at Him and kill Him as a demon; or you can fall at His feet and call Him Lord and God. But let us not come with any patronizing nonsense about His being a great human teacher. He has not left that open to us. He did not intend to.[14]

In this chapter we discussed Moses and the miracles he presented to Pharaoh to convince Pharaoh of God's superiority. I cannot resist describing the "Bridegroom of Blood"—the most bewildering mystery in the Bible. The bizarre incident takes place after God tells Moses that he must go to Egypt to lead his people out of slavery. As Moses and his family journey to Egypt, it seems that God tries to kill him. One translation reads:

> On the way, at a place where they spent the night, the Lord met Moses and tried to kill him. But Zipporah, his wife, took a flint and cut off her son's foreskin and touched his feet with it, and said "Truly you are a bridegroom of blood to me!" So He let him alone. It was then she said, "A bridegroom of blood by circumcision." (Exodus 4:24–26)

Whom is God trying to kill? Why? What is a "bridegroom of blood?" And why is Moses's wife performing an emergency circumcision of her child and touching Moses's "feet" (some translate "feet" as thigh or scrotum) with the child's foreskin? Author Kenneth Davis suggests that circumcision was believed to ward off demonic attack. Since Moses was presumably not circumcised, the smearing of the blood on him may have protected him as well.[15]

Authors Jim Bell and Stan Campbell suggest that perhaps Moses's wife wasn't fond of the Hebrew rite of circumcision and had resisted it. They also suggest that this passage might refer to Moses contracting an incapacitating disease that almost killed him, leaving his wife to do what was necessary.[16] Author J. R. Porter says that the reason this episode is so mysterious and difficult to understand is that the biblical narrator no longer knew its real meaning. It seems to be a fragment of some independent tradition and exhibits archaic features, such as representing Yahweh as a hostile night demon—and the use of a flint knife for circumcision.[17]

The King James Bible gives this translation:

> And it came to pass by the way in the inn, that the LORD met him, and sought to kill him. Then Zipporah took a sharp stone, and cut off the foreskin of her son, and cast it at his feet, and said, Surely a bloody husband art thou to me. So He let him go: then she said, A bloody husband thou art, because of the circumcision. (Exodus 4:24–26)

Again, the reader must ask why, having asked Moses to return to Egypt, should God then decide to kill him? And why should Zipporah's circumcising her son have apparently led to God's leaving Moses alone? Here are some other translations to whet your appetite:

> At a lodging place on the way, the LORD met [Moses] and was about to kill him. But Zipporah took a flint knife, cut off her son's foreskin and touched [Moses's] feet with it. "Surely you are a bridegroom of blood to me," she said. So the LORD let him alone. (At that time she said "bridegroom of blood," referring to circumcision.) (New International Version)

> Now it came about at the lodging place on the way that the LORD met him and sought to put him to death. Then Zipporah took a flint and cut off her son's foreskin and threw it at Moses' feet, and she said, "You are indeed a bridegroom of blood to me." So He let him alone. At that time she said, "You are a bridegroom of blood" because of the circumcision. (New American Standard Bible)

> And it cometh to pass in the way, in a lodging place, that Jehovah meeteth him, and seeketh to put him to death; and Zipporah taketh a flint, and cutteth off the foreskin of her son, and causeth [it] to touch his feet, and saith, "Surely a bridegroom of blood [art] thou to me;" and He desisteth from him: then she said, "A bridegroom of blood," in reference to the circumcision. (Darby Translation)

Speaking of Moses, did you know that many other myths echo the life of Moses? For example, in Mesopotamia, there was a legend of the warlord Sargon of Akkad, who, like Moses, was placed in a waterproof basket in a river for later discovery. Sargon eventually becomes King. Both the Old and New Testaments are rife with stories that first originated with other traditions. For example, history records many examples of ancient and pre-Christian religions with a savior who was crucified. Many of these individuals were known as the Son of God, the Savior, the Messiah, the Redeemer, or the Resurrected. Many had virgin births, physical ascension into heaven, the presence of magi or "wise men," and were part of a divine trinity. If you are Christian, does the existence of these pre-Christian savior legends have any impact on your Christian beliefs?

Stephen Spignesi's *The Odd Index* lists sixteen crucified saviors other than Jesus Christ.[18] His source is an 1875 book by religious scholar and historian Kersey Graves, who published *The World's Sixteen Crucified Saviors, or Christianity Before Christ.* The book gave the Christian clergy nightmares because it attempted to prove that Christianity was essentially based on legends and myths from centuries past and that the "legend" of Jesus Christ bore dozens (in some cases, hundreds) of similarities to pagan gods from as far back as the year 2000 B.C. I cannot vouch for the information provided in Graves's 1875 book, but even if a quarter of his examples of Christ legends predating Christianity are correct, this should stimulate lots of discussion. You can find the complete text of Graves's book on several Internet sites. In his preface, Graves writes:

> The Christian bible, in some respects, is superior to some of the other bibles, but only to the extent to which the age in which it was written was superior in intelligence and natural mental capacity to the era in which the older bibles were penned . . . being of more modern origin, the progress of mind had worn away some of the legendary rubbish of the past. By comparing Christ's history with those of the oriental Gods, it will be found: that Christ taught no new doctrine or moral precept; that he inculcated the same religion and morality, which he elaborated, as other moral teachers, to great extremes; that Christ differs so little in his character, preaching, and practical life from some of the oriental Gods, that no person whose mind is not deplorably warped and biased by early training can call one divine while he considers the other human; and that if Christ was a God, then all were Gods.[19]

Clearly there are many mythological heroes and gods—such as Hercules, Osiris, Bacchus, Mithras, Hermes, Prometheus, Perseus, and Horus—that have much in common with Jesus. All were said to have gods for fathers and virgins for mothers and births announced by stars. All were born on December 25 (solstice), had tyrants trying to kill them when they were infants, met with horrifying deaths, and rose from the dead. Also notable are New Testament allusions to several New Testament Jews, such as Theudas and Judas, who lived just prior to Jesus and claimed to have received revelations and miraculous powers from God. They were killed and their followers scattered (Acts

5:36–37). Similarly, the false Jewish prophet Bar-Jesus of Paphos is mentioned in Acts 13:6. Paul, while filled with the Holy Spirit, strikes Bar-Jesus blind.

Among the most fascinating "paradoxes" of the Bible occurs when two prophets, both speaking in the name of God, give opposing predictions. For example, consider the prophet Hananiah who confronts prophet Jeremiah:

> Then the prophet Hananiah took the yoke off the neck of the prophet Jeremiah and broke it, and he said before all the people, "This is what the LORD says: 'In the same way will I break the yoke of Nebuchadnezzar king of Babylon off the neck of all the nations within two years.'" (Jeremiah 28:10–11)

Jeremiah disagrees and says that he has been told by God to wear a wooden yoke on his neck to symbolize that Israel is to be subservient to Babylon. He "countermands" Hananiah in the following:

> Shortly after the prophet Hananiah had broken the yoke off the neck of the prophet Jeremiah, the word of the LORD came to Jeremiah: "Go and tell Hananiah, 'This is what the LORD says: You have broken a wooden yoke, but in its place you will get a yoke of iron. This is what the LORD Almighty, the God of Israel, says: I will put an iron yoke on the necks of all these nations to make them serve Nebuchadnezzar king of Babylon, and they will serve him. I will even give him control over the wild animals.'" (Jeremiah 28:12–14)

Despite these paradoxes or contradictions, many of the prophets probably thought they were in touch with the divine. As Marcus Borg points out in *Reading the Bible Again for the First Time*,[20] if we assume that some of the prophets were actual historical figures, it is quite possible that they had ecstatic experiences in which they truly believed, and this could account for the courage of the prophets when speaking very unpopular messages. For example, Jeremiah was so unpopular that he was beaten and lowered into a tank to starve and die.

◎ ◎ ◎

We have discussed a monotheistic God in this chapter, and in the "Some Final Thoughts" section I'll explain how Judaism evolved from monolatry (belief in the existence of many gods, but worship of only one) to monotheism. Several scholars have suggested that benevolent polytheism was, in some ways, better for humanity than monotheism. Author Robert Martin writes, "Polytheists often see one of the gods as the god of the group, the one who looks specially after their interests. In a sense, polytheism reflects and encourages a sort of tolerance and stability. A polytheistic tribe typically accepts the existence of their own special god, but also of the gods of the neighboring tribes."[21] Although this analysis is probably simplistic, it provides fertile ground for debate. (See note 14 to "Some Final Thoughts" for discussions on the physics of polytheism.)

Perhaps monotheism evolved through constant fighting for limited resources in the dry climate of the Middle East. One tribe would have to demonstrate its superiority over another by claiming its God was more powerful. The tribes probably had some common messages like: "My God can beat your God, and here is why." Moses did this, and the last plague that brought death to the Egyptian firstborns (and of all the firstborn animals) temporarily convinced Pharaoh that the God of Israel was more powerful than the Egyptian deities. In the Bible, the Israelites protected themselves from God's wrath by marking their doors with lamb's blood, which they believed would make death "pass over" their homes. One could wonder if this act symbolically limits God's omniscience. Why does He need to "see" lamb's blood to know whom to pass over? Perhaps, one might argue, it is an "angel of death" that does the killing and needs to see the blood, because the *angel* is not omniscient. Perhaps the application of blood is a symbol for Jews to demonstrate their solidarity to one another and serves as a test of their faith.

Continuing with our exploration of the relative violence stirred up by polytheism and monotheism, as well as the evolution of monotheism from polytheism, note that in Exodus 20 the monotheistic God tells Moses, "I will send my terror ahead of you and throw into confusion every nation you encounter." Pretty tough words! Obviously, the most powerful god would be the god more powerful than all other gods. This sort of god would eventually come to be thought of as infinite and omniscient. Finally, this Supergod evolves into the *only* true God for monotheists. Unfortunately, as lofty, inspiring, and mystical as this concept is, members of one monotheistic religion have often tried to convert others by force and by fighting wars. It would be intriguing if one could quantify the degree of horror (war, torture, murder) done in the name of a monotheistic God versus that done in the name of a polytheistic god. It seems possible that the monotheists would lose on this scale of justice, although they might claim to have created great beauty, art, philosophy, and kindness as well.

Of course, this is not to say that polytheists have not played one-upmanship with their gods in relation to the God of monotheists. In biblical times, we find that victorious Middle Eastern nations often transferred captured idols from defeated peoples into their own temples. This symbolized the belief that the victor's gods were superior to those of the conquered nation. For example, in the Book of Samuel, the Philistines treated the Israelite's golden Ark of the

Covenant as a captured idol and carried it to their temple to place beside a statue of their god Dagon.

Another indirect example of god competition—and the quest for omnipotence—occurs in 2 Kings 3 when Yahweh tells the Israelites He will hand them the kingdom of Moab. A battle ensues and seems to be going in the Israelites' favor. Desperate for survival, Mesha, the King of Moab, sacrifices his firstborn son and successor as an offering to Moab's national god, Chemosh. The horrifying sight of the burnt human offering so impresses and frightens the Israelites that they are forced to retreat. Even in this advanced stage of the Israelite religion, Israel appears to recognize the power of a foreign God. (Note that in 1868, archaeologists discovered the "Moabite stone" in Transjordan. This basalt pillar, dated to 830 B.C., celebrates the victory of Mesha's Chemosh over Yahweh.)[22]

Let's wrap up this chapter with a few quotes from people who might challenge the assumptions of the Revelation Gambit. Here is one from Thomas Nagel, who, in *The Last Word*, wrote on what he calls "the fear of religion itself":

> I speak from experience, being strongly subject to this fear myself: I want atheism to be true and am made uneasy by the fact that some of the most intelligent and well-informed people I know are religious believers. It isn't just that I don't believe in God and, naturally, hope that I'm right in my belief. It's that I hope there is no God! I don't want there to be a God; I don't want the universe to be like that.[23]

I wonder how Nagel would play or analyze the Revelation Gambit?

Here are a few more religious paradoxes from Paul Tillich. Try to wrap your mind around these brain twisters, written by Tillich, as you drift off to sleep on a stormy night:

- "It would be a great victory for Christian apologetics if the words 'God' and 'existence' were very definitely separated except in the paradox of God becoming manifest under the conditions of existence. . . . God does not exist. He is being-itself beyond essence and existence. Therefore, to argue that God exists is to deny him."
- "The faith which makes the courage of despair possible is the acceptance of the power of being, even in the grip of nonbeing. Even in the despair about meaning being affirms itself through us. The act of accepting meaninglessness is in itself a meaningful act. It is an act of faith. . . . The vitality that can stand the abyss of meaninglessness is aware of a hidden meaning within the destruction of meaning."

- "Absolute faith, or the state of being grasped by the God beyond God, is not a state which appears beside other states of the mind. It never is something separated and definite, an event which could be isolated and described. It is always a movement in, with, and under other states of mind. It is the situation on the boundary of man's possibilities. It *is* this boundary. Therefore it is both the courage of despair and the courage in and above every courage. It is not a place where one can live, it is without the safety of words and concepts, it is without a name, a church, a cult, a theology. But it is moving in the depth of all of them. It is the power of being, in which they participate and of which they are fragmentary expressions."[24]

◉ ◉ ◉

In this chapter, I mentioned the idea that God evolves as man "advances." Bahaullah (1817–1892), the prophet founder of the Baha'i faith, has suggested that messengers, or prophets, of God evolve as humanity changes. According to the Baha'is, the prophets even have "specially designated limitations":

> These Manifestations of God have each a twofold station. One is the station of pure abstraction and essential unity. In this respect, if thou callest them all by one name, and dost ascribe to them the same attribute, thou hast not erred from the truth. . . . The other is the station of distinction, and pertaineth to the world of creation and to the limitations thereof. In this respect, each Manifestation of God hath a distinct individuality, a definitely prescribed mission, a predestined Revelation, and specially designated limitations. Each one of them is known by a different name, is characterized by a special attribute, fulfills a definite Mission, and is entrusted with a particular Revelation.[25]

The Baha'is believe that the changing laws and concepts of religion are needed to meet the requirements of an ever-evolving humanity:

> The Prophets of God should be regarded as physicians whose task is to foster the well-being of the world and its peoples, that, through the spirit of oneness, they may heal the sickness of a divided humanity. . . . Little wonder, then, if the treatment prescribed by the physician in this day should not be found to be identical with that which he prescribed before. How could it be otherwise when the ills affecting the sufferer necessitate at every stage of his sickness a special remedy? In like manner, every time the Prophets of God have illumined the world with the resplendent radiance of the Day Star of Divine knowledge, they have invariably summoned its peoples to embrace the light of

God through such means as best befitted the exigencies of the age in which they appeared. They were thus able to scatter the darkness of ignorance.[26]

God's revelation is likened to clothing which must be changed as time progresses:

And now concerning thy question regarding the nature of religion. Know thou that they who are truly wise have likened the world unto the human temple. As the body of man needeth a garment to clothe it, so the body of mankind must needs be adorned with the mantle of justice and wisdom. Its robe is the Revelation vouchsafed unto it by God. Whenever this robe hath fulfilled its purpose, the Almighty will assuredly renew it. For every age requireth a fresh measure of the light of God. Every Divine Revelation hath been sent down in a manner that befitted the circumstances of the age in which it hath appeared.[27]

According to the Baha'is, this evolution of religion and religious message is known as "progressive revelation." Just as it would not be appropriate to give the same lessons to a toddler that one would give to an adult, religious messages must be tailored to the capacity of humans, which changes through the centuries. (We don't offer burnt lambs to God anymore or condone slavery, as the Old Testament people did. Nor do we put a child to death for cursing his or her father or mother, as it says in Exodus 21:17.)

---

Anybody can be happy in the state of comfort, ease, health, success, pleasure and joy; but if one will be happy and contented in the time of trouble, hardship, and prevailing disease, it is the proof of nobility.

—Abdu'l-bahá, *Tablets of Abdu'l-bahá*

---

Why does God value faith so highly? Faith allows religion to survive. In the New Testament, people had such faith in Peter that they believed even his shadow could cure them (Acts 5:15). Even the most ruthless of pogroms have not succeeded in eradicating faith. Communism, persecution, and torture haven't destroyed religion. If God were as obvious as a rock, then God would be just another boring daily staple.

—Dennis Gordon, personal communication

# CHAPTER 8

# The Paradox of Eden

B.C. MANSFIELD

*And the LORD God commanded the man, saying, Of every tree of the garden thou mayest freely eat: But of the tree of the knowledge of good and evil, thou shalt not eat of it: for in the day that thou eatest thereof thou shalt surely die.*

*—Genesis 2:16–17*

YOU ARE TRANSPORTED BACK IN TIME TO THE GARDEN OF EDEN. IT'S definitely a nice place to visit. Lush vegetation is everywhere. Look! Over there. To your right. That long-haired woman must be Eve!

A great blue butterfly rises from a trickling stream. It drifts toward Eve, moving like a feather floating in the breeze. Her hand goes to her face as her eyes open wide in wonder. The butterfly, floating at the height of her head, flashes various shades of blue and crimson in the bright afternoon sunlight. At the edges of the membranous wings are little sparkles, as if the light is igniting tiny dust particles in the air when the wings move through them.

Yes, Eve is happy. This is before she and Adam eat the fruit of the tree—the famous tree of knowledge of good and evil—before God kicks her out of Eden and punishes her forever with exhausting pain during childbirth.

As you watch Eve chase after the butterfly, several paradoxes are on your mind. Before Eve ate the fruit, she either knew that obedience to God is good and disobedience is evil, or she did not know. If she did not know, she cannot be blamed for disobeying God by eating the forbidden fruit. (The Bible never specifies what type of fruit it is, although today we often think of it as an apple.) If she cannot be blamed, then God should not have punished her by kicking her out of Eden and giving her pain during childbirth. In particular, God punished Eve in Genesis 3:16 as follows: "I will greatly multiply thy sorrow and thy conception; in sorrow thou shalt bring forth children; and thy desire [shall be] to thy husband, and he shall rule over thee."

On the other hand, if Eve *did* know that disobedience is evil, then she already had the knowledge of good and evil, something eating the fruit was supposed to provide her with. If she already had such knowledge, there would have been no temptation for her to eat the forbidden fruit. In addition, an omniscient God would have known Eve knew of good and evil, and He would not have made not eating or eating the fruit (and subsequently not gaining or gaining of the knowledge of good and evil) a test of her morality. Whatever the significance of the tree, the Bible indicates a behavioral change in Eve after she eats the fruit; for example, she and Adam are suddenly ashamed of their nudity: "Then the eyes of both of them were opened, and they realized they were naked" (Genesis 3:7).

The Paradox of Eden has perplexed philosophers and theologians for centuries. Could it have been unjust for God to have made such a prohibition and given a subsequent punishment? Whether or not Eve knew that obeying God was good and disobeying God was bad, God seems to have acted unfairly. Speaking strictly from a legal or logical standpoint, does this mean God acts unjustly?

The butterfly has alighted on Eve's hand. You watch her for another few moments wondering if you should warn her. But you don't want to alter history. It's too difficult to predict the consequences of your interference. You return to the future wondering if God would have permitted you to warn Eve. If you had been able to warn her, would God have let her avoid eating from the tree of good and evil?

## MUSINGS AND SPECULATIONS

*One thing I have no worry about is whether God exists. But it has occurred to me that God has Alzheimer's and has forgotten we exist.*
　　　　　　　　　　　　　　　—*Jane Wagner,* The Search for
Signs of Intelligent Life in the Universe

*A myth is a religion in which no one any longer believes.*
　　　　　　　　　　　—*James Feibleman,* Understanding Philosophy

The premise of the tree story in Genesis is that the forbidden fruit provides knowledge of good and evil. Some feel that in not knowing good from evil or right from wrong, Eve could not be aware that it would be evil to disobey God's command not to eat the fruit.

This Paradox of Eden is based on Richard La Croix's paper "The Paradox of Eden," which appeared in the *International Journal for the Philosophy of Religion.*[1] La Croix takes a firm stance: Because God punished Adam and Eve for doing something that they could not have known to be wrong or evil, God acted unjustly. If, before eating the fruit, they already knew that obeying God is good and disobeying God is bad, then they already would have possessed the knowledge of good and evil. An omniscient God would know this and, therefore, God's command not to eat the fruit of the tree of knowledge of good and evil was not a fair test of Adam and Eve's sense of right and wrong. Therefore, La Croix suggests that being just is not an essential property of God.

Another relevant opinion can be found in Rabbi Allen Podet's article "La Croix's Paradox: An Analysis" published in the same journal.[2] Podet suggests alternative ways of looking at the paradox. First of all, the paradox *assumes* that Eve's being kicked out from Eden was a punishment for disobedience. (To me this assumption seems warranted, but perhaps the Bible allows some room for interpretation here.) Podet also says that simply knowing that it is good to obey God and bad to disobey Him is just one tiny facet of "knowing good and evil." For example, eating the fruit may convey additional knowledge and additional ways of knowing. Lastly, the paradox assumes that God was testing Eve's righteousness, but God might have been testing all kinds of things such as obedience, attitudes, gullibility, or even nothing at all![3]

There is probably no episode of the Bible that has been subject to a greater variety of interpretations than the story of Adam and Eve in the Garden of Eden. Few interpretations seem to account for all the information in Genesis. Given this, the Paradox of Eden is ripe for further debate. Some of my colleagues have asked whether Eve was competent to resist the serpent who coaxed her to eat of the tree. Again, because this was the tree of knowledge of good and evil, the implication is that before eating it, Eve did not know right from wrong. How could Adam and Eve reasonably be held accountable for wrongdoing committed before they truly realized what wrongdoing was? Interestingly, the immediate effect of Eve's new knowledge of good and evil is that she knows that it is immoral to be naked. For example, the story says nothing about her eyes being open to the wrongdoing of murder or cruelty.

A related paradox, called the "Paradox of the Fortunate Fall" focuses more directly on the consequences of Adam and Eve's fall from grace.[4] If Adam and Eve had not eaten the forbidden fruit and been cast out of Eden, then humans would not have had the wondrous fortune of Jesus's redemption story. If humans had not erred, they would not have needed salvation.

In modern times, the Paradox of the Fortunate Fall has been discussed in depth by American philosophers Arthur O. Lovejoy and Herbert Weisinger.[5] Lovejoy writes,

> Adam's eating of the forbidden fruit, many theologians had observed, contained in itself all other sins; as the violation by a rational creature of a command imposed by infinite wisdom, and as the frustration of the divine purpose in the creation of the earth, its sinfulness was infinite; and by it the entire race became corrupted and estranged from God. Yet if it had never occurred, the Incarnation and Redemption could never have occurred.

For centuries, scholars have also suggested that it was fortuitous that Adam and Eve ate the forbidden fruit and subsequently fell. For example, consider the following anonymous medieval hymn that has been debated for centuries:

Adam lay ibounden [bound]
Bounden in a bond;

Four thousand winter [years]
Thought he not too long;
And all was for an appil,
An appil that he tok,
As clerkes finden
Wreten in here book.
Ne hadde the appil take ben,
The appil taken ben,
Ne hadde never our lady
A bene hevene quene [heaven's queen].
Blessed be the time
That appil take was
Therefore we moun singen [may sing]
*Deo gracias* [*Thanks be to God*].

English poet John Milton (1608–1674), in *Paradise Lost*, also raises the paradox.[6] When the archangel Michael explains the plan for Christ's redemption to Adam, Adam cries out with happiness:

O goodness infinite, goodness immense!
That all this good of evil shall produce,
And evil turn to good; more wonderful
Than that which by creation first brought forth
Light out of darkness! Full of doubt I stand,
Whether I should repent me now of sin
By mee done and occasion'd, or rejoice
Much more, that much more good thereof shall spring,
To God more glory, more good will to Men
From God, and over wrath grace shall abound. (XII. 469–78)

In particular, the angel Michael explains to Adam that the final paradise will be much better than Eden as a result of Christ:

His faithful and receive them into bliss,
Whether in Heav'n or Earth, for then the Earth
Shall all be Paradise, far happier place
Than this of Eden, and far happier days. (XII. 462–65)

Do you think the Fall was happy or a disaster for humans? Some of my Christian friends tell me that they would prefer that Eve had not fallen and that

Jesus Christ had not existed or been needed for salvation. If you take the Bible literally, how do you think humanity would have evolved had Adam and Eve not fallen?

Opinions continue to be sharply divided about the Fall. Arthur Lovejoy himself approves of the concept of the Fortunate Fall. He elaborates:

> No devout believer could hold that it would have been better if the moving drama of man's salvation had never taken place; and consequently, no such believer could consistently hold that the first act of that drama, the event from which all the rest of it sprang, was really to be regretted. Moreover, the final state of the redeemed, the consummation of human history, would far surpass in felicity and in moral excellence the pristine happiness and innocence of the first pair in Eden—that state in which, but for the Fall, man would presumably have remained. Thus Adam's sin—and also, indeed, the sins of his posterity which it "occasioned"—were the *conditio sine qua non* both of a greater manifestation of the glory of God and of immeasurably greater benefits for man than could conceivably have been otherwise obtained.[7]

On the other side of the fence are philosophers and theologians who reject the idea of the Fortunate Fall. Writer Diane McColley strongly argues that

> nothing could be more repugnant to Milton's thought than the idea that disobeying God could be good for you. In *Paradise Lost*, God's grace is fortunate, but it does not depend upon human weaknesses to manifest itself. Growth in understanding and in love is fortunate, but it results from obedience, not from sin. Mankind is liberated not by sin but by regeneration; and regeneration, although it takes men and women above the height they fell from, does so by progressively restoring the abilities they lost by falling. If Adam and Eve had not fallen, they would "by degrees of merit rais'd" have "open[ed] to themselves the way" to heaven, and God would have deigned "To visit off the dwellings of just men/Delighted" (VII. 157–58, 57); that is, they would have achieved that "far more excellent state of grace and glory than that from which [they fell]" promises to regenerate. . . . The Fall was in no way fortunate, but perverted a process of growth and fruition that might have continued through obedience and that regeneration would restore. God's means of restoration are fortunate, of course, but the disobedience was not.[8]

Writer Virginia Mollenkott is also firmly against Lovejoy's position. Like McColley, she contradicts Lovejoy's opinion that Milton expressed and supported the doctrine of the Fortunate Fall:

> Picture redemption as the "ultimate result" of the Fall. Redemption is the result of God's concern for fallen man; apart from the loving nature of God,

there is no necessary connection between the Fall and the Atonement. Redemption is therefore the remedy, not the result. . . . In other words, Milton demonstrates that once sin is a fait accompli, God manages to do something wonderful about it. There can be no doubt that to Milton the goodness of God surpasses the evil of Satan; but that is not the same thing as claiming that God's goodness to fallen man surpasses what God's goodness would have provided if man had never fallen.[9]

From the standpoint of Christianity, the Paradox of the Fortunate Fall is one of the most fundamental dilemmas. If Adam and Eve had not stumbled, perhaps the world would not need (or have needed) salvation. Did an omniscient God foresee their stumble, and if so, did He in some sense want the fall so that Jesus would one day walk the Earth? There are Christians who would suggest that God was rational in permitting the Fall because this led to redemption and a later reunion with God in Heaven. After all, the Fall and the existence of evil is only temporary. Through the benevolence of God and the wonder of Mary and the resurrection, human beings will find the Garden again.

However we may wish to interpret the Paradox of Eden and the Paradox of the Fortunate Fall, many would agree that a literal interpretation of the Bible is not the best way to extract information. Early in Genesis, before the fourth day of creation, we find "evening" and "morning" (Genesis 1:5, 8, 13)—yet the sun has not yet been created. Adam is supposed to "surely die" if he eats the forbidden fruit, yet he lives another 930 years (Genesis 5:5). The Turkish philosopher Abu Nasr al-Farabi (d. 980) believed that the Bible, Koran, and utterances of prophets are expressed as poetic metaphors in order to make the messages of actual truths appeal to and be understood by the people. Alan Dershowitz, in *The Genesis of Justice*, pays particular attention to God's promises of reward or punishment that don't seem to materialize in a literal fashion:

> God threatens, in the Ten Commandments, to punish the "iniquity of fathers on children to the third and fourth generation." He postpones punishment and reward until after the death of the sinner and saint repeatedly through the early books of the Bible, thus making consequences invisible *within a given generation*. He has learned that by threatening *immediate, specific*, and *visible* punishment—such as He did to Adam—He risks loss of credibility when these consequences do not materialize.[10]

Dershowitz suggests that the theologians of Judaism, Christianity, and Islam had to accept the "afterlife" solutions of older religions—namely, the existence of a world after death in which the good are rewarded and the bad punished. Because justice was not obvious in this world, it had to be served in a world no human could see and from which no human could return or report. On the subject of the afterlife for Christians, Professor Marcus J. Borg writes, "If you had been able to convince me at age twelve or so that there was no afterlife, I would have absolutely no idea why I should be Christian. Heaven was what it was all about."[11]

Fig. 8.1. *Adam and Eve driven out of Eden. Reprinted from Gustave Doré,* The Doré Bible Illustrations *(New York: Dover, 1974), 3.*

And the serpent said unto the woman, Ye shall not surely die: For God doth know that in the day ye eat thereof, then your eyes shall be opened, and ye shall be as gods, knowing good and evil.

—Genesis 3:2–5

Without transgression there is no knowledge.

—Philip Roth, *American Pastoral*

# CHAPTER 9

# The Brain and God:
# Who's in Charge?

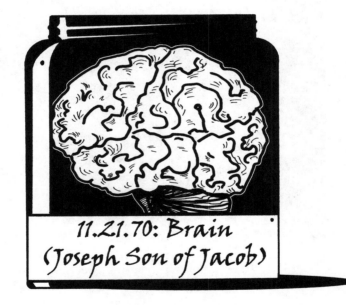

*I'm not sure if others fail to perceive me or if, one fraction of a second after my face interferes with their horizon, a millionth of a second after they have cast their gaze on me, they already begin to wash me from their memory: forgotten before arriving at the scant, sad archangel of remembrance.*

—*Ariel Dorfman*, Mascara, *1988*

YOU ARE WITH YOUR FRIEND MISS MUXDRÖÖZOL, THE EXTRATERRES-trial artist introduced in "Chapter 2: Good and Evil." Today she is showing you a rather strange collection. You walk down fluorescent corridors filled with gray, wrinkled things stored in formalin-filled jars to prevent decay.

Miss Muxdröözol motions to the brains. "I've gone back in time to gather all these."

You nod as you look at small labels on the jars. Outrageous! On your left are the brains of the Israelites, the postdiluvian patriarchs Abraham and his descendants Isaac, Jacob, and Joseph.[1]

You turn to Miss Muxdröözol, "This is utter sacrilege. You don't mean to tell me you have the brains of these famous biblical men?"

"Yes, I traveled back in time to the Mideast about two thousand years before the birth of Jesus. Do not worry. We removed their brains seconds after their death. History was not changed, and the men did not suffer because of my act. Their souls, if they existed, were not affected by what I did to their bodies after death."

You give a little tap on the jar marked "Abraham." His cerebrum jiggles like a big, dancing prune. You think about this ancient man. According to the Bible, God had promised Abraham a country especially set aside for him and his descendents. God told him, "I will make you into a great nation."

You walk a little further, wrinkling your nose at the strange chemical odors. On your right are a few clear pickle jars. You reach for the one marked "Joseph, Son of Jacob," open it, and drag your fingers lingeringly over his gray-white frontal lobes. Might there be remnants of his genius preserved in his neuronal networks—the time Joseph interpreted Pharaoh's dreams or the time he forgave his brothers for their sins against him? Could some fossil of his love toward his Egyptian wife Asenath still be trapped within the folds of flesh?

The brain: three pounds of soft matter that can take a split second of experience and freeze it forever in its cellular connections. One hundred billion nerve cells are the architecture of our experience. Is the biblical Joseph still here in the wet organ balanced in your palm? Could we reconstruct his memories? Would Joseph approve such a breach of privacy?

You replace Joseph and glance longingly at some of the other brains in Miss Muxdröözol's possession: Enoch, Irad, Mehujael, Methushael, Lamech, Adah, Jabal, Zillah. Such exotic-sounding names. She tells you that some of the brains in her collection are perfused with glycerol and frozen to −320 degrees Fahrenheit with liquid nitrogen. She hopes some day to learn from their memories. She refuses to give up hope that memories still reside in the brain cell interconnections and chemistry, much of which is preserved. Maybe she is right. After all, far back in the 1950s, hamster brains were partially frozen and revived by British researcher Audrey Smith. If hamster brains can function after being frozen, why can't ours? In the 1960s, Japanese researcher Isamu Suda froze cat brains for a month and then thawed them. Some brain activity persisted.

But what if there is an afterlife? You bang on the giant thermos bottle containing Moses's brain, causing the brain to make a splashing sound like a drunken fish. Miss Muxdröözol had frozen his brain immediately upon his death on Mount Nebo. Therefore, if there is an afterlife, he—or a brainless version of "he"—must have already experienced it by now. What would happen if his brain were revived? Would it register those new experiences?

You shake your head to change the direction of your thoughts. "Miss Muxdröözol, this collection is crazy. Have you lost your mind?"

Her body glimmers like mercury. "I am quite sane. My cryonicist friends believe that one day people can be revived if we freeze their brains today. What that means for the concept of an afterlife, I don't know."

She pauses. "Today I want to take a break from our usual discussions about God and omniscience and talk about a different kind of knowing. I want you to understand more about paradoxes of the brain, free will, time, consciousness, and causality. I'm going to drive you nuts, and by the time we're done you're going to question what it means to *know* something. These paradoxes will be biological and vast in their implications. We'll return to pure philosophy, logic, and theology tomorrow."[2]

Miss Muxdröözol sits on a wooden chair inlaid with a strange encryption:

## ᚨᛟᚲ ᚹᛁᛚᛚ ᚻᛗᚹᛗᚱ ᛒᛗ ᚼᛒᚠᛗ ᛏᛟ ᚱᛗᚼᚻ ᛏᚾᛁᛃ.

"What's that mean?" you ask.

"Never mind that. Let's start with several quick experiments with the notion of causality—that cause is followed by effect. Put up your hands whenever you like."

You pause and lift your hand.

"When we talked about omniscience, we also talked about knowing things like facts and events. I bet you think that you initiated the movement of your hand through your willpower."

"Yes, of course. I willed it, and it happened."

Miss Muxdröözol shakes her head. "You think that your psychological decision process is the trigger and prime cause of that movement. However, 0.8 seconds *before* you consciously decided to move your hands, there was an electrical signal in your brain called a *readiness potential*. Neuropsychologists have proven this. In other words, at the exact instant you *consciously* decided to move your hands, the actions had been already determined almost a second before. By monitoring your brain activity, I could have foreseen your movements before you made your conscious decisions. I could know before you know."

You fiddle with some forceps lying on a low table. "Incredible," you say. "You mean a neurologist could know that I was about to lift up these forceps before I made the conscious decision?"

Miss Muxdröözol nods. "Lesson 1: The relation between cause and effect, as you experience it, does not reflect the actual sequence of causal interdependence." She pauses. "Here's another experiment that should disrupt your notions of causality on a human scale. Come closer."

You nod. For a second your eyes focus on the mounted head of a moose that is perched above the doors of Miss Muxdröözol's museum of brains. At the left, you see a counter made of oak, soaked through with lacquers and oil. On it is a wooden statue of Dagon, one of the major Philistine gods of yore. The statue seems to be half man, half fish. Yes, Miss Muxdröözol has some odd tastes in decor.

She waves a gleaming electrode in front of you. "I'm going to insert this into your brain."

"No way!" you say. "Get that out of my face."

"The electrode is so thin, this won't hurt a bit." Without further hesitation, she inserts the wire into your brain.

She's right. It doesn't hurt.

Miss Muxdröözol looks at you. "What are you thinking? Let your mind drift."

You look toward the bottles of brains and then at Miss Muxdröözol. She smiles as she strokes her silky, rainbow-colored hair. You let your thoughts drift. "I'm thinking of the biblical story of Noah's ark. I am visualizing all the animals. I can see Noah and his sons Shem, Japeth, and Ham lifting huge pieces of wood to finish the construction. I smell animal dung. There is a rainbow in the sky."

"Okay," Miss Muxdröözol says. "This demonstrates another notion of causality and free will. I've been stimulating your brain with the electrode, and you experience this stimulation as spontaneously arising sensations rather than events I've imposed. Although I'm controlling you, you feel entirely free. Lesson 2: There are important illusions that reflect your brain's *interpretation* of causality."

This is all so unsettling. You walk away from her and into another room. Small American Indian rugs lay on the wooden floor, before a fireplace and windows. Against one wall is a large aquarium filled with red parrot fish about an inch in length. As they swim back and forth, they remind you of rubies, or perhaps the wisps and eddies of scarlet confetti.

Miss Muxdröözol follows you and brings out a huge buzzsaw. "Now I want to show you that the brain has its own time machine. Come closer."

You look at the saw in her hand. "You're not going to cut me with *that!*"

Miss Muxdröözol tosses saw to the floor. "Of course not. Just kidding."

She extends her vestigial thumb and places its opal surface on your leg. "When I touch you, your brain needs half a second for computation of the sensory signals. However, you do not perceive the touch half a second later. You immediately experience having been touched. This means that your brain antedated the experience by half a second. Think of your brain as a post office that assigns a date to a letter earlier than the actual date of the letter."

You look at your leg. "Miss Muxdröözol, you mean that my brain knows when the sensory signal arrived, and it compensates for its computation time? It creates the illusion of simultaneity?"

"Correct. Lesson 3: In order to perceive stimuli coming from the outside world in the correct order, we shift the perception backward in perceived time to the moment the stimulation actually took place. I call this the brain's time machine."

The smell of hamburgers and French fries wafts through the air. There must be a kitchen nearby. You look up and notice that on the window sill is a bronze bust of Albert Einstein. On the wall is a picture of Einstein boarding a large flying saucer.

"Miss Muxdröözol, you have some odd tastes. May I remove the electrode in my brain now?"

"Not yet. For our next experiment I want to measure your reaction time." She hands you a golden ark engraved with two cherubim, or winged angels. Inside the box is a bell with a button on top.

She looks at you. "Press this button when you perceive my touch."

She touches you, and you press the button. The bell rings.

"Sorry, Miss Muxdröözol. I pressed the button by accident."

"You did not. Here's what happened. Due to normal reaction time, you pushed the button 0.2 seconds after I touched you. However, 0.3 seconds later, I retroactively masked your conscious perception of the sensory stimulus by electrically stimulating your sensory cortex. Therefore, I canceled your perception in retrospect."

"You mean I apologized for an imaginary error. I reacted *properly* to a stimulus that I did not perceive?"

"Lesson 4: An experience at this very moment may be canceled later. There's trouble with determining simultaneity in the brain. Moreover, the notion of cause and effect becomes difficult. The temporal order of subjective events is a product of the brain's interpretational processes, not a direct reflection of events making up those processes."

The top of Miss Muxdröözol's hair glistens in the fading rays of light, and even though her large face is in shadow, the extraordinary glint of her eyes is still apparent.

In one of Miss Muxdröözol's hands is a *Cosmopolitan* magazine and a few UFO zines. Interesting combination. You sometimes find the idea of little gray men taking over the world almost comforting—perhaps they could solve some of the pollution and population problems.

Miss Muxdröözol snaps her fingers. "Next experiment. Look at this card. What do you see?"

"Two crosses separated by about 4 degrees."

### Crosses that Emit Light

"Okay, I'm going to light them in rapid succession. What did you see?"

"A single cross seems to move from one location to the other. It skated from left to right."

"What do you think will happen if I make one cross red and one cross green? What will happen to the color of the cross as it 'moves' from left to right?"

"Hmm. I think the illusion of motion will disappear, replaced by two separate flashing crosses. Or maybe the illusory 'moving spot' will gradually change from one color to the other as it moves."

Miss Muxdröözol turns on the device. "Let's give it a try." A green cross-shaped light momentarily flashes on the left followed by a red light flashing on the right.

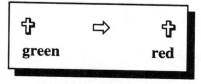

### Crosses that Emit Light

"Ooh," you say.

"What do you see?"

"First the green light seems to be moving, and then it changes to red abruptly in the middle of its (illusory) passage from left to right."

Miss Muxdröözol nods. "Okay, you saw it smoothly traveling but abruptly change color. At the halfway point between lights, it turned from green to red. Here's my question. How were you able to fill in the spot at the times and positions between the two flashes of light, *before the second flash occurred?* How and why did the light turn red before the red light came on?"

You shake your head. "Did I have clairvoyance that let me know the color of the second flash before it was experienced?"

Miss Muxdröözol waves her hand in a modified Kung Fu outward block to dismiss your lame idea. "The answer is that the imaginary content—the color change—couldn't have been created until *after* you saw the second colored light flash on."

You take a deep breath. "But if I were able to consciously identify the second spot, wouldn't it be too *late* to create the illusory color-switching and intermediate movement?"

Miss Muxdröözol opens a window to let in some fresh air. Outside you hear a few birds and the occasional croaking of frogs. "Researchers have proposed that the intervening motion is produced retrospectively, but only after the second flash occurs, and is projected *backward in time.*"

You brush back some hair that a faint breeze has caressed out of place. "I like these perception experiments," you say. "Have any other experiments we can do?"

"Certainly. Let's discuss one of my favorite temporal anomalies of consciousness. In the scientific literature, it's called the 'cutaneous rabbit.' Follow me."

Miss Muxdröözol leads you over to a velvet bench beside a painting of the Mona Lisa.

"Where did you get that?" you say.

"It's a long story. I won it in the contest described in Chapter 5."

"Chapter 5? You act as if we're in some kind of book?"

She ignores your question. "May I attach electrodes to your arm?"

You consider the question for a moment. "Sure, I'll do anything in the name of science."

She places mechanical tappers on your wrist, elbow, and upper arm. "I will now deliver a series of quick rhythmical taps. Five taps on your wrist, two at your elbow, and three more on your upper arm."

You look up from your arm. "It feels as if the taps travel in a regular sequence over equal-spaced locations on my arm—as if a little animal were smoothly hopping along the length of the arm from wrist to shoulder."

She nods. "Exactly. That's why it's called the 'cutaneous rabbit.' Cutaneous means skin. Even though I made taps at only three places along your arm, you felt as if a rabbit were hopping continuously *along* the arm."

"Miss Muxdröözol, how could my brain know that after five taps on the wrist there were going to be some taps on the elbow?"

"Neuropsychologists have determined that a person's experience of the 'departure' of the taps from the wrist begins with the second set of taps at the elbow. However, if we didn't deliver the elbow taps, you would experience all five taps at your wrist, as expected."

"Miss Muxdröözol, let me get this straight. Obviously, the brain can't know about a tap at the elbow until *after* it happens. Right?" You rub your elbow. "Maybe the brain *delays* the conscious experience until after all the taps have been 'received,' and then it revises the sensory data to fit a theory of motion and sends this time-altered version of reality to our consciousness."

Miss Muxdröözol sits down beside you. She begins to play nervously with a few of her thoracic vertebrae. She says with rare uncertainty, "You said that you thought the brain delays the conscious experience until after all the taps have been received. But would the brain always delay response to one tap in case one more came? If not, how does the brain know when to delay? I don't know the answers."

Miss Muxdröözol pauses. "Want to try another experiment? It also deals with your mind playing tricks with time."

"It sounds interesting, but each experiment is weirder than the last. They are fascinating though."

Miss Muxdröözol walks over to you with an electrode in her hand. "Hold still. I'm now placing an electrode in your left cortex."

You step back.

"It will be okay." She places an electrode in the left hemisphere of your brain. You hear a slight crunching sound as she penetrates your skull, but the pain you feel is less than a mosquito's bite. "I'm placing another electrode on your left hand. I'm stimulating your cortex before your left hand is stimulated. Did you feel the tingles in this order?"

"No. I know that the left side of the brain controls sensation on the right side of the body. I'd expect to feel two tingles: first on my right hand, induced by the brain stimulation, and then on my left hand. What I did feel was reversed. First I felt the left hand tingle, then the right."

"You see that the timing of 'mental' and 'physical' events can be all messed up." She pauses. "May I implant an electrode in your brain's motor cortex?"

"I suppose so. You wouldn't take no for an answer."

"Good. Now, I have wired you to an old-fashioned tape cassette player. On the tape is the Mormon Tabernacle Choir singing the 'Hallelujah Chorus.' I want you to press a button on the cassette player to advance the music whenever you wish."

You begin the experiment, and the tape changes songs, but—wait!—you are confused. "Miss Muxdröözol, the cassette player seems to change songs before I have even decided to make a change! It seems to anticipate my decision."

"Quite right. But I tricked you. The player's button is a dummy button, and did not have any affect on the cassette player. What actually advanced the songs was the amplified signal from the electrode in your motor cortex. Again, we see that voluntary motions are not initiated by our conscious minds! The signal occurred before your conscious intent to push the button. Scientists call this phenomenon the *precognitive carousel* because they tried this test using a carousel and slide projector. Subjects advanced slides just as they were about to push the button!"

Miss Muxdröözol removes the wire from your head, and then you sit down on a large spongelike piece of furniture. It smells like limes and occasionally purrs. Perhaps this kind of furniture is common for aliens of Miss Muxdröözol's species.

She removes a package from her pocket. "Care for some seaweed?" She folds her multiply jointed leg and begins to eat a portion of seaweed that looks like it has been shredded beforehand. The shreds wind around one another like braids of hair. "We do not eat meat on our world. At least, not anymore."

"No thanks," you say.

She looks at you with her glistening eyes. "Let's summarize. The mind plays tricks with time by making slight temporal adjustments. Today's lessons show that the brain plays with the concept of simultaneity and projects events back in time. You've also learned about cutaneous rabbits and precognitive carousels—all terminology in the serious psychological literature."

The two of you are silent for a while. Miss Muxdröözol tosses one of her vertebrae to you.

You hold the vertebra tightly in your hand. Perhaps this is a way that her species signals a desire for intimate friendship.

You look at Miss Muxdröözol. "Miss Muxdröözol, would you like to have some dinner together? I could get reservations for two at The Four Seasons. They have a vegetarian menu."

Miss Muxdröözol pauses for a few seconds considering your question. She waves her forelimbs. "Thank you for the offer, but we usually don't enjoy the food you Earthlings enjoy. Frankly, I prefer something more jumentous—"

Before she finishes, you take her hand and smile at her. "Perhaps while you are eating your seaweed, you wouldn't mind me placing electrodes on your scalp. Won't hurt a bit." You start running after her as she bolts, making silly sounds that imitate the crunching of seaweed.

## MUSINGS AND SPECULATIONS

The experiments in this chapter demonstrate how the mind plays tricks with time, and are all based on numerous different physiological experiments conducted by Wilder Penfield, Benjamin Libet, Paul Kolers, M. von Grünau, H. van der Waals, C. Roelofs, and others, and described by Daniel Dennett, Marcel Kinsbourne, and Rainer Wolf.[3] Voluntary motions are not initiated by our *conscious* minds. And the brain does seem to have a "time machine" for antedating perceptions. The brain "projects" mental events backward in time in strange ways.

I discuss these and other paradoxes of the brain in my book *Time: A Traveler's Guide*. Note that the various biological and mental paradoxes raise interesting issues about who is actually in control of our actions and seem to place organic limitations on our knowledge. The theological implications are broad. What if Eve's intent to reach for the forbidden fruit was not initiated by her conscious mind? What if God's intent to commit some act was not initiated by His conscious mind?

These topics touch on our discussions about how an omniscient God may be incompatible with free will. As many have noted, omniscience need not imply a denial of free will, because *knowing*—being conscious of—something does not *cause* something any more than knowing what the President had for breakfast invalidates the fact that he chose freely. But can one choose freely if one chooses before one is conscious of choosing? We'll discuss these topics in more depth in chapters that follow.

Figure 9.1 is a schematic illustration of the green light/red light experiment discussed in this chapter. Subjects actually report seeing the color of a "moving" cross switch midtrajectory from green to red. How are we able perceptually to fill in the empty spot between two crosses at the intervening places and times (along a path running from the first to the second flash) *before* that second flash occurs? One possible explanation is that the brain has an editing stage prior to consciousness. Perhaps there is a time delay, as is common in "live" TV or radio broadcasts, that allows the brain to package stimuli before they reach consciousness. In the brain's editing room, missing frames are filled in after the red (second) light flashes, and the brain inserts these back in perceived time like a director splicing in new frames in a videotape. By the time the finished piece arrives at consciousness, it already has its illusory continuity.

Figure 9.2 reinforces what you have learned in this chapter, namely that the time line experienced consciously by you is often quite different from the "objective" time line of events occurring in your brain or in real life. In short, the time lines do not correspond and can develop kinks and event-order differences relative to one another. Daniel Dennett and Marcel Kinsbourne believe that this nonalignment is "no more mysterious or contracausal than the realization that the individual scenes in movies are often shot out of sequence." Nevertheless, disparities among time lines should stimulate fascinating adventures and experiments in consciousness and chronology, particularly as research in computer–brain interfaces matures in the twenty-first century.

Researchers have also conducted experiments relating to time and free will. For example, a subject with brain waves monitored is asked to flex his wrist whenever he feels like it. The subject watches a rapidly moving clock and reports the exact time of his subjective intention to flex his wrist. The electrode responds about 300 milliseconds before the decision is experienced. This means that you can know a person's intent before the person does! This also certainly means that a God, even with very limited omniscience, can know a person's intent before the person does. The sensation of free will, created in memory, occurs after the fact as a convenient way to record the decision. Some might argue that free will in the religious sense, involving big moral issues, takes place on a different time scale such that this model of the brain does not apply. However, if scientists can demonstrate that some decisions are determined in the brain before we are aware of them, perhaps many or all of our decisions are predetermined.

Other time experiments involve alternately flashing police car lights that can appear to *move* back and forth. Moreover, one light appears to move toward the other a split second before the other flashes. Obviously, the brain can't predict the future and know the other light is going to flash before it does. The whole experience of movement is created after the fact. All experiences are created after the fact.

I suggest that readers interested in various temporal anomalies of consciousness read Dennett and Kinsbourne's article, "Time and the Observer: The Where and When of Consciousness in the Brain."[4]

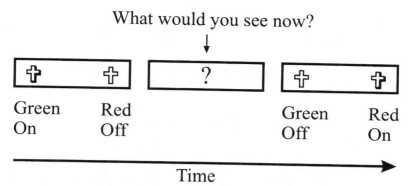

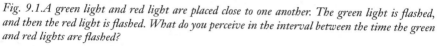

Fig. 9.1. *A green light and red light are placed close to one another. The green light is flashed, and then the red light is flashed. What do you perceive in the interval between the time the green and red lights are flashed?*

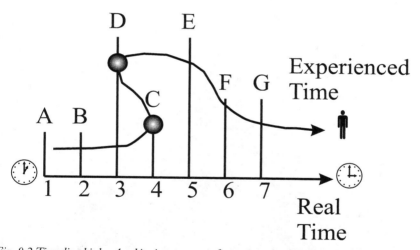

Fig. 9.2. *Time line kinks. A subjective sequence of experienced events (top line) often does not coincide with events in the brain in real time (bottom line).*

God makes an interesting point: despite the hierarchical structure of human religion, there isn't any middleman. There's only Him. . . . Peeping out at all of His interior/exterior Escher-like universe-body simultaneously as if the skin of reality was the skin of the Creator's optic nerve. Thus, His omniscience belies intimate contact with all of creation, implies a co-creator status to any sentient beings, especially nutty ones like humanity.

—Martin Olson, personal communication describing
a fragment from his *Encyclopedia of Hell*

# CHAPTER 10

# The Bodhisattva Paradox

B.C. MANSFIELD

*The Buddha, the Godhead, resides quite as comfortably in the circuits of a digital computer or the gears of a cycle transmission as he does at the top of a mountain or in the petals of a flower; to think otherwise is to demean the Buddha—which is to demean oneself.*
    —*Robert Pirsig,* Zen and the Art of Motorcycle Maintenance

YOU'VE ALWAYS WANTED TO SEE THE WORLD'S LARGEST BUDDHA statue, so you take a break from the drudgery of your regular work and travel to the Po Lin Monastery on Lantau, one of Hong Kong's outer islands. When you arrive at the mysterious shore, you can't believe your eyes. The Buddha on Lantau Island is the largest bronze statue in the world that depicts Buddha seated. It's so big that you actually see it from your airplane.[1]

Now you are on foot, hoping to reach the Buddha before sunset. All around you are winding coastal paths and tough mountain trails. Waterfalls tumble through secluded ravines.

Only minutes remain until you reach the statue. A quiet breeze touches your face and everywhere is the smell of flowers. You look ahead. There's a green hill. Two hundred and sixty-eight steps upward. And finally you are inches away from the Buddha.

The Buddha sits on a Lotus Blossom. One hand is up, the other in his lap. His pose is one of teaching. There is a nearby monastery. In the distance you can see the ocean. Occasionally, Buddhist pilgrims light small ceremonial fires that give off an exotic lilac scent.

A small man approaches you. "I am a bodhisattva." He pronounces the word "boe-di-*SAHT*-va" as he bows.

You bow back. "Sir, I am unfamiliar with that word."

"In Sanskrit bodhisattva means 'one who is destined for enlightenment.' The term originally referred to the historical Buddha, Siddhartha Gautama."

You nod and look up at the vague perpetual clouds, and then you gaze back into the man's dark eyes. He continues, "In certain blends of Buddhism, the term refers to someone like me who has passed through ten stages to spiritual perfection, but out of compassion chooses to delay the final reward, Nirvana. The reason I delay is that I want to work for the salvation of all other sentient beings. I want to help others reach perfection."

You bow again. You are impressed with his altruism. "That is very interesting."

"Yes, it is, but I have a bit of a dilemma. Maybe you can help me."

"I will try, Master."

"As I said, I cannot enter Nirvana. The reason? If I did this I would be demonstrating a selfishness that a bodhisattva cannot have."

"I understand. If you are selfish, then you are not a bodhisattva and therefore cannot enter Nirvana."

"Exactly. If I lack the selflessness, I can't enter Nirvana because that is selfish. The bodhisattva is powerless to enter Nirvana."

You motion the bodhisattva to sit next to you on a marble bench. "This reminds me of a Christian teaching. God cannot do evil things because it is inconsistent with his essence. Similarly, you, a bodhisattva, cannot perform the ultimate selfish act."

The monk looks sad. "So no one can reach Nirvana. You ordinary folks can't reach Nirvana because you are *not* bodhisattvas. And we bodhisattvas cannot because we *are* bodhisattvas. This paradox bothers me."

"Me too. Your choice to stay back in this world is ultimate proof of your selflessness. If only a bodhisattva can enter Nirvana, because only he is unselfish enough not to do so, then who truly can enter Nirvana?"

Together you gaze out to the endless oceans. The monk presses a button on the ground, and Antonín Dvořák's *Symphony No. 7 in D Minor* pours out of cracks between the granite and quartz. "Freedom," you whisper, and then you smile as orange light reflects off spirals on tessellated water, challenging the azure of an endless sky. You want to say something to the bodhisattva, something profound, something that adequately expresses your emotions.

The monk has tears in his eyes, and he stretches his arms and says, "I know. We can go anywhere. We have shattered time." He gives your hand a squeeze. You think he looks like an angel in the glorious pink rays of the sun. His hand feels warm.

You stop, for saying the truth aloud is unendurable. You know now why this tranquil life seems like an afterlife or a dream, unreal. It is because you know in your heart that it can be repeated, refined, and relived with slight alterations and sadness avoided. You feel omniscient, omnipresent, omnipotent. You will never experience pain or loneliness or horror again. All this lovely play of form and light and color on the Indian Ocean and in the eyes of men is no more than that: a playing of illusions in spacetime.

"Let's go," the monk says as your spirits flee above the Indian Ocean. Together you gaze into clear, limitless water. Your disconnected minds turn and glide above bright shining swirls of mist. You are moving toward open sea.

### MUSINGS AND SPECULATIONS

*All that is not given is lost.*

—*Indian proverb*

Okay. I know the ending of this parable got a bit out of hand. I can get carried away, and sometimes I enjoy a poetic moment. Let's return to Earth. The paradox discussed here has been discussed in depth by the philosopher Arthur Danto.[2]

Perhaps one way out of the paradox is to conclude that the concept of "selfishness" has no meaning once one is on the threshold of Nirvana. If it has no meaning, the paradox is less strong. Can you think of other resolutions to the paradox of the bodhisattvas? Perhaps Nirvana isn't chosen but attained automatically—like death in a sense.

Buddhism, more than any religion, is riddled with paradoxes. One of my favorites comes from the fourth-century Chinese Taoist Chuang Tzu:

> The fish trap exists because of the fish; once you've gotten the fish, you can forget the trap. The rabbit snare exists because of the rabbit; once you've gotten the rabbit, you can forget the snare. Words exist because of meaning; once you've gotten the meaning, you can forget the words. When can I find a man who has forgotten words so I can have a word with him?[3]

"Zen" is a Chinese way of accomplishing the Buddhist goal of experiencing the world with minimal thought, prejudice, and emotion. Unlike other forms of Buddhism, Zen holds that spiritual and mental freedom cannot be attained solely by years of practice but must come through a flash of insight called *tun-wun* in Chinese or *satori* in Japanese. In other words, Zen eschews the intellect as the main means for understanding reality. Instead, Zen requires its practitioners to meditate on paradoxes, often in the form of Zen *koans*—problems with no logical solutions—to disrupt the usual reasoning processes. For example, when Joshu, a great Zen master was asked, "When a man comes to you with nothing, what would you say to him?" his reply was, "Throw it away." Another famous koan is, "What is the sound of one hand clapping?" Koans are used to enable us to fly beyond restrictions of self and to shock the mind into enlightenment.

Musician John Cage on his CD *Indeterminacy* told a story about his Zen teacher D. T. Suzuki:

> Before studying Zen, men are men and mountains are mountains. While studying Zen, things become confused. After studying Zen, men are men and mountains are mountains. After telling this, Dr. Suzuki was asked, "What is the difference between before and after?" He said, "No difference—only the feet are a little bit off the ground."[4]

Here are some other interesting koans from several anonymous, ancient authors:[5]

- One monk said to the other, "The fish has flopped out of the net! How will it live?" The other said, "When you have gotten out of the net, I'll tell you."

- A monk said to Joshu, "Your stone bridge is widely renowned, but coming here I find only a heap of rocks." Joshu said, "You see only the stones and not the bridge." The monk said, "What is the bridge?" Joshu said, "What do you think we are walking on?"
- Some professors asked a monk to lecture to them on spiritual matters. The monk ascended a podium, struck it once with his stick, and descended. The academics were dumbfounded. The monk asked them, "Do you understand what I have told you?" One professor said, "I do not understand." The monk said, "I have concluded my lecture."
- A student said to the chief monk, "Help me to pacify my mind!" The chief monk said, "Bring your mind over here and I will pacify it." The student said, "But I don't know where my mind is!" The monk replied, "Then I have already pacified it."
- A monk asked Nansen, "Is there any great spiritual teaching that has not been preached to the people?" Nansen said, "There is." "What is the truth that has not been taught?" "Nothing," Nansen replied.
- A young monk asked his teacher, "What is the true spiritual nature of life?" His teacher picked up a bowl of water and threw it in the student's face, saying "Go wash out your mouth!"
- A monk, taking a bamboo stick, said to the people, "If you call this a stick, you fall into the trap of words, but if you do not call it a stick, you contradict facts. So what do you call it?" At that time a monk in the assembly came forth. He snatched the stick, broke it in two, and threw the pieces across the room.

Let's mention a final possible paradox. "Nirvana" is a transcendent state free from suffering and individual existence. It is an ultimate religious goal. If Nirvana is the final experience, and if it is only attained by the loss of the self, *who* is experiencing Nirvana? What is an experience without an experiencer? Nirvana implies ultimate annihilation of the individual while at the same time providing individual fulfillment in eternal life.

Another possible paradox is that Nirvana is a state that sometimes requires years of meditation to achieve. The seeker does those things necessary to reach this state. But this means we can never achieve Nirvana, a state of complete desirelessness, because to achieve Nirvana one must desire it. How can you do what is necessary to achieve Nirvana without making Nirvana the goal of your actions?[6] Perhaps the solution to the paradox is for the seeker eventually, or at the last second, to let go of the desired goal.

👁 👁 👁

In our quest to transcend our ordinary lives, which are just minuscule fragments of the vast spacetime in our universe, we have been able to figure out how the stars came into existence. We know why stars shine. We know how they produce the heavy elements necessary for our bones and brains.[7] We also have compelling theories for how the universe came into existence, by random fluctuations in the quantum foam, governed by the laws of physics. However, we are less sure about where the foam and laws came from. We are less sure about why there is ultimately something rather than nothing. Robert Lawrence made a Zenlike remark in *Closer to Truth:* "Sometimes only silence gets us closer to truth."[8]

"Silence" has always been a mystical topic in religion. The Buddha himself when confronted with paradoxes would reply with:

# silence

Timothy Ferris, in *The Whole Shebang*, similarly believes, "In a creative universe, God would betray no trace of his presence, since to do so would rob the creative forces of their independence, to turn them from the active pursuit of answers to mere supplication of God. And so it is: God's language is silence."[9] The Ismailis, members of a Muslim sect, developed a method of reading the Koran called *tawil* in which they attempted to hear a sound of a verse on several levels simultaneously, which helped them become conscious of the silence surrounding each word.

In the Hebrew Bible, have you ever wondered who is the last person with whom God speaks? The answer is Job, the human who dares to challenge God's moral authority. After the Book of Job, God never speaks again, and He is decreasingly spoken of. In the Book of Esther—a book in which the Jews face a genocidal enemy (as they did in the Book of Exodus)—God is never mentioned. Why is there a long twilight in the ten closing books of the Hebrew Bible in which God is silent? During the time of Moses, God is revealed through miracles. After the Jews are exiled to Babylon and return, there are few divine signs.

John Fowles, in *The Magus*, sums up this isolation: "There are times when silence is a poem."[10]

👁 👁 👁

When I was a child, I wandered through my father's library and came across a book by Hendrik Willem Van Loon titled *The Arts*, published in 1937. I pulled the dusty book from the shelf and was delighted to find the following philosophical gem, a conversation between a student and a wise, old teacher:

> "Master, will you not tell us what the highest purpose may be to which mortal man may aspire?"
>
> A strange light now came into the eyes of Lao-Kung as he lifted himself from his seat. His trembling feet carried him across the room to the spot where stood the one picture that he loved best. It was a blade of grass, for within itself it contained the spirit of every blade of grass that had ever grown since the beginning of time.
>
> "There," the old man said, "is my answer. I have made myself equal of the Gods, for I too have touched the hem of Eternity."[11]

Lao-Kung, like many of the ancient philosophers and writers, considered the concept of God to be intimately intertwined with the infinite. For example, Figure 10.1 is a view of Heaven from Dante's *Divine Comedy* showing the number of angels increasing to infinity the higher one ascends. Saint Augustine believed not only that God was infinite, but also that God could think infinite thoughts. According to Augustine, God "knows all numbers."

Augustine's works, along with the simple Van Loon passage, planted a seed in early childhood from which my interest in paradox and God grew. Maybe this book will contain seeds for you.

> If we are to think positively of the One, there would be more truth in Silence.
>
> —Plotinus (205–270)

> As one goes through it, one sees that the gate one went through was the self that went through it
>
> —R. D. Laing, "Knots"

> We say God is pure spirit and always was and always will be. . . . The truth is in Genesis. . . . I'll tell you what the big bang was, Lestat. It was when the cells of God began to divide.
>
> —Anne Rice, *Tale of the Body Thief*

*Fig. 10.1. Dante's view of heaven. Reprinted from Gustave Doré,* The Doré Illustrations for Dante's Divine Comedy *(New York: Dover, 1976), 134.*

Passage after passage—not only in the Gospels but throughout the Bible—tantalize, fascinate, puzzle.... The Bible is not a quiet narrative—it stirs the mind. Perhaps these mysteries are present for just this purpose—to cause us to ponder.

—Alma Guinness, *Mysteries of the Bible*

Alpha might be unidentified with the jealous God of the Old Testament, who watches over all creatures.... I demolished Alpha by invoking the ghost of Kurt Gödel, whose notorious "incompleteness of knowledge" theorem quite obviously rules out the existence of an omniscient being. However, this is an area where logic gets you nowhere. Belief—or disbelief—in Alpha appears to be irrevocably programmed into most people at an early age.

—Arthur C. Clarke, *Skeptical Inquirer*

# CHAPTER 11

# The Paradox of Pascal's Wager

*Belief is a wise wager. Granted that faith cannot be proved, what harm will come to you if you gamble on its truth and it proves false? . . . If you gain, you gain all; if you lose, you lose nothing. Wager, then, without hesitation, that He exists.*

—*Blaise Pascal,* Pensées

*The sole cause of man's unhappiness is that he does not know how to stay quietly in his room.*

—*Blaise Pascal,* Pensées

You have traveled back in time with Miss Muxdröözol, your extraterrestrial friend. The year is 1665. The place: the Jansenist monastery Port-Royal des Champs, about 30 kilometers southwest of Paris. The air is filled with the lusty odors of earth and sheep manure. In the distance is the gentle tintinnabulation of cowbells.

You watch as Blaise Pascal (1623–1662)—the famous French mathematical genius and religious philosopher—writes about a strange argument in favor of belief in God. Pascal's hair is long and his nose pointy (see Figure 11.1). His hand appears tired from writing.

Pascal looks up but does not see you because you are using the latest cloaking technology. This technology makes you invisible to anyone you visit back in time.

Miss Muxdröözol points to Pascal. "There he is. He recently nearly lost his life when the horses pulling his carriage bolted and his carriage was left hanging over a bridge above the river Seine."

*Fig. 11.1.Blaise Pascal (1623–1662), the famous French mathematical genius and religious philosopher, who developed a strange argument in favor of belief in God. (French postage stamp.)*

"Was he injured?" you whisper, although the cloaking device reduces the volume of whatever you say by 90 percent, thereby making it very unlikely he can hear you. Perhaps he thinks your voice is the whisper of the wind.

"He wasn't hurt—physically. However, the experience affected his outlook on life. He had some subsequent religious experiences in November of 1654, and he pledged his life to Christianity."

"What's he doing now?"

"I think he's starting to work on his *Pensées*, his most famous work in philosophy. It will be a collection of personal thoughts on human suffering and faith in God." Miss Muxdröözol pauses and motions you to sit down on the dusty stone floor. "Pascal did not think that reason alone could justify belief in a god. He came up with the following wager to decide whether or not we should believe based on the possible outcomes for the afterlife."

Miss Muxdröözol touches one of the tapestries on the wall depicting an ancient prophet with a long beard. The prophet appears to be looking right at you.

Miss Muxdröözol continues her explanation. "Many religions suggest that God punishes those who do not believe in Him. These atheists, at best, live in an unfulfilled afterlife and, at worst, burn in the flames of hell forever. On the other hand, God rewards believers with eternal happiness in heaven. We can summarize the potential benefits and risks of believing in God." She hands you a card that she ejects from a microprinter in her ankle:

**Table 11.1   Pascal's Belief vs. Unbelief Outcomes**

|  | *God Exists* | *God's Doesn't Exist* |
|---|---|---|
| You believe | Eternal bliss! (4) ☺ | Death is final (2) ☻ |
| You don't believe | Eternal pain! (1) ☹ | Death is final (3) ☻ |

"Tell me about the numbers in the table," you say.

"The benefits are ranked from 4 (eternal bliss) down to 1 (eternal pain). It's difficult to know how to assign harm and benefit to your beliefs for column 2 unless your belief causes you or others unhappiness. One could argue that it's better to believe in a truth (3) than a falsehood (2), but one could equally argue that believing in a falsehood has positive effects on yourself and humanity. Although the benefit values in column 2 are debatable, we don't really need to consider column 2, because you can see that believing in general has a huge potential benefit."

"I think I see where this is heading, at least as far as Pascal was concerned. If you believe it is possible (or worthwhile) to believe in something by studying a cost-benefit analysis, Pascal would advise you to choose to believe in God. Pascal himself believed that to opt for God was a win-win solution."

"Very good analysis. However, I tend toward atheism. Listen to my argument. I think I can show you how Pascal's argument is flawed."

You move a little closer to Miss Muxdröözol so that you can whisper and avoid the risk of Pascal hearing you. "Tell me more."

"I don't think there is strong evidence for God's existence. Would you say it is possible for rational people to have some reasonable doubts about God's existence?"

You pause. "Yes, it is possible. I'm an open-minded person. I also sometimes yearn to have more direct evidence of God to give all the people on Earth."

"You concede rational people could have reasonable doubts. Now, consider that God exists. It's also not too much of a stretch of the imagination to think that God likes it when His creatures use their intellects and perform experiments? He may value rationality in His creatures. Do you personally think He will damn to hell someone for using rationality?"

"No. I don't personally believe that. That would not be sufficient reason for damnation."

Miss Muxdröözol nods her head. "I think it's even possible that God could be unhappy with those who are not rational, those who believe in all sorts of things without being logical about it. For example, maybe God does not like it when people believe in psychic surgeons who claim to be able to perform surgery with no knives. Today we know these people are charlatans who hide chicken guts in false thumbs. The so-called operation looks impressively bloody."

"Yes, I have heard about those scams."

"I even think that such a God might punish believers for their credulity and reward clear thinkers that don't succumb to peer pressure and so forth. Of all the creatures on Earth, humans are the only ones that God gave the most intelligence, so obviously God wants us to use our intellect and to be freethinkers. So when we die, God will reward freethinkers. He won't be happy with people who tossed their reason away in favor of ignorance."

Miss Muxdröözol ejects another card from her body-attached microprinter. On the card is the following payoff matrix:

**Table 11.2    Miss Muxdröözol's Belief vs. Unbelief Outcomes**

|  | *God Exists* | *God's Doesn't Exist* |
|---|---|---|
| You believe | Punishment for credulity!(1) ☹ | Dead wrong (2) ☹ |
| You don't believe | Reward for rationality (4) ☺ | Dead right (3) ☺ |

Miss Muxdröözol looks at you with her huge, unblinking eyes. "Don't worry. I'll erase this when we leave. Notice that in column 2, top row, you are not too happy believing in God if He *doesn't* not exist, because that would mean you spent your life believing in an untruth. Your only rational choice is to not believe in God."

Could Miss Muxdröözol be correct?

You think about this as you gaze outside the window where the leaves on the ground are coated with a thin patina of snow that glimmers like a mirror. A squirrel is gathering nuts and placing them beneath the jawbone of an ass. Of course, it's not really a jawbone of an ass. It's your time travel machine, in camouflage mode, ready to take you home. Its bony white surface is made out of durable titanium to help it withstand the changing of the years.

You look at Miss Muxdröözol's table of values in bewilderment, wondering about the validity of Pascal's Wager.

## MUSINGS AND SPECULATIONS

*Reason's last step is the recognition that there are an infinite number of things which are beyond it.*

—*Blaise Pascal*, Pensées

Pascal's approach to belief in God was certainly revolutionary for its time, but the Church never officially accepted it. The Church usually favored a "rationalistic approach" to believing in God rather than one based on gambling. Pascal felt that we are incapable of knowing either what God is or if He exists. Reason cannot decide this latter question. The best way to figure this out is to wager.

Pascal believed that to choose God was the best bet. The risk is finite, but the gain infinite. One flaw in Pascal's argument is that it only deals with two possibilities: a particular God exists or does not exist. This premise ignores the possibilities that other gods with a host of strange characteristics could exist and that each of these gods could have different criteria (or no criteria) for salvation and damnation. For example, the New Testament God requires more for salvation than simply belief in God. One must also believe in God's son or perhaps do good deeds, be born again, and so forth. I know many Christians who think that Jews and Muslims will burn in hell, yet Jews and Muslims typically believe in God. Also, what if God does not exist, but a nearly omniscient squid from another world rules the cosmos? Its criteria for reward and punishment could differ from the biblical criteria for belief in God. All of these factors point out difficulties in considering Pascal's interesting logic.

In 1908, W. W. Rouse Ball, author of *A Short Account of the History of Mathematics*, expressed his skepticism:

> Pascal made an illegitimate use of the new theory in the seventh chapter of his Pensées. In effect, he puts his argument that, as the value of eternal happiness must be infinite, then, even if the probability of a religious life ensuring eternal happiness be very small, still the expectation (which is measured by the product of the two) must be of sufficient magnitude to make it worth while to be religious. The argument, if worth anything, would apply equally to any religion which promised eternal happiness to those who accepted its doctrines. If any conclusion may be drawn from the statement, it is the undesirability of applying mathematics to questions of morality of which some of the data are necessarily outside the range of an exact science. It is only fair to add that no one had more contempt than Pascal for those who change their opinions according to the prospect of material benefit, and this isolated passage is at variance with the spirit of his writings.[1]

To me, the biggest challenge to applying Pascal's Wager is the difficulty in understanding what is meant by God. God means something different to each person. For example, Michio Kaku, author of *Hyperspace*, differentiates between two kinds of Gods—the God of Miracles and the God of Order.[2] Many scientists use the word God to mean the God of Order, the God of mathematical and physical laws and underpinnings of the universe. Others may use the word God to refer to the God of Miracles who intervenes in our affairs, turns water into wine, answers prayers, cures the dying, inflicts plagues on His enemies, performs various miracles, helps the Israelites destroy the Canaanites, and avenges the righteous people on Earth.

During the fourteenth century, the Black Death swept Europe, littering towns with corpses. Some people thought that the Plague was the work of an angry God. (Today we know the immediate culprit was a tiny bacterium,

*Yersinia pestis*, and its proteins, which rendered the immune system ineffective.) Clearly, the belief-outcome tables in this chapter depend a lot on the characteristics of God.

👁 👁 👁

Ed Gracely (see "The Devil's Offer" in Chapter 6) wrote to me about Pascal's Wager:

> Pascal's wager involves an argument that belief in God is pragmatically justified by the possibility of an infinite gain in the afterlife, with at most a finite loss. There are many possible replies to Pascal, but they all have complications and difficulties, some of which are paradoxical. For example, not only is there a finite probability of gaining God's favor by belief, but there is also a finite probability of doing so by non-belief. And any specific religious belief, from the most sensible to the absurd, has some probability of gaining divine favor as well. Because any belief or lack of belief has some probability of gaining divine approval, they all have infinitely good implications, and the decision about belief is difficult to make. Naturally, the decisions all also have finite probabilities of divine punishment, so they also have infinitely bad implications. So now what happens to ethics? Every action (not just every belief) has some probability of divine favor/disfavor, thus they all have infinite (and equivalent) consequences. Therefore, it is difficult to choose among various actions. (This argument is purely theoretical, because most of us would agree that a 5% probability of an infinite good is, all else equal, better than a 1% probability of it.)[3]

Gracely suggests, not unlike Miss Muxdröözol, that a more reasonable argument against Pascal's Wager considers that God would be more likely to punish than to reward blind faith. Certainly, many atheists and agnostics would accept this as a possibility. However, Gracely notes that the wager might not really create faith but instead replace it:

> This "wager approach" would seem to imply that it is of great importance to convince people to give up their faith, an implausible conclusion. This method of dealing with the wager argument also leaves us needing to scrutinize every action in terms of whether the action would be, perhaps, slightly more likely than another to bring about eternal punishment (or reward). Once the mere possibility of infinite reward or punishment is admitted, it creates severe difficulties—you risk either vitiating all ethics, or being forced to pass every ethical decision through the lens of that possible consequence. I don't know that a fully consistent approach to the problem exists. This sec-

ond approach (but not the first) is unaffected if we state that heaven and hell last for $10^{100}$ years, not forever, so this becomes a problem of vastly large numbers, not truly of infinity.[4]

Gracely is also interested in the concept of infinity as it relates to sacrifices of various kinds. For example, he has suggested that we might set aside the religious perspective on Pascal's Wager and consider the fact that the human race may theoretically exist forever, and that a sacrifice made today to ensure humanity's survival may have infinite consequences:

> If this is true, you find yourself forced to regard benefits to present individuals as having no weight, compared to the small chance of saving the race. This same argument would continue forever. So we have the curious specter of a human race living forever, and focusing heavily throughout that eternity on making sure that it does so, even if this effort made life not worth living at every time point. Jan Narveson discusses this kind of problem in his essay, "Future People and Us" in the book *Obligations to Future Generations*.[5]

It seems particularly fitting to close this chapter with a recent quote from skeptic Barry McGuire:

> A world with a god is totally indistinguishable from a world without one. That is why all wager theories are totally disingenuous. Pascal leads you down a primrose path suggesting you are far better off wagering that there is a god. . . . [However, what you discover from more reading of Pascal] is that your wager must now transform into acceptance of the full array of Roman Catholic beliefs. Only this will keep you from the fires of hell. So a simple wager that there is a god will get you the same results as a wager that there isn't. Either way you will burn, baby, burn.[6]

I'm interested in the idea of cosmic omniscience in relation to the idea in Einstein's relativity theory that simultaneity cannot exist and, thus, either there can be no perception of simultaneity, or else all events, from God's point of view, occur simultaneously. The Ultimate Perceiver must perceive either all at once or via infinite different views; the Creator's living room can be seen only as One Big Thing or as an Endless Infinity of Things, but nothing in between those two equal and opposite extremes.
—Martin Olson, personal communication

CHAPTER 12

# Two Universes

B.C. MANSFIELD

*As the island of knowledge grows, the surface that makes contact with mystery expands. When major theories are overturned, what we thought was certain knowledge gives way, and knowledge touches upon mystery differently. This newly uncovered mystery may be humbling*

*and unsettling, but it is the cost of truth. Creative scientists, philoso-*
*phers, and poets thrive at this shoreline.*
　　　　　*—W. Mark Richardson, "A Skeptic's Sense of Wonder"*

Consider two universes. Universe Omega is a universe in which God does not exist, but the inhabitants of the universe believe God exists. Universe Upsilon is a universe in which God does exist, but no inhabitant believes God exists.

| Universe Omega | Universe Upsilon |
| --- | --- |

In which universe would you prefer to live? In which universe do you think most people would prefer to live?[1]

## MUSINGS AND SPECULATIONS

*When they learned to navigate the polarity barrier between the two*
*universes, they were amazed to discover our life and existence, sim-*
*ilar to theirs, in opposite reality, and over time established contact*
*across the barrier and learned to navigate and explore their anti-*
*matter counterpart—our phenomenal universe. They also learned*
*to communicate across the barrier and maintained contact with the*
*Earth man by electromagnetic means, which they carried on for*
*over 25 years.*
　　　　　*—James W. Deardorff, "The Meier Case and Its Spirituality"[2]*

I surveyed about 50 individuals regarding this question. Universes Omega and Upsilon were chosen by roughly equal numbers of people. Some respondents suggested that if people think God exists, then God is sufficiently "real." Other individuals suggested that people would behave more humanely to each another in a Universe where people believed in God. Yet others countered that an ethical system dependent on faith in a watchful, omniscient, or vengeful God is fragile and prone to collapse when doubt begins to undermine faith. Following are some comments I received.

　　Keith D. said, "I would prefer to live in Universe Omega. If the God of Upsilon is omniscient, He will know of the existence of Universe Omega and its believers, and perhaps He would save them."

Diane R. said, "I choose Upsilon. I've had enough of living in Omega already, thank you very much."

Lorraine M. said, "I vote for Upsilon; if God exists there are many possibilities to discover this existence. The idea of communing with a God that doesn't exist seems scary."

Peter A. said, "There have been many 'gods' that I wouldn't want to be in the same room with, so how believers define god is critical. Another important question is: does god provide for life after death?"

Don W. chooses Upsilon because "many wars have been fought over religion, with each side believing that God was on their side. Maybe life would be treated more preciously if death was regarded as final."

Elizabeth P. said, "I'd far rather live in the universe where people believe in God. I figure they stand a better chance of being better behaved towards their fellow beings. In the universe where nobody believes in a god that actually exists, everybody goes to hell anyway, right?"

Bets L. said, "If the inhabitants of Omega interpret the physical signs available to them as evidence of God, then does it really matter if God exists? These people would follow their belief with the semblance of moral order which would be in harmony with the physical phenomena they observe—thus, their religion would be helping to synchronize them with the natural order and to make their lives better off for their belief. Concerning Upsilon, if God exists but the inhabitants cannot discern that existence, then one would assume that their moral order would be assembled based on what they observe. If what they observe is a manifestation of God's order in the universe, then it should not matter whether they believe in God or simply observe and adapt to the universe around them. The only aspect of material difference between these two scenarios would be the question of afterlife. Again, this premise would be larger than a question of belief . . . if what really happens is re-incarnation, then it will happen whether one believes or not. If there is some sort of otherworld afterlife that is a function of the existence of God, then the question becomes one of the method God would use for judging worthiness. If God requires in Upsilon the belief in him/her in order to gain entry to the afterlife, then it would be pointless, as no one believes. God would require enough logic and order that he/she would never set up an algorithm in which the answer would be the null set. If God's algorithm were different (some measure of living a life of peace, love, acceptance, and inclusion), then it wouldn't matter whether one believed in God so much as whether one were able to assimilate and practice living according to some qualitative measures that would be visible to God, with or without the individual's belief."

Martie S. said, "A belief in God is likely to influence the behavior of the inhabitants. Those who believe in a God of the Judeo-Christian tradition—or of most of the Eastern Religion traditions—will most likely pattern their behaviors after what they perceive as 'the good.' If the God were one of love and tolerance, then the pattern of behavior in that universe would likely be of love and tolerance. Therefore, it is more likely that the Omega universe would be a more secure and enjoyable place to live."

April P. said, "A choice of being blissfully unaware or relying on blind faith? I'd prefer Universe Omega, because belief in God is an important motivator for a thinking species. It is an important element of cultural enrichment. Universe Omega would have to contain *thinking* inhabitants. Universe Upsilon would have to be inhabited by non-sentient life, because belief in god is a byproduct of being able to think. I wouldn't want to live in a universe whose inhabitants did not think."

Marsha S. said, "I'd prefer to live in Universe Upsilon where no banners are unfurled and no wars are fought in God's name. I'm also certain that God would forgive my disbelief. I think most people would choose Universe Omega because they feel a belief in a nonexistent God might guarantee some 'better' code of conduct."

Of course, my limited sample of respondents does not shed light on the overall thinking of America or the world. I urge you to ask colleagues this question. Other more exotic questions come immediately to mind, and I'm sure many of you will think of some. For example, imagine that both Omega and Upsilon exist and are inhabited by numerous intelligent races. What would happen if a wormhole opened between the two universes and allowed the inhabitants to interact and mix? What would be the outcome for the inhabitants? And how might the God of Upsilon respond?

There are only two ways to live your life. One is as though nothing is a miracle. The other is as though everything is a miracle.
—Albert Einstein, in Max Jammer's *Einstein and Religion*

*Esse est percipi.* (To be is to be perceived.)
—George Berkeley, *Treatise Concerning the Principles of Human Knowledge*

# CHAPTER 13

# Gödel's Proof of God

B.C. MANSFIELD

*Were theologians to succeed in their attempt to strictly separate science and religion, they would kill religion. Theology simply must become a branch of physics if it is to survive. That even theologians are slowly becoming effective atheists has been documented.*

—*Frank Tipler,* The Physics of Immortality

Perhaps the most interesting example of a mathematician studying cosmic questions is Austrian mathematician Kurt Gödel, who lived from 1906 to 1978. Sometime in 1970, Gödel's mathematical proof of the existence of God began to circulate among his colleagues. The proof was less than a page long and caused quite a stir.

---

### Gödel's Mathematical Proof of God's Existence

*Axiom 1.* (Dichotomy) A property is positive if and only if its negation is negative.

*Axiom 2.* (Closure) A property is positive if it necessarily contains a positive property.

*Theorem 1.* A positive property is logically consistent (i.e., possibly it has some instance).

*Definition.* Something is God-like if and only if it possesses all positive properties.

*Axiom 3.* Being God-like is a positive property.

*Axiom 4.* Being a positive property is (logical, hence) necessary.

*Definition.* A property $P$ is the essence of $x$ if and only if $x$ has $P$ and $P$ is necessarily minimal.

*Theorem 2.* If $x$ is God-like, then being God-like is the essence of $x$.

*Definition.* $NE(x)$: $x$ necessarily exists if it has an essential property.

*Axiom 5.* Being $NE$ is God-like.

*Theorem 3.* Necessarily there is some $x$ such that $x$ is God-like.

---

How shall we judge such an abstract proof? How many people on Earth can really understand it? Most logicians and mathematicians that I consulted were not able to explain all aspects of the proof, and so it is difficult to assess its significance. Is the proof the result of profound contemplation or the raving of a lunatic?

Certainly, Gödel's academic credits were impressive. For example, he was a respected mathematician and a faculty member of the University of Vienna starting in 1930. He emigrated to the United States in 1940 and became a member of the Institute of Advanced Study in Princeton, New Jersey. Gödel is most famous for his theorem, published in 1931, demonstrating that there must be true formulas in mathematics and logic that are neither provable nor disprovable, thus making mathematics essentially incomplete. Gödel's theorem had quite a sobering effect upon logicians and philosophers, because it implies that within any rigidly logical mathematical system there are propositions or questions that cannot be proved or disproved on the basis of axioms within that system, and therefore it is possible for basic axioms of arithmetic to give rise to contradictions. The repercussions of this continue to be felt and debated. Moreover, Gödel's article in 1931 put an end to a century-long attempt to establish axioms that would provide a rigorous basis for all of mathematics.

Over the span of his life, Gödel kept voluminous notes on his mathematical ideas. Some of his work is so complex that mathematicians believe many decades will be required to decipher all of it. Author Hao Wang writes in his book *Reflections on Kurt Gödel*:

The impact of Gödel's scientific ideas and philosophical speculations has been increasing, and the value of their potential implications may continue to increase. It may take *hundreds of years* for the appearance of more definite confirmations or refutations of some his larger conjectures.[1]

Gödel himself spoke of the need for a physical organ in our bodies to handle abstract theories. He also suggested that philosophy will evolve into an exact theory "within the next hundred years or even sooner." He even believed that humans will eventually disprove propositions such as "there is no mind separate from matter."

### MUSINGS AND SPECULATIONS

*The brain is a computing machine connected with a spirit.*
—*Kurt Gödel, quoted in Hao Wang,* A Logical Journey

I could not find significant information in the philosophical or mathematical literature regarding the interpretation of Gödel's proof of God. Hao Wang (1921–1995), one of the few confidants of Kurt Gödel, offered no opinion or help to readers in interpreting the proof. In fact, he states enigmatically, "I am only including [the proof] for some measure of completeness, and shall, out of ignorance, make no comments on it." I therefore consulted various mathematicians and philosophers on the Internet for their opinions. If you don't understand all of their comments, don't worry. At the least, they will give you the flavor of how current researchers in philosophy and mathematics express their thoughts on complex areas in which mathematics and theology overlap and interact. I have not eliminated repetitious information so that you can get a feel for points of agreement among respondents.[2]

Ivan R., a doctoral student in Computers and Information Sciences at The Ohio State University, comments:

The proof has an obvious problem in that it only shows the existence of a mathematical object with the property "God-like" as defined in the proof. There is no relation to the real world; it is like proving that there is no last cardinal number. Furthermore, the proof does not exclude the possibility of the existence of an infinite number of disjoint objects all with the property "God-like."

Mike M. from Western Illinois University comments:

Here's the easiest place at which the proof may be ripped apart. Nowhere is it shown that $x$ has to exist, except by this definition. Thus, we must be shown *why* this definition is correct before we accept it.

Pertsel V. from the Weizmann Institute of Science's Computation Center, comments:

I've heard the following advanced as a proof of God's existence:

1. "God" is defined as having all qualities in perfection.
2. Existence is a quality.
3. Therefore God must have this quality of existence, and so must exist.

However, the template for disproving such reasonings was given by A. G. Gein at one of the All-Soviet-Union mathematical competitions:

1. Non-existence is a quality.
2. Therefore God must have this quality of non-existence.
3. Therefore God must not exist.

Benjamin T., a mathematics graduate student at Dartmouth, comments:

Gödel's proof of God's existence seems to have a number of flaws. The main one is that it asserts a number of axioms which are not very reasonable, and the second one is that there is no guarantee that the resulting "God" has any relationship to the ordinary religious notions. (1) Axiom 1 gives a definition. It is fine. However I would like to know what a "property" is, and what "negative" means. (2) Axiom 2 seems to be missing something since if I define all properties to be both negative and positive then the two axioms are satisfied and the theorem is false. (3) Does the definition, "Something is God-like if and only if it possesses all positive properties" have any relationship to the usual notions of God? (4) I have no problem with Axioms 3 and 4. (5) What does "minimal" mean? Minimal in what sense? (6) Theorem 2, followed by the definition and Axiom 5, essentially asserts the existence of God, as an axiom. Of course if you want to do that then I could just assert that God exists.

👁 👁 👁

Sadly, Kurt Gödel starved himself to death in 1978. How could this have happened to one of the most brilliant logicians of the twentieth century? No one doubts that his contributions were great and that his life illumined many important ideas in mathematics and philosophy. The implications of his "incompleteness theorem" are vast, not only applying to mathematics but also touching on areas such as computer science, economics, and nature. At Princeton, one of his closest friends was Albert Einstein. (Gödel, unlike Einstein, avoided public debate. Gödel felt that his philosophical views were too controversial to publicize, and he disliked publishing anything he could not prove rigorously.) Toward the end of Gödel's life, when his longtime wife Adele was not with him to coax him to eat—because she was in a hospital recovering from surgery—Gödel stopped eating.[3] He was paranoid and felt that people were trying to poison him. On December 19, 1977, he was hospitalized but refused food. He died on January 14, 1978. During his life, he had suffered from nervous breakdowns and hypochondria.

Hao Wang, a professor of logic at Rockefeller University, wrote in *A Logical Journey*, "It is even possible that his quite informal and loosely structured conversations with me, which I am freely using in this book, will turn out to be the fullest existing expression of the diverse components of his inadequately articulated general philosophy."[4] In his book, Wang illustrates the quest for grand unifications of knowledge in Gödel's written speculations on God and an afterlife.

Wang's book is notable in that it contains numerous quotations from Gödel's conversations with Wang. Amazingly, Wang retained quotations that he said he did not understand, trusting that others might someday be able to decipher them—for example, "Consciousness is connected with one unity. A machine is composed of parts."

---

There is none beside me. I am the Lord, and there is none else. I form the light, and create darkness: I make peace and create evil.

—Isaiah 45:6–7

# CHAPTER 14

# The Paradox of Uzzah

B.C. MANSFIELD

*The only path to knowing God is through the study of science—and for that reason the Bible opens with a description of the creation.*
—*Maimonides*, Guide for the Perplexed *(1190)*

YOU AND MISS MUXDRÖÖZOL HAVE TRANSPORTED YOURSELVES BACK IN time to watch King David's people bringing the Ark of the Covenant to Jerusalem, David's new headquarters. The Ark is a gold-gilded wooden box constructed according to God's specifications. According to the Bible, it contains the tablets of the law given to Moses along with other important objects such as a golden urn that holds a piece of manna and Aaron's staff. On top are two golden angels with outstretched wings.

With powerful binoculars, you peer down at a vast, dry lake bed ten miles away. Wrinkled old mountains rise in the east against a blue Jerusalem sky.

You suddenly hear a screaming sound tear across the sky, a horrifying cry, a sound that shatters the desert quiet like the screeching of fingernails upon a blackboard. "What the hell is that?" you say to Miss Muxdröözol.

Miss Muxdröözol slows her horse. "My God!" she shouts. She cups her hands over her eyes to help her see into the bright sky.

There is a flash of brown as a hawk crashes into the sagebrush—a flurry of beating wings, sharp claws, raucous screeching.

Startled, you urge your horse to the right as your heart thumps like an anxious conga-drum player. Miss Muxdröözol brings her own horse to a sudden halt, an unpracticed action that nearly throws her from its saddle.

You will your heart to shift into neutral. "Nothing to worry about," you say, looking all around for traces of the bird. "Just a hawk."

You look up and see dozens of hawks gliding like windblown bits of ash high above the oak trees. Others seem to be joining them from over in Bethany and Gibeah. What are they looking for? The decaying remains of a wild dog's kill? Discarded remnants of a camel?

In minutes you are in a town on the road to Jerusalem. The crowds are cheering as they watch the grand spectacle of David's procession with the Ark. The sons of Abinadab walk behind and before the procession, while crowds walk with them, singing and playing all manner of instruments. One lady twirls as she plays a harp. Another crashes cymbals in some odd syncopated rhythm. Everyone seems happy.

And there is handsome David. When you were younger, you never knew for sure if this famous king of Israel was real or mythical. But in 1993, archaeological evidence outside the Bible seemed to substantiate the existence of Kind David. Archaeologists discovered a wall fragment at Tel Dan on the headwaters of the river Jordan. The Phoenician script, carved in stone, appears to refer to the House of David and the king of Israel.

Now David is dancing wildly, mostly naked. A happy fellow.

The road is bumpy. The Ark is on a cart pulled by oxen. One of the oxen stumbles.

"Watch out!" you whisper. You wish you could prevent the Ark from falling, but you have no right to actually cause a change in the historical record. Nevertheless, it takes a great act of willpower to hold yourself back. The sacred Ark is about to crash to the ground.

The person closest to the Ark is a man named Uzzah. As the cart tips, Uzzah reaches out to steady it—just as the Bible says. He cares desperately that the sacred object not be damaged. Bad move. Again, just as you read in the Bible, God strikes Uzzah dead immediately for touching the Ark. Well, at least that's what your Bible-believing friends say was the cause of Uzzah's death. All you know for sure is that Uzzah is on the ground and not moving. You recall the words in 2 Samuel 6:6–7:

David and the whole house of Israel were celebrating with all their might before the LORD, with songs and with harps, lyres, tambourines, sistrums and cymbals. When they came to the threshing floor of Nacon, Uzzah reached out and took hold of the ark of God, because the oxen stumbled. The LORD's anger burned against Uzzah because of his irreverent act; therefore God struck him down and he died there beside the ark of God.

According to the Bible, David becomes so angry (and scared) about what happened to this good Uzzah, that he parked the Ark in a nearby house for three months!

You are saddened by the sudden violence and must rest from your observations. "C'mon," you say to Miss Muxdröözol. "Let's go."

A few hours later, you and Miss Muxdröözol are sitting on a few boulders in an oak forest near Jerusalem. It is quiet except for the faraway sounds of shofars—primitive instruments made from the horns of rams.

Suddenly, a communicator on Miss Muxdröözol's belt begins to beep. "This must be a message," she says, "from my philosopher friend back in our time. He's a little odd. Bear with him."

A winged creature appears on the communicator's small viewscreen. "Why was God watching Uzzah and David? More generally, I am sometimes asked *why* God watches all of us. What is His purpose? I may have an answer for you. Some variations of quantum mechanics suggest that a conscious observer is necessary to bring subatomic events into concrete reality. I have my doubts that this applies to macroscopic objects, but one theory is that God is observing us to make us real. We need a conscious observer to 'collapse the wave form' and validate our existence. God has been watching and making humans real since before the times humans were conscious, during the pre-australopithecine era—that is, before the last half of the Late Miocene epoch and the beginning of the Pleistocene epoch. Every individual human also should have many watchers, just for safety, so that the person does not disappear. Miss Muxdröözol is one of your watchers."

"What?" you say, stepping back. "That's insane!"

The winged creature shakes his head. "The Copenhagen interpretation of quantum mechanics says that the only real things are observed things. God is the supreme observer, who, by watching all particles, converts their quantum potentials into real and actual states."

You think that the creature is spouting a lot of nonscientific gibberish, but one thing is certain. You do feel closer to Miss Muxdröözol. All the traveling and adventures with her are certainly worth the hardships. Anyone who hears about your journeys would certainly be enthralled by your descriptions of the exotic places and ancient Israelites, by your ability to adjust to adversity, by your humor and incisiveness, and above all by your realization that to understand your world, you have to make yourself vulnerable to it so that it can change you.

👁 👁 👁

"Miss Muxdröözol," you say, "this killing of Uzzah itself is a paradox. God's punishment of Uzzah seems a little harsh in light of the fact that an omniscient God must have been aware that Uzzah's motivation was to protect the Ark."

"That's true to some extent. Biblical scholars agree that Uzzah acted in good faith and intended to be helpful at the moment the Ark was falling."

You watch hawks gliding slowly in updrafts of air from the desert plains. Some are turning in slow, lazy circles. "Could it be God was angry that the Ark was being carried on a cart rather than by its specially designed poles?"

"I'm not sure. Maybe Uzzah recklessly gave himself privileges that he knew belonged to others. The Bible provides no definitive answer except that perhaps the Ark was so holy that there was never an excuse sufficient for touching it. Apparently, rules are rules, not to be broken."

You nod. "Perhaps the Ark itself should be thought of as killing Uzzah, not God, in the same way we would not 'blame' God if someone touched a highly radioactive source and died. Some say we must look at the *net* good done by the Ark, so even if it killed Uzzah it saved or helped many good people."

Miss Muxdröözol tosses a pebble into the air. "But Uzzah provides a deeper paradox. God is said to be omniscient and know the future. According to this theory, God knew, before the Earth was created, that Uzzah would touch the Ark. If God has foreknowledge, God will also know His *own* actions in the future, because they are part of the future of which He knows. If He does not know His future actions, including His future interactions with humans, He is not omniscient by most definitions of the word."

"If God himself has free will, could He have chosen not to kill the good Uzzah?"

"Good question. Consider this hypothetical situation. Uzzah touches the Ark. God may either kill him or let him live, but, because God already knows the future, God knows that He will kill Uzzah. God knew that centuries before Uzzah was even born. This is part of God's knowledge. But could God exercise His own free will and choose to let Uzzah live? Is this possible? Assume God is omniscient. If God has free will and does not kill Uzzah, as He does in the Bible, He is contradicting His perfect knowledge of the future. His knowledge, therefore, becomes imperfect. His future knowledge of what He has done is now incorrect; thus God is not omniscient. He cannot be omniscient and have free will."[1]

You get on your horses and ride for several minutes, enjoying the breeze and open plains. Miss Muxdröözol's lack of riding experience is counteracted by the calming chemicals she occasionally adds to the horse's anterior vena cava.

You pull your horse to a large Juniper tree. "Wonder what this is all about?" you say pointing to the tree. You bend lower. Someone, maybe a child, has carved the word *Apocatastasis* into the thick trunk of the giant Juniper. The deep gashes are weathered so that they are a shiny beige against the rough, peeling bark. What a strange word, you think.

"Don't think it's English," Miss Muxdröözol says, and then she changes the subject. "We don't have to think about ethical dilemmas that may ensue when God kills His people for what seem to us to be minor infractions. Instead, consider the *paradox of the lock*." She says the words slowly to get your full attention. "Consider the following. God has just created the universe, but because He has foreknowledge, He knows that the combination lock in my pocket, many millennia later, is shut, and that He will never open it."

Miss Muxdröözol brings a lock out of her pocket and hands it to you. "I lost the combination. God knows this. He knew one million years ago that I am throwing the lock out in the trash. Fine. I don't want the lock. However, if we posit a God that is all-powerful, can God, today, choose to open the lock?"

Miss Muxdröözol rides down a dusty trail. "Perhaps one possibility is that an omnipotent God can change the universe so that His 'changed choice' (to open the lock) is now the only choice that was ever predetermined. This scenario might protect His omniscience and His free will. But would an omniscient God always know precisely what His course of action at any given time will be?"[2]

"Perhaps it could be that God knows He will change His mind about the lock or about Uzzah, but this seems to be an indirect, unfathomable way of knowing."

Miss Muxdröözol nods. "As philosopher Valeska Scholl suggests, 'Why not make the decision you know you will make in the end, instead of choosing something when you know you will change the choice later?'"[3]

## MUSINGS AND SPECULATIONS

*There is no question about there being design in the Universe. The question is whether this design is imposed from the Outside or*

*whether it is inherent in the physical laws governing the Universe.*
*The next question is, of course, who or what made these physical*
*laws?*

               —*Ralph Estling,* The Skeptical Inquirer

Could God know He will make a choice, such as killing Uzzah or opening a
lock, and change His mind? Would this reversal be considered to be altering
the previous path of the universe and "integrating" the new choice as the
original?

Valeska Scholl, from Oklahoma City, writes,

> This necessarily creates a flaw in God. For if He knows everything that has,
> does, and will happen, He knows of this choice. He also knows the choice will
> change the universe. Thus, in making this choice, He either: (1) invalidates
> His knowledge for the instant that the universe rearranges itself or (2) makes
> the choice knowing it will erase all knowledge currently possessed of the fu-
> ture and fill it in with new knowledge of this new future. He could not possess
> both old knowledge and new knowledge regarding the path of the universe,
> for the old knowledge would be in error, and thus would invalidate his perfect-
> ness. If He took the second alternative, He would be acknowledging imperfec-
> tion in that He would know (having all knowledge) that the universe would
> change, and that all information which he currently possessed that dealt with
> those events past the point of change is erroneous (thus flawed).[4]

Perhaps one way to resolve the paradox (or to create a model humans can
understand) is to imagine God having free will in the first nanosecond of creation at which point He chose all His actions for the rest of eternity. Then,
from there on, all of history was set. The concept of changing His mind, for example, then makes no sense because there is no time in which to make such a
change. All of history is there; all of space and time is there like a big block of
ice or glass, and it includes the googolplex acts of free will on God's part. However, this fixed "block of ice" model seems insufficient to account for all the
time God repents, is surprised, or regrets His acts in the Bible. It seems that
God participates interactively with humans and learns through those interactions. If He is totally outside of time, and spacetime is like a big block of ice laid
out before His eyes, can He take an ice pick and make a change in the block of
ice? Perhaps He is changing the ice all the time, and we would probably have
no idea that He did. If we had destroyed the Earth a hundred times during the
1950s with atomic bombs, and each time God, out of love, took an ice pick and

redirected spacetime, would we know? Probably not. Instead we would remember the path of existence responsible for bringing us into the current future. Perhaps the End of Days occurs when God no longer can use His ice pick to make the required adjustments.

There are many other possibilities: God may be able to know the future, but perhaps He simply doesn't want to all the time. (I discuss a limited or "contracted" God in the "Some Final Thoughts" section.) Or, perhaps future-knowing requires God to expend some kind of heavenly effort or resource, so He doesn't always wish to expend such effort to see the future. Craig Becker from Austin, Texas, likens the universe to a big computer program in which each line of the program code contains commands or statements that govern events and laws of the universe. For example, each line of code might contain commands for the states and motions of various subatomic particles—which we can write in some kind of mathematical or abstract programming language:

```
/* God's program, version 2.0 */
⊊ ⇔↓⇑→⇒← ⇔↦↪ ⊊ ∄↑ ⇓⇒←⇐↓⇑∄⇌⇌↪ ⇐↓ ⇐↓↑⇓⇒⇌⇌⇒→ →↓
⇐↓⇑→⇒↑⇓⇌∄→⇒ ↦↩⇔↦⇒← →↩↑⇒⇑⇐↩↓⇑⇐≯ ⊊→ ⇐⇒⇒↑⇐ →↓ ↑⇒ →↦∄→
↩→ ↩⇐ ↓⇒← ⇑∄→⇒←⇒ →↓ →←⇒∄↑≩ →↓ ⇐⇒∄←⇐↦≩ ∄⇑→ →↓ ⇔↓⇑→⇒←
∄←↓⇒→ ↓⇒← ⇓⇌∄⇐⇒ ↩⇑ ∄ ⇐⇒⇒↑↩⇑⇔⇌↪ ⇌↓⇑⇒⇌↪ ⇐↓⇐↑↓⇐≯ ↑̸⇒←↦∄⇓⇐
→↦↩⇐ ↩⇐ ∄ ←⇒∄⇐↓⇑ →↦∄→ ⇓↦↩⇌↓⇐↓⇓↦⇒←⇐ ∄⇑→ ⇒↔⇒⇑
→↦⇒↓⇌↓⇔↩∄⇑⇐↦∄↔⇒
```

Craig Becker writes:

> Imagine the Universe is a big computerlike simulation, and God is running it, and occasionally He reaches in to tweak it and sits back and watches what happens. Conceivably, He could just read the "computer program code" and figure out what's going to happen by tracing the flow of "commands" in the code—but it's easier or better to just let the simulation run itself. To muddy the waters further, consider this: is there a difference between running the simulation, and God "tracing" the simulation by reading the source code? I've noticed that people tend to envision God in terms of their profession: a Carpenter thinks God is a Builder, a Biologist sees God as a Biologist, a Computer Programmer sees God as the Ultimate Programmer.[5]

Philosopher of science Dennis Gordon also likens our world to a computer program when he writes to me, "Could it be that the imperfections of humans, and disasters of nature, are the result of conflicting and interacting lines of

God's computer program? Could our universe be a computerlike simulation being performed in a 'real' universe free from the software bugs that cause all the evil and disasters?"

Another way the paradox of God's free will might temporarily be resolved is to resort to the recent theoretical idea of parallel universes that exist side by side with our own in some ghostly manner. There are many different models for parallel universes, and some theories postulate the existence of baby universes that are budding off ours, with thin wormholes connecting the various universes.[6] An older but still valid theory was proposed by Hugh Everett III in his doctoral thesis, "Relative State Formulation of Quantum Mechanics" (reprinted in *Reviews of Modern Physics*).[7] Everett outlines a controversial theory in which the universe at every instant branches into countless parallel worlds. However, human consciousness works in such a way that it is only aware of one universe at a time. Physicists call this the "many-worlds" interpretation of quantum mechanics. The theory holds that whenever the universe ("world") is confronted with a choice of paths at the quantum level, it actually follows both possibilities, splitting into two universes. These universes are often described as "parallel worlds." If the many-worlds theory is correct, then all kinds of strange worlds exist. In fact, some believe that somewhere virtually everything must be true. The theory also implies the existences of universes so strange we could not describe them. My favorite tales of parallel worlds are those of Robert Heinlein. For example, in his science-fiction novel *The Number of the Beast* there is a parallel world that appears identical to ours in every respect except that the letter "J" does not appear in the English language. Luckily, the protagonists in the book have built a device that lets them perform controlled explorations of parallel worlds from the safety of their high-tech car. In contrast, the protagonist in Heinlein's novel *Job* shifts through parallel worlds without control. Unfortunately, just as he makes some money in one America, he shifts to a slightly different America where his money is no longer valid currency, which tends to make his life miserable.

Mathematicians dating back to Georg Bernhard Riemann (1826–1866) have studied the properties of multiply connected spaces in which different regions of space and time are spliced together. Physicists who once considered this an intellectual exercise for armchair speculation are now seriously studying advanced branches of mathematics to create practical models of our universe, and to better understand the possibilities of parallel worlds and travel by using wormholes and manipulating time.

Let's return to the question of God's own free will. If God knows everything within the current universe until the point He enters the time stream and thus changes the universe (or thus creates a new one), an "all-knowing, perfect, and free-willed" God might gain knowledge of the new branch at that instant. Perhaps, at this point, the old universe persists but God is conscious only of the new one. However, this approach to knowing does not sound like omniscience. Perhaps God sees all universes. The many-worlds theory suggests that a being existing outside of spacetime might see all conceivable forks, all possible spacetimes and universes, as always having existed. How could a being deal with such knowledge and not become insane? A God would see all Earths: those where no inhabitants believe in God, those where all inhabitants believe in God, and everything in between. According to the many-worlds theory, there could be universes where Jesus was son of God and universes where Jesus did not exist. Perhaps free will for God, or saying that God can make choices, merely means He shifts His consciousness from one branch of the multiverse to another whenever He makes a choice, like a ball rolling down a forked path in a pinball machine and going right or left. Of course, how an omniscient God shifts consciousness would be difficult for us to imagine. Perhaps the universe that God does not choose simply ceases to exist.

Much of Everett's many-worlds interpretation is concerned with events on the submicroscopic level. For example, the theory predicts that every time an electron either moves or fails to move to a new energy level, a new universe is created. Currently, it is not clear to what degree quantum (submicroscopic) theories can account for reality at the macroscopic, human level. Quantum theory even clashes with relativity theory, which forbids faster-than-light (FTL) transfer of information. For example, quantum theory introduces an element of uncertainty into our understanding of the universe, stating that any two particles that have once been in contact continue to influence each other no matter how far apart they move, until one of them interacts with another particle or is observed. In a strange way, this suggests that the entire universe is multiply connected by FTL signals. Physicists call this type of interaction "cosmic glue." The holy grail of physics is the reconciling of quantum and relativistic theories.

Some physicists have suggested that higher spatial dimensions may provide the only refuge for intelligent life when our universe eventually dies in great heat or cold. Michio Kaku, author of *Hyperspace*, suggests that "in the last seconds of death of our universe, intelligent life may escape the collapse by fleeing into hyperspace."[8] Our heirs, whatever or whoever they may be, will explore these new possibilities. They will explore space and time. They will seek their salvation in the higher universes. Will God be with them?

👁 👁 👁

Let's return to the fascinating story of Uzzah. For those of you who do not read the biblical stories in a literal fashion, the writers of the story of Uzzah may have meant to *scare* people regarding the famous Ark or to instill fear and respect in the hearts of followers. Perhaps the story is meant to tell the Jews not to be careless about their faith and to fear God.

God did give many specific instructions regarding the Ark, and so did God's followers. For example, Moses, in the Book of Numbers, told people how to handle the Ark. Aaron, Moses's brother, was obliged to make special preparations when the Ark was to be moved:

> Aaron and his sons are to go in and take down the shielding curtain and cover the ark of the Testimony with it. Then they are to cover this with hides of sea cows [creatures known today as dugongs], spread a cloth of solid blue over that, and put the poles in place. (Numbers 4:5–6)

Next, Aaron and his sons were supposed to enlist the help of the Kohathites. God informed Moses and Aaron that the "Kohathites are to come to do the carrying. But they must not touch the holy things or they will die. The Kohathites are to carry those things that are in the Tent of Meeting" (Numbers 4:15). Additionally, the Kohathites were not even to look inside the Ark: "The Kohathites must not go in to look at the holy things, even for a moment, or they will die" (Numbers 4:20).

The Ark is surely nothing to be messed with. In 1 Samuel 6:19, God kills again, "But God struck down some of the men of Beth Shemesh, putting seventy of them to death because they had looked into the ark of the LORD. The people mourned because of the heavy blow the LORD had dealt them."

👁 👁 👁

Recall that the creature on Miss Muxdröözol's viewscreen said to you, "The Copenhagen interpretation of quantum mechanics says that the only real things are observed things. God is the supreme observer, who, by watching all particles, converts their quantum potentials into real and actual states." You thought of this as gibberish; however, there are philosophers and physicists today who actually put forth the controversial suggestion that God's existence is established by the "riddle of quantum observership." Timothy Ferris writes in *The Whole Shebang*, "[There is] the riddle of how the early universe could have evolved in the absence of observers. The riddle may be 'solved' by invoking God as the supreme observer."[9] Similar concepts are discussed in Robert Sawyer's novel *Calculating God*.[10] Others have reversed the roles and contended it is we who, by observing God, make Him real. According to early Islamic tradition, God once said, "I was a hidden treasure and I yearned to be known. Then I created creatures in order to be known by them."[11]

Some of the exotic physical theories we've mentioned involve unimaginably small particles. Although some people may argue that a particular submicroscopic event in the quantum world can have no practical impact on our ordinary lives, I can give many examples where this argument is false. Consider a helicopter carrying a package of the deadly botulism toxin. The package is dropped in New York City, where a device is triggered by the click of a Geiger counter. According to quantum mechanics, the precise instant of the click is purely random. Hence, a quantum event can certainly have a huge impact on our lives! Similarly, small changes in history, brought about by quantum events, can produce amplified effects through time. Imagine what would have happened if Cleopatra had sported an ugly but benign skin growth on her upper lip. The entire cascade of historical events would be different. A mutation of a single skin cell caused by a random photon of sunlight would have changed the universe.

This entire line of thinking reminds me of a quote from the New Age writer Jane Roberts: "You are so part of the world that your slightest action contributes to its reality. Your breath changes the atmosphere. Your encounters with others alter the fabrics of their lives, and the lives of those who come in contact with them."[12]

---

Millennia passed before humankind discovered that energy is the basis of matter. It may take a few more years before we prove that wisdom and knowledge are the basis of, and can actually create, energy which in turn creates matter.
　　　　　　　　　　　　　　　　—Gerald Schroeder, *The Science of God*

---

Religions need a self-contradictory God to exist. This indicates that traditional Western religion is human-centric—that religion defines the universe from humanity outward, to the point of ascribing human characteristics to God Herself. Without a human God, there is no cosmic drama.
　　　　　　　　　　　　　　　　—Andy Fielding, personal communication

# CHAPTER 15

# The Paradox of Dr. Eck

B.C. MANSFIELD

*Reflect upon God's creation but not upon his nature or else you will perish.*

—*Islamic Hadith*

CONSIDER A FINITE BEING, MR. PLEX. BY "FINITE," I MEAN THAT MR. Plex is not omnipotent and not omniscient. Let's also assume that the finite Mr. Plex carries out a particular act; in this case, he lights the fuse on a bomb.

Next consider two statements:

1. Mr. Plex lights the bomb.
2. Mr. Plex is the only being who knows that 1 is true.

Now consider an omnipotent being, Dr. Eck. Assume that by calling Dr. Eck omnipotent, we mean that Dr. Eck can create any finite being. That means that Dr. Eck can create Mr. Plex. Dr. Eck can create Mr. Plex, who performs the act of lighting a bomb, which is known only to himself and to no other being. Now consider that Dr. Eck is also omniscient. I'm sure you can see the problem. Dr. Eck's omniscience seems to mean that for any finite being and for any act, if the being does the act, then Dr. Eck knows the being did the act. If this is true, then Dr. Eck cannot create Mr. Plex. Why? If Dr. Eck created Mr. Plex, then by statement 1 Mr. Plex lights the bomb and by statement 2 Dr. Eck does not know that Mr. Plex lit the bomb. If Dr. Eck does not know that Mr. Plex lit the bomb, then Dr. Eck is not omniscient. If Dr. Eck is an omniscient being, he cannot create a being like Mr. Plex, who performs an act known only to himself and no other being.

Because an omnipotent being can create Mr. Plex and an omniscient being cannot create Mr. Plex, we have an apparent contradiction. A being who is both omnipotent and omniscient is logically impossible. Dr. Eck cannot be both omnipotent and omniscient.

The paradox in this chapter and the next was discussed in depth by Richard R. La Croix, professor of philosophy at the State University of New York at Buffalo.[1] We can pursue the paradox of Dr. Eck even further. Let us consider that Dr. Eck is *mutably omniscient*. This means that Dr. Eck at some time knows everything there is to be known at that time, while it also remains possible that at some other time there is something Dr. Eck does not know. Given this, it is possible that Dr. Eck could create on November 16, 2015, Mr. Plex, who performs the act of lighting the bomb, and this act is known only to Mr. Plex, because Mr. Plex must perform the act sometime after November 16, 2015. Once Mr. Plex lights the bomb, Dr. Eck is not omniscient. Note that the mutably omniscient Dr. Eck could create Mr. Plex *while* possessing the property of being omniscient. This seems to mean that a being can actually be both omnipotent and omniscient. Dr. Eck could create Mr. Plex. However, Dr. Eck must be mutably omniscient for this to work. Traditional religions still live with the logical impossibility of God being both omniscient and omnipotent, because the God of most religions is fully omniscient, not mutably omniscient. God is usually not considered omniscient on a part-time basis.

## MUSINGS AND SPECULATIONS

*The temper of the hot and superstitious part of mankind in matters of religion is ever to be found of mysteries, and for that reason to like best what they understand least.*
—Saint Athanasius (293–373)

The God of Jews and Christians tends to be a personal God who does many of the activities that humans do: He sees, hears, speaks, loves, judges, punishes, creates, destroys, and becomes jealous and angry. The God of mystics and traditional theists usually yearns to be known by His creatures. The Spanish philosopher Joseph ibn Saddiq (d. 1143) suggested that the only thing we can say about God is that He is incomprehensible, transcending our powers of intellect. The Spanish physician Judah Halevi (1085–1141) suggested that God could not be proved using logic; however, this did not mean that faith in God was irrational but simply that a logical demonstration of His existence had no religious value.[2]

The Koran implies that God has knowledge, but we do not know quite what this means because our human concept of knowledge is insufficient. God cannot be compared to any of the things that exist.[3]

Various philosophers and theologians have formulated definitions and attributes of God. Here's a sampling, many of which are scattered through Karen Armstrong's *A History of God*. All of these descriptions and definitions make us wonder if it is possible to know much about an incomprehensible God. What is God?

- Marcion (100–165): The God of the Jewish scriptures is cruel, exterminating large populations.
- Clement of Alexandria (150–215): Jesus has become human "so that you might learn from a man how to become God."
- Saint Basil (329–379): "It is by God's energies that we know our God; we do not assert that we come near to the essence itself, for his energies descend to us but his essence remains unapproachable."
- Gregory of Nyssa (335–395): "The true vision and the knowledge of what we seek consists precisely in *not* seeing, in an awareness that our goal transcends all knowledge."

- Pope Gregory the Great (540–604): We can make no predictions about God's behavior. "Then only is there truth in what we know concerning God, when we are made sensible that we cannot fully know anything about him."

- Scotus Erigena (810–877): God is nothing. He is more than being. Every one of His creatures is a theophany, a sign of His presence. We cannot see God as He is because God, by human standards, does not exist. We only see the God that animates our world as revealed in forests, butterflies, and the tears on a little girl.

- Abu al-Hasan ibn Ismail al-Ashari (878–941): "Allah has a body . . . Radiating with light . . . Shining as a round pearl."[4]

- Saint Anselm (1033–1109): God's existence can be proven. He is "something that which nothing greater can be thought."

- Thomas Aquinas (1225–1274): "All that man knows of God is to know that he does not know Him, since he knows that what God is surpasses all that we can understand of Him."

- Isaac Luria (1534–1572): God created sleep so we can dream. In dream states we can gain insights that are unavailable to the normal conscious mind.

- John Milton (1608–1674): According to *Paradise Lost*, Jesus and God are totally separate individuals who must talk to each other for extended periods to understand each other's intentions.

- Baruch Spinoza (1632–1677): The ancient Israelites called anything they could not understand "God," but in actuality God is inseparable from reality. God's activity in the universe is simply a description of mathematical and physical laws.

- Samuel Reimarus (1694–1768): Jesus's goal was to create a godly state on Earth, but His mission failed and He died in despair. Jesus in the Gospels never directly said He had come to atone for the sins of humanity.

- Immanuel Kant (1724–1804): Human brains can only understand things and phenomena that exist in space and time. They cannot understand other realities.

- Sigmund Freud (1856–1939): God is a projection of the unconscious. The study of psychology is necessary to decode these projections. A personal God was a father figure created by our desires for justice and love.

- Brethren of the Free Spirit (late medieval heretics): God is all that is. God is in every stone and in each limb of the human body. Every created thing is divine.[5]

- The Ranters (Christian sect in Cromwell's England, seventeenth century): Every human will return to God as a raindrop returning to a lake.

God knows all things. There is no distinction between God and humans. If God is everything, then sin is nothing. Ranters deliberately tried to demonstrate this by cursing in public and violating traditional sexual mores. Outward forms of religion are rejected. Even the Bible is not the Word of God. (Ranters paraded nude in public. Some Ranters found God within themselves, gave up work, lived in voluntary poverty, and reveled in obscenity and promiscuity.)

- Hasidism (started in the twelfth and thirteenth centuries): God has disintegrated and we must build him anew.
- God ($-\infty - +\infty$): "I am What I am."
- Jewish mystics: "Everything is in Thee and Thou art in everything; Thou fillest everything and dost encompass it; when everything was created, Thou was in everything; before everything was created, Thou wast everything."[6]
- Islamic mystics: "I [God] was a hidden treasure; I wanted to be known. Hence, I created the world that I might be known."[7]
- Bahaullah, the prophet founder of the Baha'i faith (1817–1892): "To every discerning and illumined heart it is evident that God, the unknowable Essence, the divine Being, is immensely exalted beyond every human attribute, such as corporeal existence, ascent and descent, egress and regress. . . . He is and hath ever been veiled in the ancient eternity of His Essence, and will remain in His Reality everlastingly hidden from the sight of men."

Karen Armstrong in *A History of God* writes,

Human beings are the only animals who have the capacity to envision something that is not present or something that does not yet exist but which is merely possible. The imagination has thus been the cause of our major achievements in science and technology as well as in art and religion. The idea of God, however it is defined, is perhaps the prime example of an absent reality, which despite its inbuilt problems, has continued to inspire men and women for thousands of years.[8]

The physicist Isaac Newton (1642–1727) believed in God, and he thought God purposely had prevented the gravity of all the stars from pulling them together into one giant spherical mass.[9] God had carefully dispersed the stars throughout space with sufficient intervening distances to forestall a gravitational collapse. Although he does not mention the Bible, here is what Newton had to say more generally about God's omniscience and omnipotence in his *Principia Mathematica*, published in 1687:

> This most beautiful system of the sun, planets, and comets could only proceed from the counsel and dominion of an intelligent and powerful Being. And if the fixed stars are the centers of other like systems, these, being formed by the like wise counsel, must be all subject to the dominion of One. . . . It is the dominion of a spiritual being which constitutes a God. . . . And from his true dominion it follows that the true God is a living, intelligent and powerful Being. . . . He is eternal and infinite, omnipotent and omniscient; that is, his duration reaches from eternity to eternity; and his presence from infinity to infinity; he governs all things, and knows all things that are or can be done. . . . He endures for ever, and is every where present; and by existing always and every where, he constitutes duration and space. . . . In him are all things contained and moved; yet neither affects the other: God suffers nothing from the motion of bodies; bodies find no resistance from the omnipresence of God. . . . As a blind man has no idea of colors so we have no idea of the manner by which the all-wise God preserves and understands all things. He is utterly void of all body and bodily figure, and can therefore neither be seen, nor heard, nor touched; nor ought to be worshipped under the representation of any corporeal thing. We know him only by his most wise and excellent contrivances of things. . . . [W]e reverence and adore him as his servants; and a god without dominion, providence, and final causes, is nothing else but Fate and Nature. Blind metaphysical necessity, which is certainly the same always and everywhere, could produce no variety of things. All that diversity of natural things which we find suited to different times and places could arise from nothing but the ideas and will of a Being necessarily existing.[10]

If Newton believed that space was infinite, where did God reside? Newton felt that space was formed by God's omnipresence. God is the spacetime in which we operate. God created matter by an act of will when He decided parts of space should have form.[11]

As for myself, I continually wonder what a "god" might be like. I use the analogy of my 110-gallon aquarium. I clean the water, feed the fish, turn on the lights, add medications, adjust the temperature and pH, and so forth. One might be tempted to say that to the fish, I am God. But hold on. I am not a god to the fish. Although they can sense my presence, they are not capable of considering me a god. They have no concept of God. Their minds are too small. They see a stimulus and react. If we extend the analogy to a relationship between us and a higher Being, we too would not be capable of considering that higher being as He truly is, whether God or not.

👁 👁 👁

Here are a few odd questions for further thought. Consider an omniscient Dr. Eck (ö). Then consider Dr. Ick (o), who is mutably omniscient, as defined earlier in this chapter. How difficult would it be for Dr. Ick to masquerade as Dr. Eck? Could a mutably omniscient being *appear* to be omniscient to us? What if Dr. Ick were mutably omniscient at regular intervals of time, for example, changing every ten years? For example, consider that for a period of ten years God is omniscient. For the next decade He is not omniscient, and so forth. Could you accept a God with such an oscillation? Certainly, the oscillating God would still be very impressive by mere human standards. In fact, I once wrote a science fiction tale in which the period of oscillation followed the Fibonacci sequence of numbers: 1, 1, 2, 3, 5, 8, 13, 21, 34, 55, 89, 144, 233, 377, . . . These numbers are such that, after the first two, every number in the sequence equals the sum of the two previous numbers. As you can see, the periods of time for which God is either omniscient or not omniscient become increasingly long, which tends to make the finite beings in my tale have a very confusing and complicated relationship with their God. More complex yet is a story I wrote about a God that is a hive organism consisting of omniscient and mutably omniscient members all oscillating at different rates:

### Hive God with Omniscient (ö) and
### Mutably Omniscient (alien head) Components

Although various members of the God hive were omniscient at the same time, this did not mean that they had to have identical personalities (Figure 15.1). Omniscience implies knowing all, but it does not imply responding in the same fashion to the knowledge. Various arguments broke out within the God collective, and just as with today's U.S. Senate, compromise resolutions to problems were exceedingly difficult. These kinds of interactions between the omniscients and mutably omniscients prompted one of my readers to suggest that a collective or hive might have been preferable to a "jealous" Old Testament God because, perhaps, cooler "alien heads" would have sometimes prevailed. Arguments between the omniscients and mutably omniscients might be considered not as conflict but as a form of problem solving. Given what you know about the paradox of omniscience discussed in Chapter 1, do you expect the omniscients or the mutably omniscients to win a hypothetical battle or dispute between one another?

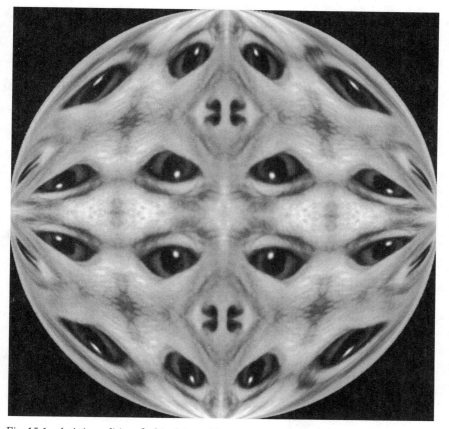

*Fig. 15.1. Artistic rendition of a hive being with omniscient and mutably omniscient components.*

Some people think of God . . . busily tallying the fall of every sparrow. Others—for example, Baruch Spinoza and Albert Einstein—considered God to be essentially the sum total of the physical laws which describe the universe.

—Carl Sagan, *Broca's Brain*

# CHAPTER 16

# The Paradox of Led Zeppelin

B.C. MANSFIELD

*There's a lady who's sure . . . she's buying a stairway to heaven.*
*—Led Zeppelin, "Stairway to Heaven"*

*The works I have written on Christian Science contain absolute truth, and my necessity was to tell it. . . . I was a scribe under orders; and who can refrain from transcribing what God indites, and ought not that one to take the cup, drink all of it, and give thanks?*
—*Mary Baker Eddy*, Miscellaneous Writing

IN THE EARLY 1970S, THE BRITISH ROCK GROUP LED ZEPPELIN released one of the most famous songs in rock and roll history—"Stairway to Heaven." Its haunting and strange lyrics have been subject to much speculation and study, some experts concluding that the song refers to the Christian apocalypse and others believing the lyrics to be meaningless. Whatever the case, "Stairway to Heaven" sheet music sales remain the biggest in the history of rock, exceeding 1 million copies. The song is 8 minutes long, and since it first was broadcast, it has had roughly 23 million minutes of airtime—almost 44 solid years.

What can Led Zeppelin possibly have to do with God and omniscience? If God is omniscient with respect to the future, then God knows everything that will ever occur. Assume that Led Zeppelin brought into existence the song "Stairway to Heaven" through hard work, trial and error, and their amazing musical expertise. Let's also assume that the song would not have existed without this group and its composing activity.

Let's start with our first assumption: God is omniscient with respect to the future. (Some have used the term "omniprescience" to refer to knowing everything in the future.) This means that God knew before the creation of the universe that Led Zeppelin would be a rock band immensely popular in the 1970s and that it would include such longhairs as Jimmy Page and Robert Plant. God also knew before the creation of the universe that, in the 1970s, Led Zeppelin would produce the phenomenon of the song "Stairway to Heaven," which did not exist until this point. Moreover, God knew that the first line of the song's lyrics would be "there's a lady who's sure all that glitters is gold." In fact, God was aware of all of the words in the song. Thus, before God created the Garden of Eden, it was possible for God to recite all the lyrics of "Stairway to Heaven."

Are you with me so far? All of this implies that if God so chose, He could have given His angels guitars and drums, and they could have performed the song in the clouds. This means that "Stairway to Heaven" existed before the creation of the Earth. God knew both that "Stairway to Heaven" existed and that it existed before He created the Earth.

However, I've started our discussion with the assumption that "Stairway to Heaven" did not exist before the 1970s. God knows the group created the song in the early 1970s and that the song did not exist, for example, in the 1930s.

Yet, God also knows that the song existed before the creation of the Earth and universe. In some strange way of thinking, this means that "Stairway to Heaven" both existed and did not exist before the Earth existed and that God knew this. This contradiction suggests that divine omniscience and the idea of musical creativity are logically incompatible.

## MUSINGS AND SPECULATIONS

*There are good grounds for thinking that the sentence "God exists" has no common meaning for theists, atheists, and agnostics if, indeed, it does have a clearly understandable meaning for any of them. One reason for thinking this way is that there are claims made by different theists that justify the view that the sentence "God exists" has no common meaning even for all theists.*
                                        *—Richard R. La Croix, "Metatheism"*

Given our strange conclusion, as La Croix once suggested, it appears that we can't subscribe to both the idea of divine omniscience and the doctrine of literary or musical creativity.[1]

We could actually leave "God" out of the picture. Consider our omniscient friend Dr. Eck. Assume he lived a million years before the creation of our galaxy. If Dr. Eck is omniscient, then every composition that will ever exist also existed before the creation of our galaxy. This includes the stirring works of Beethoven, Bach, and Brahms. Yes, all of their compositions actually existed. And a band of Dr. Eck's friends could play the Led Zeppelin song.

With God it is even possible that the musical compositions have no "beginning" at all if God lives outside of time. In any case, these scenarios suggest that the artists did not bring about the existence of the symphonies or rock anthems that they have "composed." If the compositions have no origin, perhaps they are not brought into existence by any being, not even God. Should we praise Led Zeppelin for a song they merely made manifest but did not bring into existence?

"Hold on," you say. I can hear you complaining that I am simply *assuming* that the musical compositions have no beginning. That's true. But what if we assume they do have a beginning? Assume that Dr. Eck, an omniscient being, exists. If "Stairway to Heaven" existed before Led Zeppelin, who or what act brought about its existence? This contradiction still suggests that omniscience, especially divine omniscience, and the idea of human musical creativity are logically incompatible.

What we've discussed in this brief chapter applies to all acts of creativity. I write the words for a book title:

> ## I Am Not My Wife's Hippocampus

yet if there is an omniscient God, this awesome book title existed before the creation of the universe, and I cannot be praised for its creation in any traditional sense because I did not bring the title into existence.

Some philosophers have advanced the theory that God can choose not to know certain aspects of the future and about certain "compositions" (such as in science, art, and music), which casts free will and the actual authorship of artworks in a new light. To get a fresh perspective on this question, Eric Kaplan, M.D., asks us to suppose that God's potentially perfect knowledge of future events, artworks, and so forth are represented by an immense book.[2] Imagine such a massive book, leather bound, with gold trim, titled:

> ## The Book of Everything God Can Know

As you can glean from the book's title, the book would contain all the knowledge God could possibly possess. It must then contain all of our thoughts and actions and the ultimate disposition of our souls. By analogy, God's possible "selective foreknowledge" could be represented by His choice not to look at what is written on some of the pages of the book. For example, God might avoid examining pages 24 and 666 so that His knowledge is self-limited. Dr. Kaplan writes, "However, and this is the point, whether He looks or not is irrelevant. The book has been written. It is perfect. It is done. We are 'predestined' just as completely, whether He looks or not. The existence of the book is sufficient."[3]

One counterargument to Kaplan's premise is that the book with the title *The Book of Everything God Can Know* has not been written. Kaplan's response is that the fact that the book *could* be written is sufficient. For example, at this moment, you and I do not know the 1 millionth digit of pi. This information may not be written in any book. But the knowledge of the millionth digit of pi is potentially available. The fact that you choose to exercise selective foreknowledge and not make the calculations does not alter the fact that you *could* know if you chose to. Similarly, the fact that an omniscient being *could* know this kind of information is sufficient to assure that it is determined. The same logic applies to knowing *events* in the future. No actual book needs to be written. Whether God chooses to look or not does not affect the argument. Kaplan believes that God's potential omniscience is sufficient to assure we have no meaningful moral free will. Similarly invoking a *Book of All Art God Can Experience*, we might also have trouble subscribing to the idea of divine omniscience and the doctrine of artistic creativity.

👁 👁 👁

I sometimes wonder if God's knowledge of "Stairway to Heaven" before the universe was created could be considered a "recollection" of sorts. Of course, the term "recollection" is a term we humans might use to describe a concept that has limited applicability to a being existing outside of time. (Perhaps we could use the word "precollection" rather than "recollection" in this divine context.) Nevertheless, religious people sometimes suggest that before God created the universe He was probably lonely or felt incomplete or dissatisfied. This would have been a possible motivation for His creating the universe. Leszek Kolakowski, author of *The Keys to Heaven*, comments:

> It's very difficult for us to imagine such a condition of loneliness when we consider that human loneliness is always in relation to something that once was; the loss of a reality that formerly existed and that was known. God's loneliness, before the creation of the world, was unblest even by a single recollection.[4]

On the other hand, if God knew about Led Zeppelin, Shakespeare, Picasso, and Mozart before the creation of the universe, He did have recollections of a sort—in advance. Additionally, He could simulate all sorts of beings in His own mind, much like computers today can simulate primitive organismic behaviors. In any case, what exactly is loneliness when you can see all of history and all its people before the universe is even created?

👁 👁 👁

I conclude this chapter with some fascinating facts on "Stairway to Heaven."[5]

- In 1982, a hearing of the California State Assembly consumer protection committee featured testimony from "experts" who claimed that "Stairway to Heaven" revealed startling lyrics when played backward: "I sing because I live with Satan. The Lord turns me off—there's no escaping it. Here's to my sweet Satan, whose power is Satan. He will give you 666. I live for Satan."

- On January 23, 1991, John Sebastian, owner and general manager of KLSK-FM in Albuquerque, New Mexico, played "Stairway to Heaven" for 24 hours to demonstrate his interest in a format change to rock and roll. He played the song more than 200 times, eliciting hundreds of angry calls and letters. Police came to the station when a listener reported that Sebastian probably had had a heart attack while on the job (not true). The police came again when they thought the station had been taken hostage by a terrorist.

- Dr. Robert Walser, professor of musicology at Dartmouth College and author of *Running with the Devil: Power, Gender, and Madness in Heavy Metal Music*, writes of the lyrics to "Stairway to Heaven":

We might better understand the associative powers of the lyrics by breaking them up into categories. We are presented with a number of mysterious figures: a lady, the piper, the May queen. Images of nature abound: a brook, a songbird, rings of smoke through the trees, a hedgerow, wind. We find a set of concepts (that pretty much sum up the central concerns of all philosophy): signs, words, meanings, thoughts, feelings, spirit, reason, wonder, soul, the idea that "all are one and one is all." We find a set of vaguely but powerfully evocative symbols: gold, the West, the tune, white light, shadows, paths, a road, and the stairway to heaven itself. At the very end, we find some paradoxical self-referentiality: "To be a rock and not to roll."[6]

---

When God creates [in Genesis], He stands back in wonderment and, like a human artist looking at a canvas, observes that His creations are "good," thus implying it might have turned out otherwise. An omniscient and omnipotent God would have no need to look back at what He knows will always be perfect.

—Alan Dershowitz, *The Genesis of Justice*

---

I don't want to achieve immortality through my work; I want to achieve immortality through not dying.

—Woody Allen, *Without Feathers*

# CHAPTER 17

# A Few Quick Puzzles and Surveys

*The 19th century Hasidic rabbi Menahem Mendelof Kotzk once asked some visiting scholars, "Where does God dwell?" They laughed at him and said, "God is everywhere, of course. The whole earth is full of his glory." The rabbi shook his head, then said, "God dwells wherever man lets him in."*

—*Stephen Mitchell*, The Enlightened Mind

IN THIS CHAPTER, I PRESENT A SMORGASBORD OF TOPICS THAT TOUCH briefly upon a few favorite, zany, and perplexing religious questions and surveys.

## GOD AND MIND

Jacques Boivin wrote in *The Single Heart Field Theory:* "If we wish to understand the nature of the Universe we have an inner hidden advantage: We are ourselves little portions of the Universe and so carry the answer within us."[1] Does God intentionally hide parts of the universe from us? Do you agree with physicist Stephen Hawking's statement, "God not only plays dice, but He also sometimes throws the dice where they cannot be seen"?[2] How much of the universe can our minds grasp?

Perhaps our brains, which evolved to make us run from lions on the African savanna, are not constructed to penetrate the fabric of the universe. Imagine an alien with an IQ a hundred times greater than our own. What profound concepts or areas of awareness might be available to this individual to which we are now totally closed? A dog cannot understand Fourier transforms or gravitational wave theory. Human forebrains are a few ounces bigger than a dog's, and we can ask many more questions than a dog. Are there facets of the universe we can never know? Are there questions we can't ask?

Michael Murphy discusses a related idea in *The Future of the Body:*

> To a frog with its simple eye, the world is a dim array of greys and blacks. Are we like frogs in our limited sensorium, apprehending just part of the universe we inhabit? Are we as a species now awakening to the reality of multidimensional worlds in which matter undergoes subtle reorganizations in some sort of hyperspace?[3]

The Buddha also believed that certain questions humans try to ask are "improper" or inappropriate because they refer to subjects that lie beyond the reach of words. The only way to try to understand them is through meditation, because verbal descriptions are as inadequate as describing Chopin's mazurkas, polonaises, and nocturnes using words.

As Gregory (335–395), Bishop of Nyssa, suggested, "The true vision of knowledge that we seek consists precisely in *not* seeing, in an awareness that our goal transcends all knowledge and is everywhere cut off from us by the darkness of incomprehensibility."[4] He felt that we cannot "see" God intellectually but we can *feel* His presence.

## GHOST CHILDREN

The question of the morality of abortion touches on many religious issues and on what it means to be human. Often it is argued that each unborn embryo, even if it is simply a fertilized egg, is unique and worthy of life. If you were given the opportunity of viewing a book containing millions of small photos of all the possible offspring you and your spouse could potentially produce, would you view such a book? Assuming that you could squeeze 100 small photos on a page, how big would such a book be?

This is not too difficult to compute. Let's assume that a woman's ovaries contain about 500 eggs. Let's also assume that a man produces about 6 trillion sperm in a lifetime. (This figure comes from 300 million sperm per day multiplied by 60 years.) For every possible sperm there are 500 different eggs, giving us 500 multiplied by 6 trillion possible children's photos. This is about 3,280,000,000,000,000 photos. At 100 photos per page, this would produce a book about 32 trillion pages in length.

Of the people I surveyed, only about 50 percent would choose to gaze into the book of photographs. Some respondents noted that many of the children would look so similar that they would prefer to look at a book that was reduced to a reasonable size by showing only one photo per *class* of similar appearances. Many others I surveyed indicated that they would be more interested in their genetic possibilities with regard to personality, temperament, and *talent*. One respondent noted, "What if you glimpsed a potential child so heartbreakingly beautiful, or so winning and delightful, that your real children suffered by comparison? What if you took your disappointment out on them?"

Here is a sampling of responses and summaries of responses that I received.

- Some have noted that they would like to peek at some amusing, impossible combinations such as John Lennon and Margaret Thatcher.
- Would you like to visit, for one hour, a ghost world, where you could watch and talk to your ghost children?
- If you could look at a book for the mating of two apes, would any of the trillions of potential offspring look vaguely human?
- Compute the number of ghost children for simpler organisms by searching the scientific literature for the number of sperm and eggs produced for an insect or a fish.
- The largest encyclopedia is *La Enciclopedia Universal Ilustrada Europeo-America* (J. Espasa & Sons, Madrid) totaling 105,000 pages. How much larger is the book of ghost children?

- If God is omniscient, has He already seen the book of ghost children for every person who ever lived on Earth? Has He already seen the book of all the ghost children's potential children? If you believe in an omniscient God who knows all potentialities, perhaps He has seen the faces of all of Joseph and Mary's ghost children—all the ghost children of Moses, Muhammad, Hitler, Einstein—all the ghost children of every animal and of every animal on other worlds. Perhaps there are other realities inhabited by ghost children, or perhaps God solidifies the path of reality by selecting and actualizing the ghost children, thus moving them from virtual existences into actual ones. Perhaps *you* are the ghost child of your parents in an alternate reality.

## APOCALYPSE

Robert Frost wrote, "Some say the world will end in fire. Some say in ice." Do you think there is hope for humanity surviving when the planet Earth is engulfed by the sun's expanding in 7 billion years, as scientists expect?

The Book of Revelations (8:1) says, "And when he opened the seventh seal, there was silence in heaven about the space of half an hour." Many believe that the Earth is like an inmate waiting on Death Row. Even if we do not die by a comet or asteroid impact, we know the Earth's days are numbered. The Earth's rotation is slowing down. Far in the future, day lengths will be equivalent to 50 of our present days. The moon will hang in the same place in the sky, and the lunar tides will stop.

In 5 billion years, the fuel in our sun will be exhausted, and the sun will begin to die and expand, becoming a red giant. At some point, our oceans will boil away. No one on Earth will be alive to see a red glow filling most of the sky. As physicist Freeman Dyson once said, "No matter how deep we burrow into the Earth . . . we can only postpone by a few million years our miserable end."[5]

Where will humans be, 5 billion years from now, at the End of the World? Even if we could somehow withstand the incredible heat of the sun, we would not survive. In about 7 billion years, the sun's outer "atmosphere" will engulf the Earth. Due to atmospheric friction, the Earth will spiral into the sun and incinerate.

Here is our future:

| | |
|---|---|
| Sun expands to engulf the Earth. | 7 billion years |
| Stars cease to form. All large stars have become neutron stars or black holes. | 1 trillion years |
| Longest-lived stars use up all fuel. | 100 trillion years |

If this ending seems too dismal to you, perhaps we should ask if there is hope for humanity when the sun expands to engulf the Earth in 7 billion years. To give an answer, first consider that around 4 billion years ago, living creatures were nothing more than biochemical machines capable of self-reproduction. In a mere fraction of this time, humans evolved from creatures like Australopithecines. Today humans have wandered the moon and have studied ideas ranging from general relativity to quantum cosmology. Once space travel begins in earnest our descendents will leave the confinement of Earth. Because the ultimate fate of the universe involves great cold or great heat, it is likely that *Homo sapiens* will become extinct. However, our civilization and our values may not be doomed. Who knows into what beings we will evolve? Who knows what intelligent machines we will create that will be our ultimate heirs?

I conclude this question on an upbeat note from theoretical physicist Freeman Dyson:

> Gödel proved that the world of pure mathematics is inexhaustible; no finite set of axioms and rules of inference can ever encompass the whole of mathematics; given any finite set of axioms, we can find meaningful mathematical questions which the axioms leave unanswered. I hope that an analogous situation exists in the physical world. If my view of the future is correct, it means that the world of physics and astronomy is also inexhaustible; no matter how far we go into the future, there will always be new things happening, new information coming in, new worlds to explore, a constantly expanding domain of life, consciousness, and memory.[6]

## DREAMS

Novelist S. R. Donaldson once wrote, "The dreams of men belong to God."[7] Does God dream? Can an omniscient being dream? Does God create your dreams? Do you seek God in your dreams?

Scientists have shown that virtually all mammals dream. Even the fetus in the womb dreams. If humans are made in God's image, does this mean God dreams? One of my favorite quotations on dreaming comes from Shirley Jackson: "No live organism can continue for long to exist sanely under conditions of absolute reality. Even larks and katydids are supposed, by some, to dream."[8]

Fred Alan Wolf, a theoretical physicist, said: "The ultimate mystery facing us is how matter becomes conscious. Simply put, if we argue that we are made of matter, then how does that matter seemingly produce or create images and thoughts? Or even put more crudely, how does meat dream?"[9]

## SILENCE IS A POEM

I noted earlier in this volume John Fowles's enigmatic line from *The Magus*, "There are times when silence is a poem."[10] Do you think that God's apparent silence in times of humanity's greatest need, and during times of genocide, has a significance we can understand?

According to the Bible, God took a more active role in ancient days. Why? If you believe the Bible is composed of metaphors and legends, why have our metaphors and legends changed? Could a Jesus-like individual exist today and gain followers around the world? Perhaps you believe such people exist. Who are they?

Clement of Alexandria (150–215) believed that Christians could become divine by imitating the calmness and imperturbability of God. A Christian should imitate the serenity of God by speaking quietly, never laughing wildly, sitting properly, and even burping gently. Once Christians achieve this state of quiet peace, they will find that they have a Divine Companion "sharing our house with us, sitting at table, sharing in the whole moral effort of life."[11]

Basil (329–379), Bishop of Caesarea, said that elusive religious realities could only be suggested by silence.

## NOAH'S ARK

If you believe the Bible should be interpreted literally, do you believe that Noah collected all species of Earthly organisms on his ark? How could this be achieved? For example, siphonapterologists (experts in fleas) recognize 1,830 varieties of fleas. Incredible as it may seem, there are around 300,000 species of beetles, making beetles one of the most diverse groups of organisms on earth. When biologist J. B. S. Haldane was asked by a religious person what message the Lord conveyed through His creations, he responded, "An inordinate fondness for beetles."[12]

One of my favorite books on beetles is *Dung Beetle Ecology*, which points out that a large number (about 7,000 species) of the 300,000 species of beetles live off of animal dung.[13] Did Noah bring these species on the ark? If he did, did he concern himself with the fact that animal dung is often fiercely contested? On the African savanna up to 4,000 beetles have been observed to converge on 500 grams of fresh elephant dung within 15 minutes after it is deposited. Some dung beetles fashion dung into balls and roll it away for burial. The dung-ball rollers (genus *Sisyphus*) were held sacred and immortalized by the ancient Egyptians. For these beetles, the completed dung ball is waved around as a sexual display and courtship attractor.

Did Noah or his family also take *kleptoparasitic beetles*? These are dung beetles known to steal dung from others. I bet he never could have guessed that: (1) African dung beetles bury a metric ton of dung per hectare per year; (2) in the twentieth century, dozens of species would be imported to Australia to handle the dung of cattle, which could not be effectively handled by the native species; (3) insect dung communities involve hundreds of complex ecological interactions between coprophagous flies and their parasites—insects, mites, and nematodes (an ecology probably difficult to manage on the ark!); and (4) in South Africa, more than 100 species of dung beetles occur together in a single cow pat. One gigantic species, *Heliocopris dilloni* resides exclusively in elephant dung. A few species of beetles are so specialized that they live close to the source of dung, in the hairs near an animal's anus.

You get my point! It's quite a mystery as to what the biblical authors meant when they called for Noah to take pairs of every animal on the earth. (Actually, in Genesis 6:19, God tells Noah to take "two of every kind" of creature into the ark, but in Genesis 7:2 this becomes seven pairs of all clean animals, one pair of all unclean animals, and seven pairs of each species of bird.) While pondering the mysteries of living systems and their growth and reproduction, I asked a number of colleagues several questions:

1. Given a large container enclosing two individuals of every animal species in the world, what would be the approximate total weight of all the organisms? Would this weight be more than the weight of the Empire State Building in New York City? How would your answer differ if you included every plant, bacterial, and fungal organism?

2. Assume that all other organisms on Earth were dead except for those pairs in the container in question 1, and assume that the animals were released a thousand years ago. What would you expect to be surviving today? (Assume that, where applicable, a male and female were used for each species.)

3. Assume that today it started to rain for 40 days, and the rain covered all the land on the Earth. Further assume that the flood waters receded to preflood days within several months. What would be the geopolitical changes as a result of the temporary flood? What would be the ecological changes as a result of the temporary flood?

I received a number of fascinating replies from scientists. For example, biologist Ralf Stephan estimated the weight of animals in the container to be

1,000 tons. He used a value of 10 million for the number of species and assumed an average mass of 100 grams. (Insects decrease his figure for average mass because of the huge number of insect species.) There would be no significant increase in mass as a result of including bacteria or fungi, but there would be some increase if plants were used. (How would this change if extinct species were included?) Other scientists investigated the weight problem by working in units of blue whales, the "champions in the weight department." Lou Bjostad from Fort Collins, Colorado, estimated the weight of all the animal pairs in the enclosure to be about 10 whales' worth.

Surprisingly, most biologists said that no mammals would be alive after a thousand years because approximately fifty individuals of a single species are needed to sustain genetic health. Any small population is subject to extinction from disease, environmental changes, and genetic risks—the gradual accumulation of traits with small but harmful effects. There is also the problem of making sure that there are both male and female offspring surviving. Today, species are considered endangered well before their numbers drop below fifty.

Ralf Stephan also asked for clarification of my phrase "rain covered all the land." If the phrase means that all the land including the Himalayas is covered evenly, this would require a depth of 9,000 meters in most regions. Further he asked how fast will the water rise, and is there time to put people and food into boats? He indicated that most people do not have access to a boat and that most airplanes could not land, although some might float. The most important variable for immediate survivability depends on the distribution of floating objects, because if people must swim 500–1,000 meters in cold water to reach a floating object, most will drown.

One scientist indicated that such an inundation would probably also kill most of the plant life on Earth. Even if the waters were to recede, the resultant salt deposits would prevent plants from growing for many years. The scientist suggested that, during these years, many of the seeds and plants that could live through the flood itself would die out.

Other scientists wondered about the ecological effect of the numerous dead carcasses caused by the initial flood. Some biologists recommended that the initial health of each pair of organisms be defined in the original question. Another variable to consider is whether the animals are all released in one place as opposed to being spread evenly over the planet.

One colleague noted that all the pairs of animals require food. "If one animal of species A eats one of species B, then B becomes automatically extinct (unless the male was eaten, and the pair had already initiated reproduction)."

### 5,342,482,337,666?

What is the religious significance of the numbers 5,342,482,337,666? or 611,121?

In the Urantia religion, a twentieth-century sect, these numbers have an almost divine quality. Urantia is their name for Earth. According to the sect, headquartered in Chicago, we live on the 606th planet in a system called Satania, which includes 619 flawed but evolving worlds. Urantia's grand universe number is 5,342,482,337,666. Satania has its command center on Jerusem in the constellation of Norlatiadek, part of the evolving universe of Nebadon. Nebadon in turn belongs to a superuniverse called Orvonton. Orvonton and six other superuniverses revolve around the central universe of Havona, the dwelling place of god.

Urantia followers rely on a 2,097-page holy book that they say contains the Earth's fifth revelation from God, superior to mainstream Christianity. They think it will transform the world. In their book, Lucifer, who rebelled against his superiors, is now the deposed sovereign of Satania, named after Satan, his first lieutenant.

I'm not sure how the Urantia people come up with 5,342,482,337,666. Nor does the Urantia movement disclose who wrote *The Urantia Book* that mentions the number.[14] They do believe that human minds are created at birth, but the soul does not develop until about age 6. When we die, our souls survive. Jesus Christ is number 611,121 among more than 700,000 Creator Sons.

The numbers have particularly interesting numerical properties. The prime factors are:

$$611121 = 3 \times 7 \times 29101$$

$$5342482337666 = 2 \times 829 \times 1361 \times 2367557$$

You can see that both numbers don't seem to have very many prime factors. There are some more amazing numerical properties of these numbers. For example, considering the digits of 611,121 one at a time, we find:

$$6 + 1 + 1 + 1 + 2 + 1 = 6 \times 1 \times 1 \times 1 \times 2 \times 1 = 12$$

And 12 plays a major role in many religions. For example, there are 12 signs of the zodiac. Christ chose 12 apostles. In the Revelation of John, the heavenly Jerusalem has 12 gates. There are even 12 tones in our modern 12-tone musical scale.

The factor 1361 in the grand universe number—it's the exact year during the Papacy of Gregory XI that he decided to move from Avignon to Rome, thus ending the Babylonian Captivity of the Church.

611,121 appears in a listing of decimal representations of periods (number of digits that repeat) for $1/n$ for $n = 1, 2, 3, \ldots$ :

1, 1, 1, 1, 1, 1, *6, 1, 1, 1,* 2, *1,* 6, 6, 1, 1, 16, 1, 18, 1, 6, 2, 22, 1, 1, 6, 3, 6, 28, 1,

15, 1, 2, 16, 6, 1, 3, 18, 6, 1, 5, 6, 21, 2, 1, 22, 46, 1, 42, 1, 16, 6, 13, 3, 2, 6,

18, 28, 58, 1, 60, 15, 6, 1, 6

In fact, 611,121 is the very first string of digits starting with a number other than 1. In other words, examining the decimal representations of fractions, 1/1, 1/2, 1/3,1/4, 1/5, 1/6, and so on, it's not until 1/7 that we get a "period" of 6, since 1/7 = 0.142857142857, which repeats every 6 digits. The next 2 in the sequence indicates that 1/11 = 0.0909090 repeats every 2 digits.

Could the Urantia movement have known about the unusual characteristics of their number for Christ? What other startling numerical characteristics do these large numbers have?

## LIMITED OMNISCIENCE

Aliens descend to Earth and abduct you while your car is stopped at a red light on a dark highway. While you are aboard their ship, they ask you two somewhat lengthy questions:

*We are interested in omniscience on a limited level. You may choose ten books from any one field of human knowledge, and we will give you perfect memory and understanding of the contents of these books. (By "field of knowledge," we mean books from defined areas such as: math, physics, chemistry, geology, business, philosophy, sociology, medicine, law, religion, or other subjects for which colleges might have majors.) From what single field of knowledge would you choose the ten books?*

*You may choose ten books from any one field of our knowledge, and we will give you perfect memory and understanding of the contents of these books. (By "field of knowledge" we mean books from defined areas such as: math, physics, chemistry, geology, business, philosophy, sociology, medicine, law, religion, or other subjects for which colleges might have majors.) From what single field of alien knowledge would you choose the ten books?*

What are your answers to these questions? What do you think most humans answer? How would your answer to the last question change if the aliens concluded with, "Our warning to you is that no Earthling has ever desired to go home once they acquired this much alien knowledge?"

I informally surveyed about fifty colleagues. Here are the most commonly chosen Earthly knowledge fields, sorted from most frequently given response to least frequently given response: physics, mathematics, philosophy, medicine, psychology, sociology, history, languages, business, literature, religion, electrical engineering, chemistry, and botany.

Here are the most commonly chosen alien knowledge fields, sorted from most frequently given response to least frequently given response: physics, philosophy, mathematics, engineering (including aerospace engineering), sociology, biology, religion, history, and literature.

One respondent even considered "architecture" as a field he would choose. He wondered, "How much of a civilization's culture is reflected in the engineering (and architecture) of the culture? Would it be possible to analyze a civilization based solely on their engineering accomplishments and derive what their thoughts, values, and lifestyles were?"

April P. writes to me,

From human fields, I would choose total knowledge of medicine. From alien fields, I would choose total knowledge of their sociology, psychology, or religions. I would *not* choose fields such as mathematics, physics, or chemistry because these fields contain universal truths, and the alien's knowledge in these areas would be similar to ours, especially in mathematics. (I would rather know about their social and cultural interactions.) I would not choose philosophy because aliens would most likely ponder similar questions to ours and arrive at similar logical answers. I suspect most men answering this question would choose knowledge of physics while women would opt for the emotional and sociology fields.

## CONDITIONAL OMNISCIENCE

If an alien gave you a pill giving you "conditional omniscience," would you take it? The term *conditional omniscience* means that you can see or know anything you want to see or know. Most people I surveyed said "yes," but the power did make them nervous. In a sense, the pill would serve as a "truth machine." You would know what your spouse, girlfriend, or boyfriend was *really* thinking, which could have serious emotional consequences. Many respondents told me that they would enjoy using their powers for a variety of prosaic purposes, such as: to understand how to invest money, to gain respect, to know just the right lines to use to "pick up" members of the opposite sex, to avoid dangerous situations, and to win in physical combat. Others had more lofty goals, such as to gain knowledge that would enable them to cure diseases, increase human happiness worldwide, prevent world hunger, extend life, end wars. Some would use the power to try to understand the ultimate questions: Why are we here? How did the universe form? Is there a God or afterlife? Is there intelligent life on other planets? Are miracles possible? Who really killed Nicole Brown Simpson?

---

What matters in the world is not so much what is true as what is entertaining, at least so long as the truth itself is unknowable.
—Pierre Larousse, *Grand Dictionnaire Universel*

---

If God does not exist, all is permitted.
—Fyodor Dostoyevsky, *The Brothers Karamazov*

---

"God" is a vague concept. It might refer to some kind of hyperspatial entity that is addicted to creating universes and watching them develop and who is just as remote from us as we are from tiny programs running on our computers. That entity might have a god of its own, and so on. Proving or disproving that such a demiurge exists is just as interesting as disproving the presence of omnipotent invisible peacocks in my backyard.
—Jan Willem Nienhuys, *Skeptic*

---

In the tradition of Pascal, perhaps a new wager can be posed. If mortal life is all that exists for individuals, we lose nothing by seeking to make that life as meaningful and rewarding as possible. But if eternal life exists, we have lost nothing by seeking a fulfilling existence here on Earth. Thus, one might wager on the richness of life here and now.
—John Avise, *Skeptical Inquirer*

# Some Final Thoughts

B.C. MANSFIELD

*God is a fire, and we are all tiny flames; and when we die, those tiny flames go back in to the fire of God.*
—*Anne Rice,* Tale of the Body Thief

*Even an omniscient being could not know the last digit of pi.*
—*Anonymous*

BELIEF IN AN OMNISCIENT GOD AND THE PROMISE OF HEAVEN ARE IM-
portant ideas to adherents of great monotheistic religions such as Christianity, Judaism, and Islam. These beliefs pervade much of Western culture and are clearly
evident in the United States. Although the United States has an exalted position
with respect to other democratic countries in every branch of modern science and

technology, polls over the last few years also place the United States first in be-lief in life after death among these same countries.[1] This is notable, because these beliefs are generally considered to be beyond the domain of traditional science for two reasons: the beliefs are untestable using the scientific method, and yet, conversely, no scientific evidence exists that could cause a religious person to discard his or her "theories" about heaven, God, or the afterlife in order to develop other theories that do not include these concepts.

Recent surveys indicate:

- The U.S. ranks highest, along with Iceland and the Philippines, for per-cent of believers in heaven (63 percent of the U.S. population).
- The U.S. ranks highest for percent of believers in hell (50 percent of the population).
- The U.S. ranks highest for percent of believers in life after death (55 percent).
- The U.S. ranks lowest on knowledge of human evolution (44 percent).
- 84 percent of Americans believe that God performed miracles.
- 77 percent of Americans believe saints or God can cure people of tradi-tionally incurable diseases.[2]

Indeed, science and religion are *both* thriving in America, although I suspect that the most scientifically literate people and the most religiously fundamental people usually reside in different groups with little overlap.

Not only do many *lay people* believe in God, but various *scientists* have used evidence from physics and astronomy to conclude—not to prove—that God exists. Note, however, that the scientists' "God" may not be the God of the Is-raelites who smites the wicked but rather a God that established various math-ematical and physical parameters that permitted life to evolve in the universe. Some scientists feel we exist because of cosmic coincidences or, more accu-rately, because of seemingly "finely tuned" numerical constants that permit life. Those individuals who believe in this *anthropic principle* suggest these numbers found in basic physics and in chemistry formulas are near miracles that possibly suggest an intelligent design to the universe. Here are just a few examples of where religion and science can converge.

We owe our very lives to the element carbon, which was first manufac-tured in stars before the Earth formed. The challenge in creating carbon is get-ting two helium nuclei in stars to stick together until they are struck by a third.[3] It turns out that this is accomplished only because of internal resonances, or energy levels, of carbon and oxygen nuclei. If the potential carbon resonance level were only 4 percent lower, carbon atoms wouldn't form. Were the oxygen resonance level only half a percent higher, almost all the carbon would disappear as it combined with helium to form oxygen.[4] This means that human existence depends on the fine-tuning of these two nuclear resonances. Upon learning of these resonances, the famous astronomer Sir Fred Hoyle said that his atheism was shaken:

> If you wanted to produce carbon and oxygen in roughly equal quantities by stellar nucleosynthesis, these are just the two levels you have to fix. Your fixing would have to be just about where these levels are actually found to be. . . . A common sense interpretation of the facts suggests that a superintellect has monkeyed with physics, as well as with chemistry and biology, and there are no blind forces worth speaking about in nature. The numbers one calculates from the facts seem to me so overwhelming as to put this conclusion almost beyond question. . . . Rather than accept that fantastically small probability of life having arisen through the blind forces of nature, it seemed better to suppose that the origin of life was a deliberate intellectual act.[5]

Robert Jastrow, the head of NASA's Goddard Institute for Space Studies, called this the most powerful evidence for the existence of God ever to come out of science.[6] Other amazing parameters abound, such as those related to the "anthropic principle."[7] If all of the stars in the universe were heavier than three solar masses, they would live for only about 500 million years, and life would not have time to evolve beyond primitive bacteria. Stephen Hawking has estimated that if the rate of the universe's expansion merely 1 second after the Big Bang had been smaller by even one part in a hundred thousand million million, the universe would have recollapsed.[8] The universe must live for billions of years to permit time for intelligent life to involve. On the other hand, the universe might have expanded so rapidly that protons and electrons never united to make hydrogen atoms. If our universe were only six times smaller than it is today, it would be one thousand times hotter, and no rocky planets would form.[9] If our galaxy contained the same number of stars but happened to be one hundred times smaller, the increased density of stars would lead to high probabilities that other stars would enter our solar system and alter the planetary orbits.[10]

Physicist Paul Davies has calculated that the odds against the initial conditions in the universe being suitable for later star formation were "1" followed by a thousand billion billion zeroes.[11] Paul Davies, John Barrow, and Frank Tipler estimated that a change in the strength of gravity or of the weak force by only one part in $10^{100}$ would have prevented advanced life-forms from evolving.[12] There is no a priori physical reason why these constants and quantities should possess the values they do. This has led the one-time agnostic Paul Davies to write, "Through my scientific work I have come to believe more and more strongly that the physical universe is put together with an ingenuity so astonishing that I cannot accept it merely as a brute fact."[13] Of course, these conclusions are controversial, and an infinite number of random (nondesigned) universes could exist, ours being just one that permits carbon-based life. Some researchers have even speculated that child universes are constantly budding off from parent universes and that the child universe inherits a set of physical laws similar to the parent's, a process reminiscent of biological evolution of life on Earth.[14]

Continued efforts to reconcile science and religion have led to increased interest in scientific theories of how matter and energy were first created in our universe. Are there any meaningful correspondences of these new theories to religious creation texts such as the Old Testament's Genesis? One of the latest and most mind-boggling theories of cosmogenesis suggests that all the matter and energy in our universe was created when a four-dimensional fragment of another universe wrinkled, floated through 5-D space, and then imprinted itself on our universe. Charles Seife eloquently describes this model, called the *ekpyrotic model:*

> In [effectively] five-dimensional space float two perfectly flat four-dimensional membranes, like sheets drying on parallel clotheslines. One of the sheets is our universe; the other a "hidden" parallel universe. Provoked by random fluctuations, our unseen companion spontaneously sheds a membrane that slowly floats towards our universe. . . . The floater speeds up and splats into our universe, whereupon some of the energy of the collision becomes the energy and matter that make up our cosmos.[15]

Some have likened the ekpyrotic "membrane creator" from the hidden universe to the "Spirit of God" in the second line of Genesis, which reads, "Now the earth was formless and empty, darkness was over the surface of the deep, and the Spirit of God was hovering over the waters." The formless, dark, and empty Earth corresponds to our universe prior to the four-dimensional membrane splat that created matter and energy in our universe. The "hovering" corresponds to the floating of the membrane. Moreover, the ekpyrotic model suggests that at any moment another membrane could peel off, float toward our universe, and destroy us all. Some physicists say they already see signs of our impending demise presaged by the accelerated expansion of our universe. The possible doom at our doorsteps, predicted by a highly scientific model of our universe, corresponds with various biblical prophecies of apocalypse and the End of Days. Obviously, fitting theoretical physics to biblical passages involves extreme flights of fancy, but I enjoy the endless debates and mind-stretching dialogue that result. If, 100 years from now, scientists are able to demonstrate the existence of a mutably omniscient, ekpyrotic God from the fifth dimension (Figure S.1), what would this mean for Moses, Jesus, Muhammad, and other prophets of yore? Will robotic rabbis of the twenty-first century contemplate a hybrid oöoö God (such as discussed at the end of Chapter 15), a God that oscillates at 60 hertz? In 200 years, will androids dream of ekpyrotic sheep?

*Fig. S.1. Artistic rendition of an ekpyrotic, omniscient hive God*

I sometimes dream that a century from now a spaceship from Earth discovers remnants of advanced life-forms on Ganymede, one of the water-containing moons of Jupiter. What has happened to the beings? No one knows. Some hypothesize that they have long ago evolved into structures that our eyes do not recognize as life. Others speculate that the beings have been consumed by alien carnivores and then digested and expelled in another dimension. In reality, the life-forms have reached such a high spiritual and scientific state that they metamorphosed into high-frequency omniscient hives with names like El, Elohim, El-Elyon, El-Shadai, Kadosh, and Melekh. They oscillate between omniscience and mutable omniscience, glow with a light beyond ultraviolet, flicker like invisible filaments in the fabric of spacetime. In their dreams they create new universes in dozens of dimensions. In some of these universes, Adam has tentacles or Eve has wings, but no matter what their appearance, the new life-forms have minds that permit them to commune with their ekpyrotic hive creators.

But enough poetry. Let's return to contemporary theories of physics. We can go even further and think about the wild implications for multiple universes and what they say about our power in relation to God's. The Stanford University physics professor Andrei Linde has speculated that it might be possible to create a new baby universe in a laboratory by violently compressing matter at high temperatures—in fact, 1 milligram of matter may initiate an eternal self-reproducing universe.[16] What would be the economic or spiritual gain from creating a universe, considering it would be extremely difficult, if not impossible, to enter the new universe from ours? Would God care if we created such universes at will? Andrei Linde and writer Rudy Rucker have discussed methods for encoding a message for the new universe's potential inhabitants by manipulating parameters of physics, such as the masses and charges of particles, although this would be a precarious experiment given the difficulty of manipulating these constants in such a way that both codes a message and permits life to evolve.

While on the topic of multiple universes, recall in Chapter 5, on Newcomb's Paradox, we discussed possible limits to God's omniscience. Here we discussed Martin Gardner's suggestion that many paradoxes could be avoided if God were regarded as omniscient only in the sense that He knows all that can be known, "allowing for parts of the future to be in principle unknowable." In light of the possibility of multiple universes that we just discussed, perhaps the term *omniscient* takes on a new meaning, and the God of the Old Testament might be omniscient only in the sense that He knows all that can be known about a single universe—not all universes.

Why is it that most humans believe in some kind of religion and religious prophet? One secular answer is that we are predisposed toward supernatural beliefs because we, like all animals, are pattern-seeking machines. Creatures with the ability to recognize patterns in nature are often the creatures able to find food and mates or escape from dangerous animals. In many species, sexual selection produces males with elaborate patterns on body parts. For example, many male birds have colorful plumage. Even the Yucca moth, with only a few ganglia for its brain, can recognize the geometry of the yucca flower from birth. However, even with all the pattern detection that has evolved, the evolutionary process has not forced life-forms to be able to detect the true *cause* of the patterns. In some sense, it is better to "detect" patterns that aren't really there than to miss patterns that might get you into trouble, like the shadows of hawks before they attack. Because we are programmed to respond quickly to patterns, to search for patterns, and to "find" patterns in the chaotic world around us, we often accept nonexistent patterns and attribute fantastic causes after the acceptance. As Michael Shermer suggests in *How We Believe*, we are more gullible than skeptical by nature.[17] Perhaps our love of patterns is one reason why prophets who continually predict the end of the world on particular dates still manage to retain their followers even when the dates pass. For example, the Jehovah's Witnesses have predicted doomsday for 1874, 1878, 1881, 1910, 1914, 1918, 1920, 1925, etc., but the erroneous predictions do not seem to dampen the enthusiasm of their followers. Similarly, several authors predicted that the world could end in 1999, and each author used a different, vague quatrain of Nostradamus to make the prediction. Whatever their motivation, the authors found patterns in the chaos of Nostradamus's poetic words. Nostradamus's works have been in print ever since their first publication centuries ago, and I suspect that they will continue to be cherished for centuries to come.[18] Nostradamus was never thought to be omniscient like God, but many people have ascribed to Nostradamus the ability to know and see beyond ordinary horizons of time and space.

James Alcock, a professor of psychology at Glendon College, York University, Toronto, suggests that our brain is a belief-generating machine that produces beliefs without any particular respect for what is real or true and what is not.[19] Perhaps this is why humans are so inclined to believe in omniscient beings without scientific verification. Alcock says that this belief engine in our brains selects information from the environment, shapes it, combines it with information from memory, and produces beliefs that are generally consistent with beliefs already held. Evolution by natural selection does not select directly on the basis of reason or truth; it selects for reproductive success. A caveman might believe that evil ancestral spirits would attack if he left the cave at night. If the caveman were motivated by the search for truth, he may have left the cave at night and been killed by a nocturnal carnivore. Compare the dead caveman with one who believed in and feared ancestral evil spirits without question and was therefore more likely to live and reproduce. Seeking truth does not always promote survival, and erroneous belief can be beneficial.

Yes, fear can be a good thing, if it doesn't go too far. Fear is a cohesive force binding people and nations. It obviously prevents people from taking dangerous risks. God may have acquired omniscience because the priesthood or other authority wanted people to fear God. A God who knows everything, watches everything you do, knows when you are sinning, knows when you are merely *thinking* against the established order, is a powerful "control" factor. For example, biblical stories often promote a respect for certain established orders and fear of authority. Small infractions are often severely punished, for example: God kills Uzzah for touching the Ark of the Covenant in an attempt to stop it from falling to the ground (2 Samuel 6:6–7), and God kills Onan for spilling his semen on the ground (and not impregnating his brother's wife, whose husband God had killed around Genesis 38:10). God's mass murders are throughout the Bible, but in addition to committing murder, God also directs others to kill in His name. In Exodus, the death penalty is commanded for such diverse sins as murder, working on the Sabbath day, cursing one's parents, practicing witchcraft, sacrificing to other gods, adultery, converting from Judaism to another faith, not obeying God, and so forth. (See Appendix C for a more complete list of killings by God.)

In the Bible, there is little or no talk about equal rights, rights of the individual, abolishment of slavery, or inducements to improve the self-esteem of the individual. Above all, people must "be not highminded, but fear" (Romans 11:20). So, we can see why an omniscient God might have evolved. An omniscient (and omnipotent) God has the ultimate capacity to cause terror in the minds of believers, coax obedience to the priesthood or authority, and encourage the formation of strong clans and nations that, by natural selection, survive in competitions with their neighbors. American philosopher Anton Thorn writes about his dislike of the omniscient God concept:

> Consider the psychological ramifications of belief in an omniscient God. An individual accepting belief in such a being would never be able to know privacy in the most private haven of his existence: his own mind. While the priest himself may not claim omniscient privilege to the minds of his flock, the priest is ever ready to remind the believer of the all-seeing eye of their voyeuristic God. There is possibly no greater paralyzing psychological fear than belief in a being who can know one's own private thoughts, feelings, impulses and motivations. The priests who invented and developed prototypical god-beliefs well knew to include this notion of omniscience as a means of compulsion, as a tool of enslavement, as a force ensuring obedience to the priests' own whims.[20]

The priests have always welcomed fear, and the Bible makes it clear that God desires fear.[21] This is evident, for example, in Ecclesiastes 3:14: "I know that, whatsoever God doeth, it shall be for ever: nothing can be put to it, nor any thing taken from it: and God doeth it, that men should fear before him." Fear is one of the most prevalent emotions in the Bible, continually drummed into its readers:

- "Come, my children, listen to me; I will teach you the fear of the LORD." (Psalms 34:11)
- "The LORD Almighty is the one you are to regard as holy, he is the one you are to fear, he is the one you are to dread." (Isaiah 8:13)
- "The fear of the LORD is pure, enduring forever. The ordinances of the LORD are sure and altogether righteous." (Psalms 19:9)
- "It is a fearful thing to fall into the hands of the living God." (Hebrews 10:31)

For many more examples of fear in the Bible and other religious sources, see Appendix J, which provides analyses on the fine line between respect and fear.

Obviously, the combination of omniscience and fear or reward is a particularly powerful motivator. In the Sermon on the Mount, Jesus seems to remind people that God is closely watching their every move:

- "But when you give to the needy, do not let your left hand know what your right hand is doing, so that your giving may be in secret. Then your Father, who sees what is done in secret, will reward you." (Matthew 6:3–4)
- "And when you pray, do not keep on babbling like pagans, for they think they will be heard because of their many words. Do not be like them, for your Father knows what you need before you ask him." (Matthew 6:7–8)
- "But when you fast, put oil on your head and wash your face, so that it will not be obvious to men that you are fasting, but only to your Father, who is unseen; and your Father, who sees what is done in secret, will reward you." (Matthew 6:17–18)

Other New Testament passages suggest that God is always watching:

- "Nothing in all creation is hidden from God's sight. Everything is uncovered and laid bare before the eyes of him to whom we must give account." (Hebrews 4:13)
- "For God is greater than our hearts, and he knows everything." (I John 3:20)

Do you think that verses like these were used by priests to control their followers? Perhaps more important than what *God* knows is how our *perception* of God's supposedly infinite knowledge affects us. For example, how does the sense that God is watching us and knowing our thoughts affect membership in a particular religion, and how does it affect our relationships with members of other religions?

Fear often accompanies the prophets' relations to God. When Muhammad, founder of Islam, first had his visions of God, he felt oppressed, smothered, as if his breath were being squeezed from his chest. Later he heard a voice calling his name, but when he turned to find the source of the voice, no one was there. The local Christians, Jews, and pagan Arabs called him insane. Legend had it that Muhammad as a child had fits. When he was 5 years old he told his foster parents, "Two men in white raiment came and threw me down and opened up my belly and searched inside for I don't know what." This description is startlingly similar to the alien abduction experience described by people with temporal lobe epilepsy (TLE) resulting from unusual electrical activity in the brain.

Note that the overriding emotion experienced by Muhammad, Moses, and Saint Paul during their religious visions was not one of rapture and joy but rather of fear. When Moses heard the voice of God from a burning bush, Moses hid his face and was frightened. Luke and Paul both agreed that Paul suffered from an unknown "illness" or "bodily weakness" that Paul called his "thorn in the flesh." Famous biblical commentators have attributed this to either migraine headaches or epilepsy. Paul did once have malaria, which involves a high fever that can damage the brain. Other psychologists have noted that probable candidates for a temporal lobe epilepsy diagnosis include Moses, Flaubert, Saint Paul, and Dostoyevsky, who were all famous for their rages.[22]

In my book *Strange Brains and Genius*, I argue for the possibility that many of the deepest religious experiences result from epileptic-like phenomena. However, psychologist William James argued that religious states are not less profound simply because they can be induced by neural anomalies:

Even more perhaps than other kinds of genius, religious leaders have been subject to abnormal psychical visitations. Invariably they have been creatures of exalted emotional sensitivity liable to obsessions and fixed ideas; and frequently they have fallen into trances, heard voices, seen visions, and presented all sorts of peculiarities which are ordinarily classed as pathological. Often, moreover, these pathological features have helped to give them their religious authority and influence. To plead the organic causation of a religious state of mind, then, in refutation of its claim to possess superior spiritual value, is quite illogical and arbitrary [because] none of our thoughts and feelings, not even our scientific doctrines, not even our *dis*-beliefs, could retain any value as revelations of the truth, for every one of them without exception flows from the state of the possessor's body at the time. Saint Paul certainly once had an epileptoid, if not an epileptic, seizure, but there is not a single one of our states of mind, high or low, healthy or morbid, that has not some organic processes as its condition.[23]

Writer Eve LaPlante is just one of a growing number of writers and researchers who believe in TLE-induced religious experiences.[24] For example, Professor Michael Persinger from Ontario does research on the neurophysiology of religious feelings and believes that spiritual experiences come from altered electrical activity in the brain. David Bear from Harvard Medical School believes that "a temporal lobe focus in superior individuals (like van Gogh, Dostoyevsky, Muhammad, Saint Paul, and Moses) may spark an extraordinary search for the entity we alternatively call truth or beauty."[25]

👁 👁 👁

In many countries, belief in an omniscient being is as prevalent today as it was a thousand years ago. Today, certain religious people often claim that there are no real coincidences or accidents, that an accident may only seem to be a random event because of our superficial knowledge, and that there is actually a hidden, deeper meaning and connectedness linking all events that only God has the special powers to discern.[26] Certainly, religious people often love to find structures and patterns, even if these patterns cannot be studied using close scientific scrutiny. British astrophysicist Stephen Hawking has mused, "Ever since the dawn of civilization, people have not been content to see events as unconnected and inexplicable. They have craved an understanding of the underlying order of the world."[27]

I think that our brains are wired with a desire for religion and belief in an omniscient God. If so, the reasons for our interest, and the rituals we use, are buried deep in the essence of our nature. Religion is at the edge of the known and the unknown, poised on the fractal boundaries of history, philosophy, psychology, biology, and many other disciplines. Because of this, religion and paradoxes of omniscience are important topics for contemplation and study. Even with the great scientific strides we will make in this century, we will nevertheless continue to swim in a sea of mystery. Humans need to make sense of the world and will surely continue to use logic and religion for that task. What patterns and connections will we see in the twenty-first century? Who and what will be our God?

👁 👁 👁

Lewis Browne, in his book *This Believing World: A Simple Account of the Great Religions of Mankind*, suggested that the concept of an omniscient God came into being gradually with the notion of monotheism.[28] Judaism evolved from *monolatry* (belief in the existence of many gods, but worship of only one) to strict *monotheism* around the time of the prophet Jeremiah in the seventh and early sixth centuries B.C. As Judaism developed, the powers of the Hebrew God grew correspondingly stronger until He became omniscient, omnipotent, and omnipresent. The strict monotheism in Jeremiah's day is suggested by the following biblical statements that deny the very existence of other gods:

> Why should I forgive you? Your children have forsaken me and sworn by gods that are not gods. (Jeremiah 5:7)

> O LORD, my strength and my fortress, my refuge in time of distress, to you the nations will come from the ends of the earth and say, "Our fathers possessed nothing but false gods, worthless idols that did them no good. Do men make their own gods? Yes, but they are not gods!" (Jeremiah 16:19–20)

During the early days of Judaism, the First Commandment, "You shall have no other gods before me" (Exodus 20:3), has little meaning if the Jews do not actually believe in the existence of other gods. God does not say that no other gods exist, but just that the Jews should practice monolatry and consider Him above all others. (Note 14 discusses the physics of polytheism.)

Let's review. We can best understand the evolution from monolatry to a single, omniscient God by going back in time to around 1300 to 1000 B.C. According to Exodus, the Hebrews became a nation and adopted a national god on Mount Sinai, a granitic peak of the south-central Sinai Peninsula. As we said, the religion of the Jews, which started around 1000 B.C., was initially monolatrous. Moses told his people to worship Yahweh, but there is not one shred of evidence that the early Jews denied the existence of other gods. In fact, the story of the Jews' flight from Egypt frequently mentions other gods. The initial religion of God's chosen for about 200 years was monolatrous.[29]

The term *henotheism* is also used to describe the early religion of the Yahweh followers. Henotheism refers to the supremacy of a single God without denying the existence of others. (Technically, monolatry differs from henotheism, in which multiple gods may be worshiped but one of the many has a higher ranking.) Evidence indicates that the Hebrews frequently changed religions, often several times in a single lifetime during their settlement of the land of milk and honey. Not until the eighth and seventh centuries B.C. did prophets like Amos, Hosea, and Isaiah make Yahweh the only God of the universe.

As we discussed in Chapter 6, the Old Testament afterlife was not one of rewards and punishments. There was only a strange house of dust, called Sheol, to which all souls went after their death. The souls stayed in Sheol for a while and then disappeared from existence forever. One should be just in order to create a happier society but not to gain a reward in the afterlife.[30]

◉ ◉ ◉

Let's return our attention to omniscience and the definitions of God. In the Introduction, we focused on one working definition: God is He who created the universe and is "all-powerful, all-knowing, and all-good." Skeptics, of course, argue about the existence of such a God. For example, William L. Rowe, author of "The Problem of Evil & Some Varieties of Atheism," suggests that the existence of widespread suffering is not consistent with an omniscient, omnipotent God. He writes:

> It seems quite unlikely that *all* the instances of intense suffering occurring daily in our world are intimately related to the occurrence of a greater good or the prevention of evils at least as bad; and even more unlikely, should they somehow all be so related, that an omnipotent, omniscient being could not have achieved at least some of those goods (or prevented some of those evils) without permitting the instances of intense suffering that are supposedly related to them. In the light of our experience and knowledge of the variety and scale of human and animal suffering in our world, the idea that none of this suffering could have been prevented by an omnipotent being without thereby losing a greater good or permitting an evil at least as bad seems an extraordinarily absurd idea, quite beyond our belief.[31]

Religious people counter by suggesting that the universe is as good as it can get, and it is impossible to create a better universe; otherwise God is not all-powerful.

Some theologians have asserted that the future is laid out before God like a landscape, and therefore God has foreknowledge of all events. However, as we discussed in Chapter 14, for a God truly to have freedom and to have free actions, His future must not be fully known in advance, because there must be the possibility for God to change His mind. Certainly, the biblical God appears to have limited foreknowledge, or perhaps a kind of foreknowledge that humans cannot understand. For example, God's decision to destroy his evil creations during the great flood implies that God does not have foreknowledge of all things. Some argue that God cannot have foreknowledge of all things because this implies God could not freely alter His actions, to be free to choose. Freedom means the capacity to choose between alternatives. Do you think God has free will? For people who believe that we were "saved" by the death of Jesus, another big question is whether God knew about Jesus before He created the Earth. We discussed this topic in Chapter 8 while examining the "Paradox of the Fortunate Fall."

The polytheistic gods of yore were clearly not omniscient. They could keep secrets from each other. Followers of animistic religions sought specific knowledge from the god of streams, or the god of animals, or the god of mountains—and each god had knowledge the others did not have.

👁 👁 👁

Karen Armstrong, in *A History of God*, writes about theologians who have limited God's power so that He is far from omniscient and omnipotent. For example, philosopher Hans Jonas (1903–1993) suggested that after the horrors of the Auschwitz concentration camp, humans can no longer believe in an omnipotent God. (Jonas's mother died at Auschwitz.) To Jonas, when God created the universe, He voluntarily limited himself and shared the weakness of human beings. Our mission, therefore, is to restore God's power by praying and studying the Torah. On the other hand, the Roman Catholic theologian Hans Kung prefers a more optimistic analysis. He suggests that we shouldn't have faith in an ineffective God but rather in a powerful God who made people strong enough to pray in Auschwitz.[32]

Hans Jonas's theory of a God with limited powers deserves more attention. Drawing from cabalistic traditions, Jonas says that God surrendered Himself to the Universe and contracted until His power diminished. Think of a balloon deflating. God is the balloon. According to this theory, God suffers in history and even risks being destroyed by human evil. The reason that God was silent about Auschwitz was that He simply could not speak or make changes in history. God could not act. Of course, Jonas's contracted God raises many questions. Can a powerless, defenseless God empower people to act morally?[33]

Usually people like to think of God's activities or qualities as attracting people to do good. Some might argue that, indeed, a lot of good came out of Auschwitz. Without Auschwitz and the ensuing silence in heaven, there would have been little future for the Jews or the world. There would be no Israel, no Einstein in America, no spread of democracy through much of the world. Persecution has strange effects and often unites people. As just one ironic example, the diminished persecution of Jews in America has led to a 50 percent intermarriage rate that will lead the American Jewish faith to virtual oblivion in a few generations.

Hans Jonas writes about his theory of the contracting God in *The Phenomenon of Life:*

> In the beginning, for unknowable reasons, the ground of being, or the Divine, chose to give itself over to the chance and risk and endless variety of becoming. And wholly so; entering into the adventure of space and time, the deity held back nothing of itself; no uncommitted or unimpaired part remained to direct, correct, and ultimately guarantee the devious working-out of its destiny in creation. God renounced His own being, divesting himself of His deity—to receive it back from the Odyssey of time weighted with the chance harvest of unforeseeable temporal experience; transfigured or possibly even disfigured by it. In such self-forfeiture of divine integrity for the sake of unprejudiced becoming, no other foreknowledge can be admitted than that of possibilities which cosmic being offers in its own terms: to those, God committed His cause in effacing Himself for the world. . . . With the appearance of man, transcendence awakened to itself and henceforth accompanies his doings with the bated breath of suspense, hoping and beckoning, rejoicing and grieving, approving and frowning—and, I daresay, making itself felt to Him even while not intervening in the dynamics of His worldly scene: for can it not be that by the reflection of its own state as it wavers with the record of man, the transcendent casts light and shadow over the human landscape?[34]

If I interpret Jonas correctly, he further suggests that suffering enriches God's experience of the universe:

> Yet it is precisely through the briefly snatched self-feeling, doing, and suffering of finite individuals, with the pitch of awareness heightened by the very press of finitude, that the divine landscape bursts into color and the deity comes to experience itself. . . . Whatever variety evolution brings forth adds to the possibilities of feeling and acting, and thus enriches the self-experiencing of the ground of being. Every new dimension of world-response opened up in its course means another modality for God's trying out his hidden essence and discovering himself through the surprises of the world-adventure. . . . If this is true for the broadening spectrum of diversity as such, it is even truer for the heightening pitch and passion of life that go with the twin rise of perception and motility in animals. The ever more sharpened keenness of appetite and fear, pleasure and pain, triumph and anguish, love and even cruelty—their very edge is the deity's gain. Its creatures, by merely fulfilling themselves in pursuit of their lives, vindicate the divine venture. Even their suffering deepens the fullness of the symphony. Thus, this side of good and evil, God cannot

lose in the great evolutionary game. I have been speaking of a suffering God which immediately seems to clash with the Biblical conception of divine majesty.[35]

Jonas believes in a God who suffers along with His creation. For example, God is disappointed when His chosen people are unfaithful. But through His contraction of power, God is no longer alone. He is with His creations. He experiences the world and is affected by it. He has entered the time stream to become something more like us.

To Jonas, God changes as a result of His interactions. God has memories. He takes risks. Jonas believes that the fact of our imperfect world implies one of two things: either that a God does not exist (though several could exist) or that the God has given some control over to another agency outside Himself, though created by him. This Other has a power and authority to act on its own. For reasons we cannot fathom, God has "forgone the guaranteeing of his self-satisfaction by his own power, after he has first, by the act of creation itself forgone being 'all in all.'"[36]

All of this suggests that if there is a God, He does not have the medieval qualities of omnipotence and omniscience that lead to countless paradoxes. The God of Jonas needs freedom, and, with ultimate knowledge and power, paradoxically God could have little knowledge and power. What is a force without resistance, light without dark? True power is exercised only in relation to something that itself has power. Power is the capacity to overcome something. But if objects have even the slightest power against God, then He is not all-powerful.

From a purely theological standpoint, Jonas also sees problems with an omnipotent God. He says, "Only a completely unintelligible God can be said to be absolutely good and absolutely powerful, yet tolerate the world as it is. Put more generally; the three attributes at stake—absolute goodness, absolute power, and intelligibility—stand in such a logical relation to one another that the conjunction of any two of them excludes the third."

I suppose it is easy enough for us to resolve some of Jonas's dilemmas by suggesting that God need not be intelligible or that He may be intelligible only at times when He interfaces with humans, such as when He provided humans with the Ten Commandments. Jonas resolves the issue by suggesting that God has divested Himself of any power to interfere with the physical course of the universe. He only appeals to us by being a symbol of unfulfilled goals.

Isaac ben Solomon Luria (1534–1572), rabbi and mystic, founded an influential school of Jewish mystical thought today called Lurianic Kabbalah.

Luria's ideas have much in common with Jonas's. According to Lurianic Kabbalah, God's contraction, or *tzimtzum*, is a withdrawal and self-limitation. With
each act of tzimtzum, nature gains additional freedom. To make room for the
world, the hidden God *En-Sof* (Infinite; literally, No-End) of the beginning had
to contract Himself so that empty space (vacated by En-Sof) could expand outside of Him. From this nothing, God created the universe. Without this retreat
into Himself there could be no "other" outside God, and only His continued
contracted state preserves the finite things from losing their separate being. In
other words, in order to make room for the physical universe and our existence,
En-Sof vacated a region within Himself. By this act of tzimtzum he created a
space where he is not. One way to visualize the empty space created by God's
withdrawal is to imagine a central circle (our universe) surrounded by En-Sof:

**God (En-Sof)**
**Contracting to Create the Universe**

Karen Armstrong, in *A History of God*, notes that En-Sof did not abandon the
empty space entirely. A "thin line" of divine light penetrated this circle in the
form of "primordial man."[37] In the Talmud, the rabbis believed that God had
made worlds in addition to ours and destroyed them before He created our
present one.[38]

According to Lurianic Kabbalah, Adam's fall in the Garden of Eden scattered God's divine light. As long as the divine sparks are separated and lost in
matter, God is incomplete.[39] Luria believed that through prayer and careful attention to the Torah, Jews could help restore the sparks of Adam and redeem
the universe. We can reform God and make him anew.

Jonas's theory goes further than those advanced in Lurianic Kabbalah. To Jonas, the contraction is total as far as God's power is concerned. He has given up all his power so we can exist. Having given all of Himself to the finite, evolving universe, God has no more to give: it is humanity's turn to give to him.

The notion of a limited God is not a rare concept these days. Dutch theologian Anton van Harskamp writes:

> In The Netherlands it is quite normal for educated Christians, both Catholics and Protestants, to cut the traditional relation between God and Power. They consider the concept of divine power as a dangerous concept, once constructed by foolish priests and evil leaders as an ideological tool to keep the faithful silent and meek. However, [to my mind] a powerless God is no God.[40]

(See note 40 for more information on God's powerlessness through self-destruction.)

Clearly, if we rely on the Bible, God is far from omniscient. In scene after scene God changes His mind, is surprised, or relents when sufficient persuasion is given. Various examples are give in the Appendices. As mentioned in Chapter 1, some notable examples of nonomniscience are given in Job when God has no idea where Satan has been:

> One day the angels [in Hebrew, "the sons of God"] came to present themselves before the Lord, and Satan also came with them. The LORD said to Satan, "Where have you come from?" Satan answered the LORD, "From roaming through the earth and going back and forth in it." (Job 1:7)

Probably, whoever wrote the powerful story of Job did not consider God omniscient. It appears that He is completely uninformed about Satan's activities. Psychologist Carl Jung speculates that God is so entranced by His creation that He *forgets* entirely about His omniscience.[41]

In Exodus, the people of Israel rebelled against God by making and worshiping a golden calf. In Exodus 32:9, God tells Moses He wishes to destroy Moses's people: "I have seen this people, and behold, it is a stiff-necked people; now therefore let me alone, that my wrath may burn hot against them and I may consume them." Moses responds to God, in verses 11–13, with a desperate prayer for his people, and finally he persuades God to relent—not because the people are worthy of forgiveness but because God would be diminished in the eyes of the Egyptians if God killed His Chosen. Moses reminds God, "Your name will be profaned among the Egyptians, and your word to the fathers will fall." God agrees and gives up His initial plan—instead of destroying all the people, He appoints the sons of Levi to kill 3,000 men (Exodus 32:25–29) and sends a plague among the people (Exodus 32:35). This is certainly evidence of God changing His mind.

Another good example of God changing His mind, at least temporarily, occurs in the story of Sodom and Gomorrah. God decides to wipe out the people in Sodom, where Abraham's nephew Lot has settled. Before God has a chance to destroy the town, Abraham bargains with Him, persuasively arguing that God should not kill the innocent with the guilty. (What would have happened if Noah had tried this bargaining approach with God in order to save more people's lives?) After much back-and-forth haggling with Abraham, God agrees that if there are twenty righteous men in Sodom, He won't destroy the town. This is the first instance in Judeo-Christian history of a man challenging God to be just. Unfortunately, aside from the members of Lot's family, twenty can't be found, so God sends two angels in human form to warn Lot of Sodom's imminent destruction. When a mob of Sodomites want to have sex with the two angelic strangers, Lot attempts to bargain with the crowd by offering his two virgin daughters to be raped by the mob:

> Before they had gone to bed, all the men from every part of the city of Sodom—both young and old—surrounded the house. They called to Lot, "Where are the men who came to you tonight? Bring them out to us that we can have sex with them."
>
> Lot went outside to meet them and shut the door behind him and said, "No, my friends. Don't do this wicked thing. Look, I have two daughters who have never slept with a man. Let me bring them out to you, and you can do what you like with them." (Genesis 19:4–8)

Presumably, Lot is offering to let the mob gang-rape and sodomize his virgin daughters. And Lot is supposed to be a holy person favored by God! From our limited, human viewpoint, "righteousness" in the Old Testament does not appear to be measured by how a man treats his wives or daughters.

After God has destroyed the people of Sodom and nearby Gomorrah, Lot's daughters realize God has not left them any men for husbands. To solve the problem, they get Lot drunk and take turns having sex with their father (Genesis 19:23–29). They become pregnant. You probably didn't learn in Sunday school that Lot not only offered his daughters to be brutalized by a mob but also committed incest (although the Bible does give Lot an excuse in that his drunkenness made him unaware of his incest). Obviously, the biblical concept of morality is very malleable and difficult to understand.

As a final example of God changing His mind or being surprised, consider that in the Book of Samuel, God tells the prophet Samuel that He will send a man named Saul who will "govern His People" (1 Samuel 15–17). However, when Saul later does not totally destroy the Amalekites and all their animals, God is "grieved that He had made Saul king over Israel." Clearly, God is depicted as being surprised and saddened by His decision to make Saul leader of the Jews and by Saul's less than total destruction of human and animal life.

These perplexing examples, of course, are just a few among hundreds from the Bible. Often in these kinds of "paradoxes of omniscience," our supposed free will to choose right from wrong shifts the responsibility of evil from God to humans, but at the same time it also seems to deny God divine omniscience.

As we have discussed in this book, it does not appear from the Bible that God already knows that Eve will eat the apple, that humans will be banished from the Garden of Eden, that Cain will kill Abel, and that people will be so wicked that they will all be destroyed, except for Noah's family. Genesis tells us that God *repented* of making the world. Would a God know in advance that he would repent (i.e., regret) making the world and go ahead with creation anyway? The biblical answer seems to be "yes," although the mystery of God's apparent change of heart will probably never be fully understood by humans.

👁 👁 👁

For a moment, let's focus on the concepts of *temptation* and *sin* and how these create paradoxes when we consider God's omniscience and humans' free will. This precise subject has been tackled by Dr. Joseph Fulda, a philosopher, author, and educator.[42] Fulda suggests that while God does not control the autonomy of free-willed agents, He completely controls the environment within which they act. In his article "The Mathematical Pull of Temptation," Fulda advances a theory of temptation that can be used to show how God can be used to "rescue" His omniscience in the face of free-willed agents.[43]

Let's tackle the subject of temptation directly. Traditional religion seems to suggest that we are all tempted by desires. The temptation seems to be in proportion to the object of desire (money, power, gazing into the forbidden Ark of the Covenant or at Pamela Anderson Lee, etc.). However, Fulda suggests that the tempting object is not necessarily the dominant consideration in explaining our handling of the temptation.

Consider a simple experiment with two hypothetical trials, a "red" trial and a "black" trial. Imagine you are in a $5 \times 5 \times 5$ foot cement cubicle. Nothing is in the room except a red handle protruding from the wall:

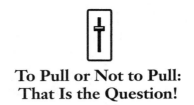

# To Pull or Not to Pull:
# That Is the Question!

You are in the room for 24 hours. Pulling the red handle at any time initiates a cascade of sinful events that culminate in your obtaining the object of your temptation. This can be done in private so your family and friends won't ever know about it. In fact, after your release, no one on Earth will ever know about the event except you.

For a moment, think of some sinful temptations that would actually strongly appeal to you. For example, if you are a married man, think of the temptation of spending a few hours with a woman depicted in *Playboy* magazine. If you are a married woman, think of the temptation of spending a few hours with Robert Redford, Brad Pitt, or any man other than your spouse. If neither of these temptations appeals to you, think of others. Think of gazing into the Ark of the Covenant, something that God forbade, but that you are curious about. Perhaps your religion does not permit drinking wine, so wine could be your temptation. Perhaps you feel it is sinful merely to look at a videotape of naked people or to receive $1 million, unearned, so in these examples the tape or money could be the object of temptation. However slight the pull of the temptation behind the red handle, very few people can resist its *continuous* lure, particularly if the outcome is extreme pleasure, power, or relief from pain. I'll explain this further in a moment.

Fulda also arranges the converse experiment, which he calls the black trial. You are outside your cement cubicle and have already been promised the object of your temptation. Now, you are placed back in the cubicle with a black handle protruding from the wall. Again, you're stuck in the room for 24 hours. Moving the black handle just once disrupts the sequence of events that would otherwise produce for you the object of your temptation. If you move the black handle, you have resisted the temptation. Fulda suggests that however strong the pull of the tempting object, the continuous "pull of conscience" over time nearly guarantees that you will leave the cubicle having pulled the black handle.

Let's assume that you are a very righteous person. You normally resist sinful temptations. In fact, you are so good that in your ordinary life if you were presented with a temptation 100 times, you would resist 99 times. Given this 1/100 chance of succumbing, let's further assume that the temptation is presented to you 10 times in a minute and that you are conscious for 15 hours in a day. In this scenario, this means you are presented with $10 \times 60 \times 15 = 9,000$ occurrences of the temptation in a day. Simple probability calculations show that for 9,000 presentations in the red trial, you are virtually certain (with a $1-.99^{9000}$ probability) to succumb. (Here a probability of 1 means absolute certainty of succumbing, and 0 means no chance of succumbing.) Likewise, even if in the black trial you are easily swayed by temptation and would select the tempting object 99 times out of 100 presentations of the object, the same probability calculations suggest that for the 9,000 chances you will have to resist, it is virtually certain ($1-.99^{9000}$) you will resist. This is the same as saying that your likelihood of succumbing to temptation with the black handle is $a^b$, or $0.99^{9000}$, which is unimaginably small. Notice that in either case, the number $a$ in $a^b$ doesn't matter too much when given a large number of opportunities $b$ to succumb or resist. It's just a question of mathematics. Put another way, the object of temptation is not the dominant force in your succumbing. However small your temptation to pull the red handle is it is likely that you will not resist. With the red handle, you are as weak as your weakest moment, while with the black handle you are as strong as your strongest moment: it just takes one pull at one moment to trigger the cascade of events.

What does this mean for God? Even if we have free will, God's omnipotence places Him in control of our opportunities and our environment, both of which are related to the parameter $b$. Our free will places us in control of the likelihood $a$ of succumbing or resisting an opportunity. Perhaps if you have a very strong character, you can resist temptation and $a$ increases in the red trial. But your interaction with God is controlled by $a^b$. Because the variable $a$ is not very important when compared to $b$, which dominates the mathematics of temptation, God is in charge of your choice matrix. Fulda writes:

> God sets up the opportunity structure within which we sin or do good, and He can force an outcome out of even truly free actors, and even when He does not force an outcome, it may be plain to Him as a simple result of His knowledge of both $a$ and $b$ and his complete control over $b$. Since we would not expect forcing or prior-knowledge-without-forcing for each of man's actions, our solution remains partial, but it does suggest an avenue of thought and research on this millennia-old problem.[44]

So, if Eve had been tempted with the apple thousands of times, no doubt she would have given in. On the other hand, if God had wanted to ensure that Eve would avoid the forbidden fruit, a black handle scenario would have virtually guaranteed it. The relevance of free will appears to be diminished in our temptation-handle scenarios. As U.S. mathematician Norbert Wiener wrote in

*The Human Use of Human Beings*, "Control is nothing but the sending of messages which effectively change the behavior of the recipient."[45]

👁 👁 👁

It is time to sum up this book. We've examined several apparent logical problems with omniscience that suggest that God *cannot* be omniscient in the traditional religious use of the word if logic, as we know it, is a valid way of characterizing the universe. Several appendices, such as Appendix K, delve into this further. Various logical problems are also magnified if God interacts with His predictions, with His people, and with free will, as apparently happens many times if we are to believe even just a small percentage of the Bible.

The word *omniscient* comes from the medieval Latin *omniscientia* and did not appear in English use until 1604. Although "omniscience" never appears in the Bible, the idea that God has the capacity to know anything He desires is well documented, as we have discussed several times (see also Appendix B). Hebrews 4:13 reads: "And before [God] no creature is hidden, but all are naked and laid bare to the eyes of the one to whom we must render an account." And Psalm 139 states:

> O Lord, you have searched me and known me. You know when I sit down and when I rise up; you discern my thoughts from far away. You search out my path and my lying down, and are acquainted with all my ways. Even before a word is on my tongue, O Lord, you know it completely. (Psalms 139:1–4)

Clearly, according to the Bible, God is *supposed* to know it all. Certainly the Christian God is described as having the power to do all things. "For with God nothing shall be impossible" (Luke 1:37). In Luke 18:27 we find, "And he said, The things which are impossible with men are possible with God." This omnipotence implies that God has the *power* to know all of the future. But, as philosopher and theoretical physicist Joseph Francis Alward notes, "Having the power to know all of the future is not the same as knowing all of the future. The God described in the Bible has the power to know as much of the future as He wishes, of course, but does He—or did He—want to know all of it?"[46] Similarly, we discussed in Chapter 15 how traditional religions do not resolve the paradox of the logical impossibility of God being both omniscient and omnipotent, because the God of religions is fully omniscient, not mutably omniscient (a term defined in Chapter 15). The God of religion is usually not considered omniscient on some days and not others. I say "usually" because there do exist philosophers who suggest the biblical God is omniscient only when He wants to be. Would a God who is omniscient only sometimes still be considered an omniscient being? Our thinking on these matters is easily twisted like taffy in a taffy puller. Let us examine the verse Romans 8:29:

> For whom He foreknew, He also predestined to be conformed to the image of His Son, that he might be the firstborn of many brethren. Moreover whom He predestined, these He also called. [The New International Version translates this as, "For those God foreknew he also predestined to be conformed to the likeness of his Son, that he might be the firstborn among many brothers. And those he predestined, he also called."]

Alward says that the Romans phrase "For whom He foreknew, He also predestined" implies there are two categories of people: those "for whom he *did* foreknow and predestinate," and those for whom he did *not*. If this is what this passage means, then this might indicate that God did not have foreknowledge of all things. Alward suggests that the only kind of omniscience suggested in the Bible is knowledge of past and present. God knows some future events but not all future events. The Bible makes it clear in a number of places that its God does not know some of the future.

If God is omniscient or mutably omniscient, how does God reason? Of course, this is a presumptuous question for us limited humans to ask. Can a dog understand how humans might reason? Anton Thorn from San Francisco says that the question is moot:

> The very task of reason is to proceed from previously validated knowledge to evaluate new knowledge claims according to its congruity with that previously validated knowledge, with the intention of validating new knowledge as a result. A being said to be omniscient by nature does not have to go through this drawn-out process as there would never be any new knowledge for it to acquire or validate; it simply knows because it already knows. No means or method of knowledge is at all applicable in the case of an omniscient being.[47]

Following Thorn's line of thought, God does not reason. What would it mean for God to "acquire" knowledge? David King, in *Guide to Objectivism*, writes:

> The concept of omniscience is the secret wish-fulfillment of every mystic. To acquire one's knowledge, by a process of struggle and effort, is abhorrent to the mystic. But to know everything, to know it instantaneously and without effort, to know it causelessly without any specific means of knowing it, or acquiring one's knowledge, or holding one's knowledge, this is the mystics'

passionate dream. The concept of omniscience is a psychological monument to the mystics' hatred of effort.[48]

Of course, literal omniscience makes little sense, because some questions are logically unanswerable or meaningless, like what is the last digit of pi? Practical or applied omniscience must therefore mean knowing everything that is knowable. Xyla Bone, in her opus *I Am My Husband's Hippocampus*, writes:

> Finally, think of what literal omniscience implies. I hold a rock in my hand. It contains silicon atoms. God must know the past of each atom of silicon, their birth in stars, and their constituents way back to the beginning of time. But wait, He must know much more. He must know the atomic positions that change every picosecond. He must know the state of all their electrons, the history of their quarks and electrons, the quantum states, the vibrations of the strings. Oh God, and every ripple of the quantum foam. Tell me, is this the same God, who in Exodus 21:28–33, gave Moses the law "If an ox gores a slave, the owner shall pay the slave owner thirty shekels of silver, and the ox shall be stoned"? Is the God of Gluons and Galaxies the same God concerned with Israeli oxen dung?[49]

And what about the Bible itself? One way of thinking suggests the primary purpose of the Bible today is to be an alternate-reality device. It gives its readers a glimpse of other ways of thinking and of other worlds. It is also the most mysterious book ever written. We don't know the ratio of myth to history. We don't know all the authors. We are not always sure of the intended message. We only know that the Bible reflects and changes humankind's deepest feelings. The Bible is the hammer that shatters the ice of our unconscious. Dan Platt, of the IBM Watson Research Center, once told me, "The Bible is at minimum an interesting model of human understanding—of how we reach across cultures to understand each other and learn about what we hold as sacred. I have the notion that that kind of interface is the most visible place to look for God."

A lot of our discussions in this book have been playful. We have enjoyed games in which we play chicken with omniscient beings, wager about the afterlife, watch as the mystery of Eden unfolds, and so forth. However, the question of limited omniscience and the notion of a finite God have had serious consequences in history, and I do not wish to make light of the suffering and anguish that have accompanied these questions among ancient and modern philosophers. Some have said that God's thoughts are so perfect that His thinking and His doing are one and the same act. The ancient Greek philosophers believed that God could not possibly talk to humans and be concerned with daily events in human lives. The French philosopher Voltaire (1694–1778) likewise thought it unlikely that the God of the Bible would be very interested in the affairs of creatures residing within the thin film of life that coats the planet Earth, although Voltaire seems to have believed in the existence of God. Others believed that God had deliberately turned His back on humans. In his book *Night,* Nobel laureate Elie Wiesel describes his experiences in the Nazi concentration camps. In one scene, a young boy is hanged. The boy is too light for the rope to kill quickly and cleanly. The boy hangs for over half an hour, lingering between life and death, gasping for breath. The Nazis require the other prisoners to watch the unrelenting horror.

> The boy's tongue is still red. His eyes still see.
> One of the prisoners whispers, "Where is God now?"
> And Wiesel answers, "Here He is—He is hanging here on this gallows."[50]

---

Abraham teaches God an important lesson about the individualization of justice. The teacher becomes the student and the student the teacher. After all, somebody had to straighten God out about justice before matters really got out of hand.

—Alan Dershowitz, *The Genesis of Justice*

---

The largest size imaginable, the entire universe, is 10 with 29 zeros after it (in centimeters). The smallest size describes the subatomic world, and is 10 with 24 zeros (and a decimal point) in front of it. Humans are right in the middle. Does this return us to a privileged place?

—Sharon Begley, "Science Finds God," *Newsweek*

---

Great indeed, we confess, is the mystery of our religion.

—1 Timothy 3:16

# Appendices

B.C. MANSFIELD

*I [God] will smash them one against the other, fathers and sons alike. I will allow no pity or mercy or compassion to keep me from destroying them. . . .*

*Now go, attack the Amalekites and totally destroy everything that belongs to them. Do not spare them; put to death men and women, children and infants, cattle and sheep, camels and donkeys.*

—*Jeremiah 13:14, 1 Samuel 15:3–4*

*Science seemed to have disposed of the Creator God, and biblical scholars have proved that Jesus had never claimed to be divine. As an epileptic, I had flashes of vision that I knew to be a mere neurological*

*defect: had the visions and raptures of the saints also been a mere*
*mental quirk? Increasingly, God seemed an aberration, something*
*that the human race had outgrown.*

—*Karen Armstrong*, A History of God

## A. CAN GOD CHANGE HIS MIND?

WE'VE DISCUSSED HOW DIFFICULT IT IS TO UNDERSTAND HOW THE
biblical God might be omniscient and at the same time appear to change His
mind or repent of (i.e., regret) His actions. Think about it, and you'll see this
can create various paradoxes. Other biblical enigmas arise as God apparently
changes His character through time. Do you think God changed as He evolved
from the Old Testament "angry" God (who tells the Jews to show no mercy
and kill infants) to the New Testament God more predisposed to mercy and
love? Can God change?

One of the most clear examples of God's changing His mind occurs in 2
Kings 20:1. God tells King Hezekiah, "Put your house in order, because you
are going to die; you will not recover." A few lines later, God changes His mind
and tells the prophet Isaiah, "Go back and tell Hezekiah . . . 'I have heard your
prayer and see your tears. I will heal you.'" And Hezekiah recovers.

Here are some other examples of God apparently changing His mind.
We've discussed a few of these, but I include them here for thoroughness:

- The Lord was grieved that he had made man on the earth, and his heart
  was filled with pain. So the LORD said, "I will wipe mankind, whom I
  have created, from the face of the earth—men and animals, and creatures that move along the ground, and birds of the air—for I am grieved
  that I have made them." (Genesis 6:6–7)
- Forty more days and Nineveh will be overturned. . . . [However] When
  God saw what they did and how they changed their evil ways, he had
  compassion and did not bring upon them the destruction he had threatened. (Jonah 3:4 and 3:10)
- I am grieved that I have made Saul king, because he has turned away
  from me and has not carried out my instructions. (1 Samuel 15:11)
- Then Abraham approached the Lord and said: "Will you sweep away
  the righteous with the wicked? . . . What if there are fifty righteous people in the city [Sodom]? . . . Will not the Judge of all the earth do
  right?" The Lord said, "If I find fifty righteous people in the city of
  Sodom, I will spare the whole place for their sake." (Genesis 18:23)

- "I [God] have seen this people [who made the golden calf], and behold, it is a stiff-necked people; now therefore let me alone, that my wrath may burn hot against them and I may consume them." [Moses responds to save his people] "Your name will be profaned among the Egyptians, and your word to the fathers will fall." . . . Then the Lord relented and did not bring on his people the disaster he had threatened. [Instead of destroying the whole people, God tells the sons of Levi to kill 3,000 men and sends a plague among the people.] (Exodus 32:9–35)
- "Perhaps they will listen and each will turn from his evil way. Then I will relent and not bring on them the disaster I was planning because of the evil they have done." (Jeremiah 26:3)
- "If you stay in this land, I will build you up and not tear you down; I will plant you and not uproot you, for I repent over the disaster I have inflicted on you." (Jeremiah 42:10)

## B. BIBLICAL SUGGESTIONS
## THAT GOD IS OMNISCIENT

Although the Bible does not use the word *omniscient*, there are many lines that suggest God sees or knows all:

- The Lord searches every heart and understands every motive behind the thoughts. If you seek him, he will be found by you; but if you forsake him, he will reject you forever. (1 Chronicles 28:9)
- For God is greater than our hearts, and he knows everything. (1 John 3:20)
- Nothing in all creation is hidden from God's sight. Everything is uncovered and laid bare before the eyes of Him to whom we must give account. (Hebrews 4:13)
- I know what is going through your mind. (Ezekiel 11:5)
- Now we can see that you [Jesus] know all things and that you do not even need to have anyone ask you questions. This makes us believe that you came from God. (John 16:30)
- The eyes of the Lord are in every place, beholding the evil and the good. (Proverbs 15:3)
- My eyes are on all their ways; they are not hidden from me, nor is their sin concealed from my eyes. (Jeremiah 16:17)
- Can any hide himself in secret places that I shall not see him? . . . Do not I fill heaven and earth? (Jeremiah 23:24–25)

- Neither is there any creature that is not manifest in his sight: but all things are naked and opened unto the eyes of him with whom we have to do. (Hebrews 4:13)

Here are hints of God's knowledge of the future:

- [David says] . . . your eyes saw my unformed body. All the days ordained for me were written in your book before one of them came to be. (Psalm 139:16)
- This man was handed over to you by God's set purpose and foreknowledge; and you, with the help of wicked men, put him to death by nailing him to the cross. (Acts 2:23)
- For whom He foreknew, He also predestined to be conformed to the image of His Son, that he might be the firstborn of many brethren. Moreover whom He predestined, these He also called. (Romans 8:29)
- [God's elect] have been chosen according to the foreknowledge of God the Father. (1 Peter 1:2)
- He indeed was foreknown before the foundation of the world, but was manifest in these last times for you. (1 Peter 1:20)
- [God] make known the end from the beginning, from ancient times, what is still to come. I say: My purpose will stand, and I will do all that I please. (Isaiah 46:10)
- Lord, you know all things; you know that I love you. (John 21:17)
- Known to God from eternity are all His works. (Acts 15:18)
- God is greater than our hearts, and He knows everything. (1 John 3:20)

## C. THIRTY EXAMPLES OF GOD ENTERING THE TIME STREAM AND AIDING MASS KILLING

*A five-second summary of the entire Old Testament: "I, God, am angry at you Jews for worshipping other gods, and, therefore, I will have your enemies destroy you."*

—*Anonymous*

Generally not known to most of my colleagues, and perhaps to most people, is the fact that the biblical God frequently aided in mass exterminations of people.[1] Of course, the one well-known example is God destroying the entire population of Earth, except for Noah's family, during the flood. His paradoxical love for and disgust with His chosen people provides ample room for fertile debates. Some have argued that in the face of so much killing by God, the question of humans' free will becomes particularly problematic. What is the essence of free will if God is always punishing infractions? Consider a ruler who says, "You are free to choose *A* or *B*, but if you choose *B* I will kill you instantly." While it's technically true that you are free to choose, any traditional association of personal freedom is abruptly decoupled from the notion of free will. For example, if a religious minority were persecuted and not permitted to practice their religion today, we would say they were not "free" to practice their religion, although technically they would be "free" to make the choice and suffer the consequences—such as death, torture, or imprisonment.

According to the Bible, God's most frequent method of coercing or punishing the Jews is to have their enemies triumph over them. For example, we are told that the reason Jerusalem fell to the Babylonians is that God was angry and therefore brought the Babylonians to kill the Jews—men, women, and children:

> But they mocked God's messengers, despised his words and scoffed at his prophets until the wrath of the LORD was aroused against his people and there was no remedy. He brought up against them the king of the Babylonians [Nebuchadnezzar], who killed their young men with the sword in the sanctuary, and spared neither young man nor young woman, old man or aged. God handed all of them over to Nebuchadnezzar. (2 Chronicles 36:16–17)

In other words, the biblical reason the Jews are exiled from Judah and the Temple is destroyed is that this is God's judgment upon a rebellious people. Similarly, we find:

> I [God] am going to bring disaster on this place and its people—all the curses written in the book that has been read in the presence of the king of Judah. Because they have forsaken me and burned incense to other gods and provoked me to anger by all that their hands have made, my anger will be poured out on this place and will not be quenched. (2 Chronicles 34:24–25)

Before we delve into the killing, the following scene from Ezekiel is perhaps the most anti–free-will statement in the Bible. God is speaking to the Israelites, who prefer (freely choose) a different way of life than what God proscribes:

> "You say, 'We want to be like the nations, like the peoples of the world, who serve wood and stone.' But what you have in mind will never happen. As surely

as I live, declares the Sovereign Lord, I will rule over you with a mighty hand and an outstretched arm and with outpoured wrath. . . . I will take note of you as you pass under my rod, and I will bring you into the bond of the covenant. I will purge you of those who revolt and rebel against me." (Ezekiel 20:32–35)

If humans do have free will, there certainly seems to be significant coercion related to the choices we make.

Now let us consider mass killing and genocide. Here are some standard, commonly known examples:

- And every living substance was destroyed which was upon the face of the ground, both man, and cattle, and the creeping things, and the fowl of the heaven; and they were destroyed from the earth; and Noah only remained alive, and they that were with him in the ark. (Genesis 7:23)
- Then the LORD rained down burning sulfur on Sodom and Gomorrah—from the LORD out of the heavens. (Genesis 19:24)
- At midnight the LORD struck down all the firstborn in Egypt, from the firstborn of Pharaoh, who sat on the throne, to the firstborn of the prisoner, who was in the dungeon, and the firstborn of all the livestock as well. (Exodus 12:29)
- Moses stretched out his hand over the sea, and at daybreak the sea went back to its place. The Egyptians were fleeing toward it, and the Lord swept them into the sea. The water flowed back and covered the chariots and horsemen—the entire army of Pharaoh that had followed the Israelites into the sea. Not one of them survived. (Exodus 14:27–28)

Here are some less commonly known examples of mass murder:

- When the LORD your God brings you into the land you are entering to possess and drives out before you many nations—the Hittites, Girgashites, Amorites, Canaanites, Perizzites, Hivites and Jebusites, seven nations larger and stronger than you—and when the LORD your God has delivered them over to you and you have defeated them, then you must destroy them totally. Make no treaty with them, and show them no mercy. (Deuteronomy 7:1,2)
- Then Moses said to them, "This is what the LORD, the God of Israel, says: 'Each man strap a sword to his side. Go back and forth through the camp from one end to the other, each killing his brother and friend and neighbor.'" The Levites did as Moses commanded, and that day about three thousand of the people died. (Exodus 32:27)

- And fire came out from the LORD and consumed the 250 men who were offering the incense. (Numbers 16:1–40)
- The LORD said to Moses and Aaron, "Separate yourselves from this assembly so I can put an end to them at once." . . . Aaron stood between the living and the dead, and the plague stopped. But 14,700 people died from the plague, in addition to those who had died because of Korah. (Numbers 16:21–49)
- At that time we took all his towns and completely destroyed them [Canaanites]—men, women and children. We left no survivors. (Deuteronomy 2:34)
- The LORD said to Moses, "Do not be afraid of him, for I have handed him over to you, with his whole army and his land. Do to him what you did to Sihon king of the Amorites, who reigned in Heshbon." So they struck him down, together with his sons and his whole army, leaving them no survivors. And they took possession of his land. (Numbers 21:34–35)
- The LORD said to Moses, "Take all the leaders of these people, kill them and expose them in broad daylight before the LORD, so that the LORD's fierce anger may turn away from Israel." So Moses said to Israel's judges, "Each of you must put to death those of your men who have joined in worshiping the Baal of Peor." Then an Israelite man brought to his family a Midianite woman right before the eyes of Moses and the whole assembly of Israel while they were weeping at the entrance to the Tent of Meeting. When Phinehas son of Eleazar, the son of Aaron, the priest, saw this, he left the assembly, took a spear in his hand and followed the Israelite into the tent. He drove the spear through both of them—through the Israelite and into the woman's body. Then the plague against the Israelites was stopped; but those who died in the plague numbered 24,000. [God killed 24,000 Israelites who slept with Moabite women!] (Numbers 25:1–9)

You get the picture. God's mass killings stupefy the mind. The following table shows some more body counts.

**Table Appendix C.1**

| Who | Where | How Many |
| --- | --- | --- |
| All the males and kings of the Middianites. Wives and children sold into slavery. | Numbers 25:16–17 and Numbers 31:7–8 | Many |

**Table Appendix C.1** *(continued)*

| *Who* | *Where* | *How Many* |
|---|---|---|
| Two kingdoms on the east side of the Jordan | Numbers 32 | Many |
| The Ammonites | Deut. 2:19–21 | Many |
| The Horims | Deut. 2:22 | Many |
| Citizens of Jericho | Joshua 6 | They "utterly destroyed all in the city, man and woman, young and old, and ox . . . with the edge of the sword." |
| People of Ai: men, women, children | Joshua 8:1–30 | 12,000 |
| All the people of Makkedah, Libnah, Gezer, Eglon, Hebron, Gaza, Askerlon, Ekron. . . . | Joshua 10 and Judges 1:18–19 | "Joshua left none remaining but utterly destroyed all that breathed, as the Lord God of Israel commanded." |
| Moabites | Judges 3:20 | 10,000 |
| Perizzites, Canaanites | Judges 1:4 | 10,000 |
| Midianites | Judges 8:10 | 120,000 |
| Bethshemesh | 1 Samuel 6:19 | 50,070 (God may have killed this number partly because they looked into the Ark) |
| People from Dan to Beersheba | 2 Samuel 24:15 | 70,000; "So the LORD sent a plague on Israel. . . ." |
| Sons of Aaron | Leviticus 10:1–2 | 2 killed for "offering strange fire before the Lord" |
| Israelites | Numbers 11:1 | Many, for complaining |
| Israelites | Numbers 11:31–33 | "God smote them with a very great plague." |
| A man caught picking up sticks on the Sabbath | Numbers 15:35–36 | 1; God orders death by stoning. |
| Assyrians | 2 Kings 19:35 | 185,000 (by an angel of the Lord) |

Although the Ten Commandments forbid murder, the Old Testament appears to contain numerous murders by God or aided by God in which innocent women and children are killed. How do you reconcile this conflict? Also, some scholars have wondered about the size of these numbers. It would be interesting to determine the approximate populations of the Middle East during biblical times to discover whether these impressive body counts exceed the local population numbers.

A fascinating and little-known story of the "bronze snake" occurs in the Old Testament after Moses leads his people out of Egypt. After God helps the Jews completely destroy a Canaanite town in Hormah, the Jews travel from Mount Hor along a route to the Red Sea, and they grow impatient along the way. As a punishment, God kills many of the Jews with poisonous snakes until Moses protects them by building a bronze snake atop a pole. Moses tell the people they must stare at the snake in order to live:

> They spoke against God and against Moses, and said, "Why have you brought us up out of Egypt to die in the desert? There is no bread! There is no water! And we detest this miserable food!" Then the LORD sent venomous snakes among them; they bit the people and many Israelites died. The people came to Moses and said, "We sinned when we spoke against the LORD and against you. Pray that the LORD will take the snakes away from us." So Moses prayed for the people. The LORD said to Moses, "Make a snake and put it up on a pole; anyone who is bitten can look at it and live." So Moses made a bronze snake and put it up on a pole. Then when anyone was bitten by a snake and looked at the bronze snake, he lived. (Numbers 21:3–9)

Later Moses's bronze snake, also known as Nehushtan, becomes a thing of evil:

> He [Hezekiah] broke into pieces the bronze snake Moses had made, for up to that time the Israelites had been burning incense to it. It was called Nehushtan. [*Nehushtan* sounds like the Hebrew for *bronze*, *snake*, and *unclean thing*.] (2 Kings 18:4)

The killing by God continues in the New Testament. Perhaps the most poignant example occurs during the time of the early Church, which established a community that provided for the needs of fellow Christians. The pooling of property and land was supposed to be voluntary. However, in Acts 5, God kills Ananias for giving Peter only half the money from the sale of Ananias's land. Ananias is punished for this deception and falls down dead. Peter subsequently asks Ananias's wife Sapphira if the money her husband had given Peter was the total amount from the sale of the land. When she says "yes," God also kills her instantly. "Great fear seized the whole church and all who heard about these events" (Acts 5:11). Biblical scholars suggest that Ananias and Sapphira were killed not because they withheld money from the Church but rather because they lied to God. Similarly, in Acts 12:25 we find that "because Herod did not give praise to God, an angel of the Lord struck him down, and he was eaten by worms and died."

## D. CAN A JUST GOD SUPPORT CANNIBALISM AND CHILD SACRIFICE?

*All our ideas of the justice and goodness of God revolt at the impious cruelty of the Bible. It is not a God, just and good, but a devil, under the name of God, that the Bible describes.*
    —*Thomas Paine*, The Age of Reason

In Chapter 7 we discussed the biblical mystery of the "Bridegroom of Blood"— the most perplexing story in the Bible. It takes place after God tells Moses that he must go to Egypt to lead his people out of slavery. As Moses and his family journey to Egypt, it seems that God tries to kill him.

Before discussing cannibalism and child sacrifice, let me tell you about another perplexing tale—that of Balaam in Numbers 22. When the Israelites travel to the plains of Moab and camp along the Jordan River, King Balak is terrified by the hoards of newcomers. He asks Balaam, a Mesopotamian wizard, to curse the Israelites. Something has gone wrong in the retelling, however, because throughout the story, Balaam appears to be a God-fearing man, and he does only as he is told. Balaam decides to seek God's counsel, and is told to go with King Balak's men and await further instructions: "That night God came to Balaam and said, 'Since these men have come to summon you, go with them, but do only what I tell you'" (Numbers 22:20).

Balaam obeys, and God gets angry:

Balaam got up in the morning, saddled his donkey and went with the princes of Moab. But God was very angry when he went, and the angel of the LORD stood in the road to oppose him. Balaam was riding on his donkey, and his two servants were with him. (Numbers 22:21–22)

Obviously something is missing from the narrative. God's anger is unexplained in light of Balaam's following orders. Shortly thereafter, Balaam's ass (i.e., his donkey) starts to talk to him.

Perhaps the most serious of paradoxes in the Bible relates to the question of whether or not children should be punished for their parents' perceived sins.

On the one hand, several times in the Old Testament God says children should *not* be punished for the transgressions of family members. For example, in Deuteronomy 24:16 we find, "The fathers shall not be put to death for the children, neither shall the children be put to death for the fathers: every man shall be put to death for his own sin." This policy is reiterated in 2 Kings 14:6. Similarly, in Ezekiel 18:20 we find,

> The soul who sins is the one who will die. The son will not share the guilt of the father, nor will the father share the guilt of the son. The righteousness of the righteous man will be credited to him, and the wickedness of the wicked will be charged against him.

However, God violates this edict of personal responsibility throughout the Old Testament. In Exodus 34:7 we find, "God punishes the children and their children for the sin of the fathers to the third and fourth generation." Similarly, in 1 Kings 21, we find that the angry King Ahab is not punished for his role in the death of Naboth, but that his son will suffer instead: "Because Ahab has humbled himself, I [God] will not bring this disaster in his day, but I will bring it on his house in the days of his son." In 2 Samuel, God kills David's baby for David's sin:

> Nathan replied [to David], "The LORD has taken away your sin. You are not going to die. But because by doing this you have made the enemies of the LORD show utter contempt, the son born to you will die." After Nathan had gone home, the LORD struck the child that Uriah's wife had borne to David, and he became ill. David pleaded with God for the child. . . . He fasted and went into his house and spent the nights lying on the ground. The elders of his household stood beside him to get him up from the ground, but he refused, and he would not eat any food with them. On the seventh day the child died. (2 Samuel 12:13–18)

Perhaps the most well-known example of punishment of children for the sins of their parents is in Genesis, when God punishes Eve by inflicting the pain of childbirth on all future generations of women. He punishes Adam by requiring *all* men to toil for their food. Following are other references to punishing future "innocent" generations:

- The Lord is long-suffering, and of great mercy . . . visiting the iniquity of the fathers on the children unto the third and fourth generation. (Numbers. 14:18).
- A bastard shall not enter into the congregation of the Lord; even to the tenth generation shall he not enter. (Deuteronomy 23:2)

- During the reign of David, there was a famine for three successive years; so David sought the face of the Lord. The Lord said, "It is on account of Saul and his blood-stained house; it is because he put the Gibeonites to death." (2 Samuel 21:1)

- Nevertheless, death reigned from the time of Adam to the time of Moses, even over those who did not sin by breaking a command, as did Adam. (Romans 5:14)

- [God speaking to Moses] Say to Aaron: "For the generations to come none of your descendants who has a defect may come near to offer the food of his God. No man who has any defect may come near: no man who is blind or lame, disfigured or deformed; no man with a crippled foot or hand, or who is hunchbacked or dwarfed, or who has any eye defect, or who has festering or running sores or damaged testicles. No descendant of Aaron the priest who has any defect is to come near to present the offerings made to the Lord by fire. He has a defect. . . . because of this defect, he must not go near the curtain or approach the altar, and so desecrate my sanctuary." (Leviticus 21:21)

- The Lord had closed up every womb in Abimelech's household because of Abraham's wife Sarah. (Genesis 20:18)

- When David saw the angel who was striking down the people, he said to the Lord, "I am the one who has sinned and done wrong. These are but sheep. What have they done? Let your hand fall upon me and my family." (2 Samuel 24:17)

- I the Lord thy God am a jealous God, visiting the iniquity of the fathers upon the children unto the third and fourth generation of them that hate me. (Exodus 20:5, Deuteronomy 5:9)

- I let them become defiled through their gifts—the sacrifice of every firstborn—that I might fill them with horror so they would know that I am the Lord. (Ezekiel 20:26)

I feel particularly saddened when King Darius of Persia kills the wives and children of some bad men, even though the wives and children do not seem to have sinned:

> At the king's command, the men who had falsely accused Daniel were brought in and thrown into the lions' den, along with their wives and children. And before they reached the floor of the den, the lions overpowered them and crushed all their bones. (Daniel 6:24)

The Bible gives us no sense, from God or from Daniel, of the wrongness of torturing innocents. The only thing we hear after this act in Daniel 6 is that God "rescues and saves" and that Daniel becomes prosperous. We never weep for the children whose bones were crushed by the savage beasts.

Numerous passages in the Bible seem to indicate that God is not omniscient. Consider for example:

- I, the Lord, will go down and see if what they have done is as bad as the outcry that has reached me. If not, I will know. (Genesis 18:21)
- So Satan went forth from the presence of the Lord. (Job 1:12 and 2:7)

Here are some other little-known oddities:

- *Beating of slaves is permitted:* "If a man beats his male or female slave with a rod and the slave dies as a direct result, he must be punished, but he is not to be punished if the slave gets up after a day or two, since the slave is his property." (Exodus 21:20–21)
- *Women must marry their rapists:* "If a man happens to meet a virgin who is not pledged to be married and rapes her and they are discovered, he shall pay the girl's father fifty shekels of silver. He must marry the girl, for he has violated her. He can never divorce her as long as he lives." (Deuteronomy 22:28–29)

Let's end this subsection with apparent requests from God for child sacrifice, cannibalism, or rape:

- Do not hold back offerings from your granaries or your vats. You must give me the firstborn of your sons. Do the same with your cattle and your sheep. Let them stay with their mothers for seven days, but give them to me on the eighth day. (Exodus 22:29–30)
- She and the girls went into the hills and wept because she would never marry. After the two months, she returned to her father and he did to her as he had vowed. (Judges 11:30–40) [Jephthah the Gileadite sacrifices his daughter to God.]
- Nothing that a man owns and devotes to the Lord—whether man or animal or family land—may be sold or redeemed; everything so devoted is most holy to the Lord. No person devoted to destruction may be ransomed; he must be put to death. (Leviticus 27:28–29)

- In my anger I will be hostile toward you, and I myself will punish you for your sins seven times over. You shall eat the flesh of your sons, and the flesh of your daughter shall you eat. (Leviticus 26:28–29)
- Hear the word of the Lord, O kings of Judah and people of Jerusalem. In this place I will ruin the plans of Judah and Jerusalem. . . . I will make them fall by the sword before their enemies. . . . and I will give their carcasses as food to the birds of the air and the beasts of the earth. . . . I will make them eat the flesh of their sons and daughters, and they will eat one another's flesh during the stress of the siege imposed on them by the enemies who seek their lives. (Jeremiah 19:1–9)
- In your midst fathers will eat their children, and children will eat their fathers. I will inflict punishment on you and will scatter all your survivors to the winds. (Ezekiel 5:10)
- I will make your oppressors eat their own flesh; they will be drunk on their own blood, as with wine. (Isaiah 49:26)

In the Book of Numbers, we find that 32,000 captured virgin women were to be given to soldiers, and 32 of the women God wanted for Himself:

Moses and Eleazar the priest did as the Lord commanded Moses. The plunder remaining from the spoils that the soldiers took was 675,000 sheep, 72,000 cattle, 61,000 donkeys and 32,000 women who had never slept with a man. . . . And the half, the portion of those who had gone out to war, was. . . . 16,000 people, of which the tribute for the Lord was 32. (Numbers 31:31–40)

Readers should consult Dennis McKinsey's "Biblical Errancy" web site, book, and related web sites for additional examples.[1]

## E. AQUINAS'S GOD AND MAXWELL'S DEMON

*Atheist: "I don't believe in God."*
*Abdu'l-Baha: "I don't believe in the God that you don't believe in."*

In a 1971 issue of the journal *Manifold*, Tim Poston published "Aquinas's God versus Maxwell's Demon," an unusual article on thermodynamics and God.[1] The Second Law of Thermodynamics states that in any isolated system, entropy (disorder) must always increase. (The term "isolated" is important because entropy can decrease locally at the expense of greater increase elsewhere.) The Second Law is evident in the shuffling of cards: it is easier to randomly shuffle cards *out* of a particular sequence than into it. As the cards are shuffled, information is lost.

The following is excerpted, with permission, from Poston's article, which attempts to show that God's omniscience implies the Second Law of Thermodynamics:

> We consider a bit of mathematical theology, as follows:
>
> 1. God is omniscient.
> 2. Hence, He knows the position of every particle at every time.
> 3. Hence, He is observing every particle at every time. (Indeed, particle existence depends upon this observation, cf. the writings of Bishop Berkeley.)
> 4. Hence, He is gaining information about all parts of the Universe at all times and in all places.
> 5. Hence, he is increasing the entropy of the Universe in all times and in all places.
> 6. Hence, the entropy of the Universe increases in all times and in all places. (This is the Second Law of Thermodynamics. Q.E.D.)
> 7. *Corollary* 1. The Axiom of Choice implies the Second Law of Thermodynamics.
> 8. *Corollary* 2. God can raise the dead.
>    Proof: Death and decay involve increase of entropy. God can reverse these processes by means of sacrifice of some of His immense store, accumulated as above, of confidential information.
> 9. *Corollary* 3. God will die.
>    Proof: The Universe will end with a war producing chaos (The Revelation of Saint John the Divine), after which God will put it together again as chaos, after which God will put it together again as a whole using all His information. It will then remain perfect (in contrast to the present state). Hence God will cease to observe it, hence He will cease to satisfy the definition of Himself (*Summa Contra Gentilla*, Saint Thomas Aquinas), hence He will cease to exist.

## F. CAN AN OMNISCIENT BEING LOSE HIS TEMPER?

Can an omniscient being, who knows the future and sees all, lose his temper? The Bible has many apparent instances of God losing his temper. Here are just a few:

- "The anger of the Lord was hot against Israel and he sold them into the hand of Mesopotamia's king" (Judges 3:8);
- "The Lord shall swallow them up in his wrath, and the fire shall devour them" (Psalm 21:9);
- "The anger of the Lord was kindled against Israel" (2 Kings 13:3);

- "Again the anger of the Lord was kindled against Israel" (2 Samuel 24:1);
- "The Lord is a jealous and avenging God; the Lord takes vengeance and is filled with wrath. The LORD takes vengeance on his foes and maintains his wrath against his enemies" (Nahum 1:2);
- "The anger of the Lord was hot against Israel" (Judges 2:20);
- "See, the Lord is coming with fire, and his chariots are like a whirlwind; he will bring down his anger with fury, and his rebuke with flames of fire. For with fire and with his sword the Lord will execute judgment upon all men, and many will be those slain by the Lord" (Isaiah 66:15–16);
- "Therefore this is what the Sovereign LORD says: In my wrath I will unleash a violent wind, and in my anger hailstones and torrents of rain will fall with destructive fury" (Ezekiel 13:13);
- "I will turn you over to them for punishment, and they will punish you according to their standards. I will direct my jealous anger against you, and they will deal with you in fury. They will cut off your noses and your ears, and those of you who are left will fall by the sword. They will take away your sons and daughters, and those of you who are left will be consumed by fire" (Ezekiel 23:25).

As with the numerous examples of the biblical God saying he is extremely jealous, it is easy to argue that these examples of emotions are simply *metaphors* so that we limited humans can learn right from wrong. However, those who take the Bible literally may wish to ponder how an omniscient God experiences emotions.

### G. THE PARADOX OF THE FLOOD

John Paulos in his remarkable book *Innumeracy* discusses the volume of water rained down upon the earth during the flood in the Book of Genesis.[1] Considering the biblical statement "all the high hills that were under the whole heaven were covered," Paulos computes that half a billion cubic miles of liquid had to have covered the earth. Because it rained for 40 days and 40 nights (960 hours), the rain must have fallen at a rate of at least 15 feet per hour. Paulos remarks that this is "certainly enough to sink any aircraft carrier, much less an ark with thousands of animals on board."

Other ecological and biological paradoxes of the flood are discussed in Chapter 17.

## H. SAINT AUGUSTINE AND *THE CITY OF GOD*

*St. Augustine declared he had seen acephalic creatures, with eyes in their breasts. . . .*
—Glasgow Herald, *December 31, 1924*

*Love with care—and then what you will, do.*
—*Saint Augustine*, Confessions

Saint Aurelius Augustinus Augustine was born in the year 354 and became the bishop of Hippo in Africa from A.D. 396 to 430. His mother, Monica, was Christian since girlhood. His father Patricius became Christian later in life.

Saint Augustine's life was not always one normally associated with a saint. As a teenager, he became the unwed father of a boy he named Adeodatus. Augustine's mother, Monica, was determined to find Augustine a proper marriage partner and get him married. Monica eventually found a "suitable" bride who was not quite of marriageable age, and dismissed Adeodatus's mother, Augustine's true love. The whole incident distressed Augustine, who proclaimed, "Give me chastity, but not yet!" Instead of marrying immediately, he found another girlfriend. (This chronology is not meant to disparage Saint Augustine, who was also a brilliant and spiritual man.)

Interestingly, it seems that the existence of the set of all natural numbers is sanctioned by Saint Augustine, who often speaks of the relationship between numbers and God in his book *The City of God*. Here he addresses God and infinity:

> The answer to the allegation that even God's knowledge cannot embrace an infinity of things:
>
> Then there is the assertion that even God's foreknowledge cannot embrace things which are infinite. If men say this, it only remains for them to plunge into the depths of blasphemy by daring to allege that God does not know all numbers. It is certainly true that numbers are infinite. If you think to make an end with any number, then that number can be increased by the addition of one. More than that, however large it is, however great the quantity it expresses, it can be doubled; in fact, it can be multiplied by any number, according to the very principle and science of numbers.
>
> Every number is defined by its own unique character, so that no number is equal to any other. They are all unequal to one another and different, and the individual numbers are finite, but as a class they are infinite. Does that mean that God does not know all numbers, because of their infinity? Does God's knowledge extend as far as a certain sum, and end there? No one could be insane enough to say that.

Now those philosophers who revere the authority of Plato will not dare to despise numbers and say that they are irrelevant to God's knowledge. For Plato emphasizes that God constructed the world by the use of numbers, while we have the authority of Scripture, where God is thus addressed, "You have set in order all things by number, measure, and weight." And the prophet says of God, "He produces the world according to number"; and the Savior says in the Gospel, "Your hairs are all numbered."

Never let us doubt, then, that every number is known to him "whose understanding cannot be numbered." Although the infinite series of numbers cannot be numbered, this infinity of numbers is not outside the comprehension of him "whose understanding cannot be numbered."

And so, if what is comprehended in knowledge is bounded within the embrace of that knowledge, and thus is finite, it must follow that every infinity is, in a way we cannot express, made finite to God, because it cannot be beyond the embrace of his knowledge.[1]

## I. DOES GOD MAKE MISTAKES AND LEARN?

There is evidence in the Book of Genesis that God makes mistakes and learns—which is certainly not the characteristic one normally attributes to an omniscient being.[1] This mistake and learning process is most apparent in three of God's actions: the creation of Eve to end Adam's loneliness, the destruction of humankind through the flood and the subsequent promise never to destroy humankind again, and the destruction of the Tower of Babel. For example, after God creates Adam, He perceives a problem, a mistake of sorts. God says, "It is not good that the man should be alone" (Genesis 2:18). God remedies the problem by creating Eve to be Adam's companion. Micah B. Harper notes, "Were God omniscient, He would have known before He created Adam that it was not good for Adam to be alone, and because Adam was to be the pinnacle of creation, He would have created Eve first."

One reason that God destroys humanity in the flood is that He saw "how great man's wickedness on the earth had become" (Genesis 6:5). Translations of Genesis 6:5 say variously that God was sad or sorry that He created humans, which tends to imply a mistake or change of mind for God. After the flood, God also appears sorry and promises that "never again shall all flesh be cut off by the waters of a flood, and never again shall there be a flood to destroy the earth" (Genesis 8:11). Micah B. Harper believes that the flood is both "an attempt to rectify an earlier mistake and a mistake in itself, and the outcome of the whole happening is the education of God." While this opinion may be controversial, it is logically apparent that if God's intent with the flood was to stamp out evil, it did not work well, because the rest of the Bible contains descriptions of evil acts.

Equally perplexing is the story of the Tower of Babel. God interrupts the great building project and scatters humans "over the face of all the earth" (Genesis 11:8). In some sense, God is attempting to correct another mistake. God appears nervous about human accomplishments, saying, "This is only the beginning of what they will do; and nothing that they propose to do will now be impossible for them" (Genesis 11:6). It is not clear what God is referring to. Is it the arrogance of people? Or is it their newly formed power and knowledge in general?

If God is not certain what will happen as a result of His own actions, then it appears He is experimenting and learning throughout Genesis. If He is only giving the *illusion* to us that He is learning, then why give us that illusion?

## J. GOD WANTS FEAR

In the "Some Final Thoughts" section of the book, we discussed the pervasive scriptural mandate to fear God. More often than requiring love or any other emotion, the biblical God in both the Old and New Testament requires us to fear him. The paradox for humans is understanding how to both love and fear God. Although some might interpret the word *fear* to mean "respect" rather than "be afraid of"—reverence rather than terror—there are a sufficient number of examples of the word *fear* that lead us to wonder what is really meant. The frequent close association of the word *fear* with words like *cursed, trembling, dread,* and *terror* leads me to believe that many times the biblical God wants true fear.[1] When do you think respect crosses over into the realm of terror?

- "Who knows the power of your anger? For your wrath is as great as the fear that is due you." (Psalm 90:11)
- "I feared the anger and wrath of the LORD, for he was angry enough with you to destroy you." (Deuteronomy 9:19)
- "The fear and dread of you will fall upon all the beasts of the earth and all the birds of the air." (Genesis 9:2)
- "'Should you not fear me?' declares the LORD. 'Should you not tremble in my presence?'" (Jeremiah 5:21–23)
- "'I am the God of your fathers, the God of Abraham, Isaac and Jacob.' Moses trembled with fear and did not dare to look." (Acts 7:32)
- "You have put me in the lowest pit, in the darkest depths. Your wrath lies heavily upon me; you have overwhelmed me with all your waves. Why,

O LORD, do you reject me and hide your face from me? From my youth I have been afflicted and close to death; I have suffered your terrors and am in despair. Your wrath has swept over me; your terrors have destroyed me. All day long they surround me like a flood; they have completely engulfed me. You have taken my companions and loved ones from me; the darkness is my closest Friend." (Psalm 88:6–18)

- "But I will show you whom you should fear: Fear him who, after the killing of the body, has power to throw you into hell. Yes, I tell you, fear him." (Luke 12:5)
- "Therefore, my dear friends, as you have always obeyed—not only in my presence, but now much more in my absence—continue to work out your salvation with fear and trembling." (Philippians 2:12)
- "Moses said to the people, 'Do not be afraid. God has come to test you, so that the fear of God will be with you to keep you from sinning.'" (Exodus 20:20)
- "Yet because the wicked do not fear God, it will not go well with them, and their days will not lengthen like a shadow." (Ecclesiastes 8:13)
- "By faith Noah, when warned about things not yet seen, in holy fear built an ark to save his family. By his faith he condemned the world and became heir of the righteousness that comes by faith." (Hebrews 11:7)
- "And fear not them which kill the body, but are not able to kill the soul: but rather fear him which is able to destroy both soul and body in hell." (Matthew 10:28)

It is interesting that humankind's ancient religious journey began with fear of the unknown and the attempts to control this fear through magic and placating invisible spirits. Humans had to contend with disease, famine, ruthless enemies, lightning, and floods. Religion matured, and fear evolved into faith. Fear of nature soon became replaced by fear of God.

Note that even very modern religions such as the Baha'i faith occasionally have the same elements of fear as the religions of yore. Bahaullah (1817–1892), the Baha'i prophet founder, said, "The essence of wisdom is the fear of God, the dread of His scourge and the apprehension of His justice and decree." I suspect that the Baha'is would liken humans to children who must first fear the wrath of their parents so that they do not cross a dangerous road. Fear was perhaps necessary during the primitive stages of humanity to encourage respect. I have a hypothesis that as religions progress (e.g., Judaism → Christianity → Islam → Baha'i), the word *fear* is decreasingly used, and when it is used it increasingly means reverence rather than terror.

## K. TWO PROOFS THAT GOD
## IS NOT ALL-KNOWING?

Philosopher Peter Kirby has put forth an argument, outlined as follows, that appears to limit either omniscience or free will. Do you agree with his logic? If not, what flaws do you find?

In the following eleven steps, "*A*" refers to any given action, for example, "I will paint my fingernails red tomorrow." "~*A*" refers to the opposite of that action, for example, "I will not paint my fingernails red tomorrow."

1.  God's knowledge cannot be wrong.
2.  God knows that I will do *A*.
3.  If I have free will, then (I can do *A*) and (I can do ~*A*).
4.  If I can do ~*A*, then it is possibly true that I will do ~*A*.
5.  If it is possibly true that I will do ~*A*, then God's "knowledge" that I will do *A* is possibly false.
6.  If God's knowledge that I will do *A* is possibly false, then God's "knowledge" can be wrong.
7.  Therefore, God's knowledge that I will do *A* is not possibly false.
8.  Therefore, it is not possibly true that I will do ~*A*.
9.  Therefore, I cannot do ~*A*.
10. Therefore, it is false that (I can do *A*) and (I can do ~*A*).
11. Therefore, I don't have free will.

According to Kirby, anyone who accepts premises 1–6 will logically reach the conclusion of the nonexistence of free will. Any other person, or even God Himself, could be substituted for "I" in this argument. Kirby writes:

> Some try to refute this argument by suggesting God is outside of time, whatever that may mean. However, if these same people suggest the possibility that God interacts with this universe and makes prophecy (even becoming incarnate once), it would seem that God is "inside time" from time to time, so this line of defense must be rejected. Even granting the plausibility of being "outside time," the theist is still faced with the problem of God's own free will. If God has free will and makes choices, then God must have a future. Does God know His own future? If so, then God is not free. If God does not know His own future, God cannot be said to be truly omniscient. If God has not future, than He is not omniscient.[1]

Some may reject Kirby's argument by suggesting that because God does not *force* you to take a certain course, you have free will. But free will as defined in the Kirby argument has a rigorous and simple definition. Free will means the ability to do $A$ and the ability to do $\sim A$. Kirby's argument states that omniscience implies the lack of free will, not that omniscience implies that the omniscient being is making choices for you. The omniscient being could very well be powerless and unable to interact with the physical world, but this does not affect the argument.

On the other hand, some have likened the possible conflict of free will and omniscience to the game of chess. Often each chess player knows exactly how the other will react to each move. The chess argument suggests that God similarly knows how people will react to events. Humans could make many accurate predictions if they had sufficient information. A being with infinitely accurate input information could run many simulations and make many more predictions about the future than we can. But neither the chess player nor God is causing the players to make particular moves. Using the chess analogy, in order for God to make predictions about the future, He need not even be able to see the future.

While on the topic of divine foreknowledge and free choice, let us consider the following argument by Boethius (475–524), a Roman scholar, Christian philosopher, and author of the famous *De consolatione philosophiae* (The Consolation of Philosophy). In this work he makes the following argument:

> Just as when I know that a thing is, that thing must necessarily be; so that when I know that something will happen, it is necessary that it happen. It follows, then, that the outcome of something known in advance must necessarily take place.[2]

Edward Wierenga, professor of religion at the University of Massachusetts, has also had a long-term interest in omniscience, foreknowledge, and free will and has analyzed the Boethius passage, which he feels suggests the following argument:

1. If God knows that $S$ will do $A$, then it must be the case that $S$ will do $A$.
2. If it must be the case that $S$ will do $A$, then $S$ isn't free with respect to $A$.

Therefore,

3. If God knows in advance that $S$ will do $A$, then $S$ isn't free with respect to $A$.[3]

Again, this seems to take away human free will if there is an omniscient God. (In Wierenga's analysis, to say that a being $S$ is *omniscient* would mean that for every proposition $p$, if $p$ is true then $S$ knows $p$.) C. S. Lewis, author of *Mere Christianity*, tackles this question with the standard notion of God being outside of time:

> Everyone who believes in God at all believes that He knows what you and I are going to do tomorrow. But if He knows that I am going to do so-and-so, how can I be free to do otherwise? Well, here, once again, the difficulty comes from thinking that God is progressing along the Time-line like us: the only difference being that He can see ahead and we cannot. Well, if that were true, if God foresaw our acts, it would be very hard to understand how we could be free not to do them. But suppose God is outside and above the Time-line. In that case, what we call "tomorrow" is visible to Him in just the same way as what we call "today." All the days are "Now" for Him.[4]

We can analyze Edward Wierenga's three-step argument. Let $K$ stand for "God knows in advance that $S$ will do $A$." Let $D$ stand for "$S$ will do $A$." Let $F$ stand for "$S$ isn't free with respect to $A$." Let "Nec" stand for "it's necessary that." Given these definitions, we can create two interpretations for the 3-step argument:

Interpretation 1
(1') Nec(If $K$ then $D$)
(2) If Nec($D$) then $F$
(3) If $K$ then $F$

Interpretation 2
(1") If $K$ then Nec($D$)
(2) If Nec($D$) then $F$
(3) If $K$ then $F$

(1') is true. But the argument after (1') is invalid. The argument with (1") as its first premise is valid. It is of the form: If $p$ then $q$; If $q$ then $r$; If $p$ then $r$. But (1") is false. According to Wierenga, just because God knows a proposition, it doesn't follow that the proposition is necessarily true. So there are two interpretations of Boethius's argument. Under one interpretation the argument has all true premises, but it's invalid. Under the other interpretation the argument is valid, but its first premise is false. Both interpretations, therefore, are defective. So the Boethius argument doesn't establish the incompatibility of divine foreknowledge and human free action.

## L. SIXTY-FOUR WAY-OUT QUESTIONS TO PONDER

I continually plague my colleagues with questions related to spirituality. You read about some of them in Chapter 2, in which I asked friends and strangers, "What could a being do to make you believe He was God?" Other surveys are mentioned in Chapter 17. The following are additional questions for which I have solicited answers for many years. Think of these zany questions as koans that can provide hours of fun coffee-table conversations as well as serious topics for meditation. Try a few on friends.

- A being tells you that your current life is actually the afterlife, and it will last for as long as you wish. If you desire, you will not age or get sick. Does this statement bring you happiness or sadness?
- God comes up to you and says, "If you request it, I will increase the natural life span of humans to 1,000 years. Will you make such a request of me?" What is your answer?
- God comes up to you and asks, "Do you wish to know if there is life after death?" What is your answer?
- God says, "I can give you control over your dreams at night and make them as real as your experiences in life. Would you like such a power?"
- Michael, God's warrior angel from the Bible and Koran, floats with feathered wings into your home and asks, "What is the most important question I can ask humanity and what is the best possible answer you can give?" What is the safest reply you can give? Be careful—your everlasting life hangs in the balance.
- A being tells you that God exists, but He is one among many Gods. You are urged to practice henotheism—believing in the supremacy of a single god without denying the existence of others (see "Some Final Thoughts," which describes the henotheism of Moses and other early Jews). How does this affect your life?
- God appears before you and asks, "What is the most profound question you can ask me?"
- God says, "I will give you the ability to speak and understand a thousand languages, on the condition that every other human's IQ is slightly diminished. Do you accept my gift?"
- God says, "I will give all humans the ability to turn water into wine and stones into bread, if you request it." Do you request it?
- God says, "You now have five senses. I will give you another sense each week for a year, if you request it." Do you request it? Why?

- You are touring a holy shrine when suddenly God appears and asks, "Which will give you more pleasure: if lightning bugs could twinkle in color, or if humans would speak kind thoughts every other time they have them?"

- You are walking through the town of Bethlehem, birthplace of Jesus. You see a light in the sky, and hear God's voice thundering down. "Which do you choose," He asks, "sunshine could cure cancer, or the shadows of humans can do half of humanity's work? For example, the shadow of a gas station attendant can pump gas while the attendant works on another car."

- Would you rather have the gift of understanding or of persuasion?

- Neo-Jungian Clarissa Pinkola Estes asserts that if Mary, Mother of Jesus, were born today, "Mary would be a teenage girl-gang leader." As shocking as this may sound, one wonders what occupation Jesus or any prophet would have if born today. Would they be involved with computers, biotechnology, or the entertainment industry, or would they be farmers and fishermen? Would a Jesus in the twenty-first century be exploring other planets and stars?

- Humans will be modified to exist on another planet. Do you choose Pluto or Saturn? Why?

- God says, "Which is best? You can bottle time and save it until you need a little extra or every human gets four loving hugs a day."

- God says, "Which is best? Photographs and memories stay vivid through the years or all rodents achieve human-like intelligence for a week, allowing us to finally converse as equals with another species."

- You are exploring Nazareth, the historic city of Lower Galilee in northern Israel. As you walk through a field you are accosted by seven rodents. One of the rodents whispers "Yeshua," the name of Jesus in the Hebrew language. Another appears to be wearing a crucifix. What is your reaction? Is this experience sufficiently paranormal to alter any of your religious beliefs?

- God hands you two books. In a deep, stentorian voice, God asks, "Which book do you choose?" Each page of the first book contains the words, "This page intentionally left blank." Each page of the second book contains the words, "This page not intentionally left blank."

- You are walking through the world's largest cathedral church, Saint John the Divine in New York City. Suddenly you hear a hushed voice, look up, and see a vision of the angel Gabriel. "I lay before you a blank book which you can fill at will with your own desires and each will come true;

however, you cannot ask to know the future. I also offer you a book of knowledge of the future, but you must turn at most one page a day, and as you do you lose one page of memory of your past. Choose the book you wish to keep."

- God says, "I will give humans one of the following gifts. You decide. I will give everyone unlimited money, unlimited energy, or unlimited information."

- God says to you, "Answer this question with 'yes' or 'no': Will your next word be 'no'?" What is your response?

- God says, "Which do you prefer: being a rich person in a poor country, or a poor person in a rich country?"

- God says, "Which do you prefer: being a dog who looks human, or being a human who looks like a dog?"

- God says, "If you request it, I will tell you whether I am real or merely the result of abnormal electrical activity in your brain's temporal lobes." What is your request?

- God says, "What is better for humans—people who won't break the rules or people who will break the rules?"

- God says, "Some theologians suggest God created man, and other theologians say man created God. Which scenario gives the best chance for a fulfilling afterlife?"

- God says, "Which do you consider a greater punishment? Every time you cough, someone within a fifty-mile radius from where you now stand will die—or every time you laugh, someone at random on Earth will die."

- If the Pope suddenly said today that the moon was made of green cheese, how many people would believe him? 1,000? 100,000? 1 million? Would this mean that the moon, in fact, is made of green cheese?

- Is the desire to believe different from the search for the truth?

- God gives you a piano. For each note you play, someone will die. What classical piece do you choose? God gives you another piano. For each note you play, someone will experience unparalleled ecstasy. What classical piece do you choose? God gives you a piano. Every time you play an E-flat note, scientists will discover a cure for a new disease. What classical piece do you choose?

- If archaeologists discovered the bones of Jesus, thereby disproving the notion of physical resurrection, would Church authorities prefer to suppress this information rather than have it become widely known?

- You are staring at a painting of the Roman Catholic saint Mother Francis Xavier Cabrini (1850–1917), the first United States citizen to be canonized. As you gaze into her eyes, God appears and says, "Recently, some of my creations have complained that women are subservient to men in the Old and New Testaments. Of all the creatures I have created, which animals exhibit the greatest degree of liberation for the female?"

- Sometimes creationists push to have their religious beliefs about the origin of the universe taught in public schools as science. Which version of creation do you think should be taught in schools, if any: Biblical, Babylonian, Native American, or Zulu? If none, why not?

- If God were humanoid, would God be ambidextrous?

- If you could ask one question of God, what would it be? Close your eyes and ask it now. How did that feel? Did you get an answer? Are you getting an answer as you read "these words"?

- If God had created an Earth with two identically shaped landmasses, for example two square continents, the effects on the world and religion would be profound because they would suggest the presence of a creator. What effect would the existence of a perfect square or circular continent have on religion and science?

- During the time of Moses, the Hebrews called God "Yahweh." Though special to the Israelites, he was one of many Gods. It was Isaiah who proclaimed that Yahweh was the only God, and this was to be a Jewish secret. How would the geopolitics of today's Earth be changed if this message had never spread throughout the world, and monotheism had never been practiced?

- In the Book of Genesis, God turns Lot's wife into a pillar of salt. What geopolitical effect would this have on today's world if God turned evil people into pillars of salt?

- Some historians say that if there were no Saint Paul, there would be no Christianity today. Do you agree?

- God says, "I will eliminate the emotion of your choice so that you will never experience this emotion again." What emotion do you choose?

- Some philosophers, such as George Berkeley, suggest that our senses deceive us and that we are merely creations of another Being's thoughts. This Being is God. But what if God is only another being's thoughts? If you consider the above philosophy possible, then could our own thoughts also spawn other beings in alternate universes? If so, what happens when we stop thinking? Is the key to survival that some being continue thinking?

- God appears before you and asks you to change places with one person in the Bible. Who would you choose?

- God walks up to you and says, "You and I are real, aren't we?" What is your response? What is the best way to determine what things are real and what things are not real?
- Novelist S. R. Donaldson once wrote, "The dreams of men belong to God." Does God dream? Can an omniscient being dream?
- If Jesus, Moses, Muhammad, Buddha, and Confucius were gathered in a room, who would be the first to speak? What would he say?
- You died yesterday. Today, you arrive at Heaven and you find that the Waiting Room is about the size of New York State, and there are literally millions of people milling about, living in shacks with little to do all day. Angel Michael approaches you and says, "This was easier in the old days when only a thousand people died each month, but now we can hardly process the number of entrance applications. If you like, we can give you cable TV with a single channel so that you can pass the time." What channel do you choose?
- God says, "The world is becoming overcrowded and I plan to flood it as I did with Noah. Make an ark to hold 20 people." Who do you choose to bring with you? Your parents? A physician? A musician? Pamela Anderson Lee or Brad Pitt?
- You are entering the kingdom of Heaven. A sign on the pearly gates says, "Out to Lunch. Back in Ten Minutes." What are your thoughts while you wait?
- Visitors from the stars descend to Earth. If you had to choose either a priest, a rabbi, or a mullah to make "first contact" with the visitors, whom would you chose?
- Beings from another dimension come to Earth and you have the choice of giving them one of four gifts: the Old Testament, a calculus book, a Beethoven recording, or a book of mystical poetry by Persian poet Rumi. Choose.
- Would you prefer there to be no God or that God be part of a hive organism consisting of numerous interconnected beings? Would you prefer one God, no God, or many Gods?
- God gives you the ability to change certain physical properties of your bedroom windows. As a result, you are able either to gaze out and watch biblical events, or to gaze out and watch the world in the year 3000. Which do you choose?
- An angel flies into a field, approaches you, and says, "In Universe One, there is 'life after death,' but there is no God. In Universe Two, there is no 'life after death,' but God exists. In which universe would you prefer to live? In which do you now live?"

- God says, "If I were to change places with you for a day, what would be your first act as a God?"
- The year is 2020. A bearded man appears on Fifth Avenue in New York City and performs miracles. He claims to be a prophet of God. While being interviewed by Peter Jennings of ABC News, he makes Peter Jennings disappear. As a result of this miracle, do you think the bearded man could start a worldwide religion with a million followers?
- It is said that taking a dose of vitamin B-12 before sleep can cause spectacular intensification of colors in dreams. B-12 can even produce colors in dreams of people who never before had polychrome dreams. If you were to have a vision of God as a result of taking the B-12, would you value the vision less because a drug was required, or would you consider the drug an aid to breaking through this world into the next?
- You are traveling through a remote part of New Guinea and find that natives are worshiping a discarded Sony PlayStation. Do you try to convince them that videogame unit is not divine?
- God says, "I can give humans the ability to fly, on the condition that humans would have to lay eggs." Would you accept it?
- God says, "If there were one thing I could let you see me do, what would it be?"
- God says, "In order to shake things up and give humans a feeling of awe and wonder, I will turn the Earth from a sphere into the shape of a doughnut." Do you accept?
- God says, "If you request it, I will triple humankind's intelligence and kindness on the condition that all women will have only one ovary instead of two." Do you make this request?
- If all human religious thought, history, and knowledge were lost in a cataclysm, what single statement would preserve the most information for the next generation of creatures?
- God says, "Why you are reading this book?" What is your response?

You make the assumption that the Bible is a "sacred book." It isn't. To the vast majority of the human race it's one of many ancient mythological accounts that predated a better understanding of reality that we now call science.

—James Randi, "Twas Brillig . . . ," *Skeptic*

# Notes

*Can any hide himself in secret places that I shall not see him? saith the Lord. Do not I fill heaven and earth?*

*—Jeremiah 23:24*

## INTRODUCTION

1. Karen Armstrong, *A History of God* (New York: Ballantine, 1994), xx.
2. Michael Shermer, *Why People Believe Weird Things: Pseudoscience, Superstition, and Other Confusions of Our Time* (New York: W. H. Freeman, 1998), 10.
3. Steven J. Brams, *Superior Beings: If They Exist, How Would We Know?* (New York: Springer-Verlag, 1983), 14–15.
4. Quoted in Karen Armstrong, *A History of God*, 186.
5. Quoted in Michael Shermer, *Why People Believe Weird Things*, 10.
6. Austin Cline, "Omniscience," http://www.atheism.about.com/religion/atheism/library/weekly/aa063099.htm.
7. *Encyclopedia Britannica*, http://www.britannica.com.
8. Rene Dubos, *A God Within* (New York: Scribner, 1972), 3–4.
9. Marcus J. Borg, *Reading the Bible Again for the First Time* (New York: HarperCollins, 2001), 34–35.

## CHAPTER I: THE PARADOX OF OMNISCIENCE

1. Let's return briefly to our scenario with Dr. Eck. My colleague Eric Kaplan has pointed out that knowledge is not quite the same as power. You can know something, but not be able to change it. In the case of Dr. Eck, if you know Dr. Eck is omniscient, then by deciding not to swerve you can "force" Eck to chicken out (i.e., swerve), and you win. However, if Dr. Eck were really omniscient he would know your strategy and see that the game of chicken can have no meaning if both sides know what the other will do in advance. Thus, the omniscient Dr. Eck would refuse to play a game of chicken with someone who knew he was omniscient. To have the scenario be most effective, you would have to be able to force Dr. Eck to play against his will. And if you could do that, then Dr. Eck would not be truly omniscient, because there would be something he did not know—namely, how to prevent you from forcing him to play a silly game against his will. On the other hand, could

an omniscient Dr. Eck know all facts but be dumb and not be able to make use of the facts in a logical way? Could an omniscient being know only about *possible* things? If there were no possible way to prevent you from forcing him to play chicken, then he could still be omniscient while not knowing how to avoid the game. Finally, if Dr. Eck became omniscient *after* he started racing toward you, then he would certainly lose in your game of chicken.

2. The March 31, 1997, *Newsweek* survey is discussed in Wade Roush, "Herbert Benson: Mind-Body Maverick Pushes the Envelope," *Science* 276 (April 18, 1997): 357–360.

3. Kenneth C. Davis, *Don't Know Much About the Bible* (New York: William Morrow, 1998).

4. Alan Dershowitz, *The Genesis of Justice* (New York: Warner Books, 2000), 65.

5. John Denton, "Neanderthal = Nephilim?" http://www.ftech.net/~bric/rp.no38.html.

### CHAPTER 2: GOD AND EVIL

Epigraph note: Albert Einstein, address at the Princeton Theological Seminary, May 19, 1939; published in Albert Einstein, *Out of My Later Years* (New York: Philosophical Library, 1950).

My colleague Eric Kaplan notes that while Einstein captures an important paradox in the Judeo-Christian conception of God, Einstein does not accurately state the problem. Einstein seems to suggest that because God *can do* anything (i.e., He is omnipotent), that He *does* everything. But just because God *can* make a person be good or bad, this does not mean that He *does*. In the standard Judeo-Christian framework, God gives humans free will. There need not be a direct contradiction between God's omnipotence and our free will.

However, if God is the creator of the universe and life, then, like the manufacturer of an airplane, God may have some responsibility for defects in design. In some sense, a father is the "manufacturer" of his son. Yet, we do not suggest that the father should avoid disciplining the child because the father is, in effect, passing judgment on himself. Of course, we would admonish the father if the punishment were overly harsh or if the father punished the child knowing that the child had no choice in his action.

Kaplan believes that for Einstein's argument to be effective, God must be not only powerful and good but also omniscient. If God is omniscient, the very fact that He knows our thoughts and actions millennia before our births makes it difficult for some to understand why He would punish or reward us for choices that may have been foreordained—regardless of whether He ever directly influenced any of those choices. Such punishment or reward for what we could not help might be, as Einstein says, in contradiction to his supposed goodness.

1. Interested in learning more about Miss Muxdröözol? See my book *The Stars of Heaven* (New York: Oxford University Press, 2001).

2. Robert M. Martin, *There Are Two Errors in the the Title of This Book* (Ontario, Canada: Broadview Press, 1992), 175.

3. In Alan Turing's test, a human questioner sits in a room opposite a teletype or computer terminal. Hidden from the questioner is a computer and another human being. The questioner interviews both and tries to determine which is human and which is a computer. If the computer can fool the questioner, the computer is considered to be intelligent.

## CHAPTER 3: CAIN AND ABEL'S DILEMMA

1. Steven T. Kuhn, "Stanford Encyclopedia of Philosophy: Prisoner's Dilemma," http://plato.stanford.edu/archives/spr1999/entries/prisoner-dilemma/; Ariel Dolan, "Prisoner's Dilemma," http://www.aridolan.com/ad/adb/PD.html.

2. Janet Chen, Su-I Lu, and Dan Vekhter, "The Flood-Dresher experiment," http://www.stanford.edu/~jjchen/game/flood.html. See also William Poundstone, *The Prisoner's Dilemma* (New York: Anchor, 1992).

3. William Poundstone, *The Prisoner's Dilemma*, 106–108.

4. Ibid. Game theory suggests that the lower left cell (0,0.5) is the "rational outcome." Theorists call it a Nash equilibrium point. After playing the game 100 times, there was no evidence of any instinctive preference for this point.

5. Janet Chen, Su-I Lu, and Dan Vekhter, "The Flood-Dresher experiment." See also William Poundstone, *The Prisoner's Dilemma*.

6. William Poundstone, *The Prisoner's Dilemma*, 123.

7. Ibid.

8. Jonathan Blumen, "The Prisoner's Dilemma," *The Ethical Spectacle* 1 (September 1995), http://www.spectacle.org/995/.

9. Ibid.

10. Steven J. Brams, *Negotiation Games: Applying Game Theory to Bargaining and Arbitration* (New York: Routledge, 1990). Also see, "Negotiation and Game Theory," http://math.holycross.edu/~dbd/games/assignments/discussion14/discussion14.html; Ariel Dolan, "Prisoner's Dilemma," http://www.aridolan.com/ad/adb/PD.html.

11. Dennis McKinsey, "God's shortcomings," http://members.aol.com/chas1222/bepart56.html; Dennis McKinsey, "Biblical Errancy," http://members.aol.com/ckbloomfld/index.html.

12. Marcus J. Borg, *Reading the Bible Again for the First Time* (New York: HarperCollins, 2001), 8.

13. Ibid., 28.

## CHAPTER 4: THE PARABLE OF ALGAE

Epigraph note: John Fowles, "The Green Man," *Antaeus*, No. 57, ed. Daniel Helpurn (New York: The Ecco Press, Autumn 1986), 247.

1. This kind of logic is discussed further in Robert M. Martin, *There are Two Errors in the the Title of This Book* (Ontario, Canada: Broadview Press, 1992), 12.

2. Ibid., 20.

3. Ibid., 13.

4. Edward Kasner and James Newman, *Mathematics and the Imagination* (Redmond, Washington: Tempus, 1989), 103. Originally published by New York: Simon & Schuster, 1940.

5. David Eugene Smith, *A History of Mathematics in America Before 1900* (Chicago: Open Court, 1934).

## CHAPTER 5: NEWCOMB'S PARADOX AND DIVINE FOREKNOWLEDGE

1. Martin Gardner, *Knotted Doughnuts and Other Mathematical Entertainments* (New York: Freeman, 1986), 158.

2.  William Lane Craig, "Divine Foreknowledge and Newcomb's Paradox," *Philosophia* 17 (1987): 331–350; see also at: http://www.leaderu.com/offices/bill-craig/docs/newcomb.html.

3.  Robert Nozick, "Newcomb's Problem and Two Principles of Choice," in *Essays in Honor of Carl G. Hempl*, ed. Nicholas Rescher, Synthese Library (Dordrecht, Holland: D. Reidel, 1969), 115–116. Robert Nozick, cited in Martin Gardner, "Mathematical Games," *Scientific American* (March 1974): 102.

4.  Isaac Levi, "A Note on Newcombmania," *Journal of Philosophy* 79 (1982): 337–342. Richmond Campbell and Lanning Sowden, *Paradoxes of Rationality and Cooperation: Prisoner's Dilemma and Newcomb's Problem* (Vancouver: University of British Columbia Press, 1985).

5.  See the collection of columns in Martin Gardner, *Knotted Doughnuts*.

6.  Maya Bar-Hillel and Avishai Margalit, "Newcomb's paradox revisited," *British Journal for the Philosophy of Science* 23 (1972): 301.

7.  Martin Gardner, *Knotted Doughnuts*, 161.

8.  Quoted in ibid., 168.

9.  Maya Bar-Hillel and Avishai Margalit, "Newcomb's Paradox Revisited"; William Lane Craig, "Divine Foreknowledge and Newcomb's Paradox."

10. George Schlesinger, *Aspects of Time* (Indianapolis: Hackett, 1980), 79, 144.

11. Dennis M. Ahern, "Foreknowledge: Nelson Pike and Newcomb's Problem," *Religious Studies* 75 (1979): 489. Also see analysis in William Lane Craig, "Divine Foreknowledge and Newcomb's Paradox."

12. Ibid.

13. William Lane Craig, "Divine Foreknowledge and Newcomb's Paradox."

14. Ibid.

15. Martin Gardner, *Knotted Doughnuts*, 171. Also see, Martin Gardner, *The Night Is Large* (New York: St. Martin's Griffin, 1996), 437.

16. Ibid.

17. William Poundstone, *Labyrinths of Reason* (New York: Anchor, 1988), 257.

18. John Milton, *Paradise Lost* (New York: Penguin, 2000), Book III, lines 116–118.

19. Karen Armstrong, *A History of God*, 309.

20. Clifford Pickover, *Time: A Traveler's Guide* (New York: Oxford University Press, 1998).

21. Fabre D'Olivet, *Cain: A Dramatic Mystery in Three Acts by Lord Byron* (New York: Kessinger Publishing, 1997).

22. Anne Rice, *Memnoch the Devil* (New York: Ballantine, 1997).

23. Clifford Pickover, *Time: A Traveler's Guide*.

24. Milton Esterow, *The Art Stealers* (New York: Macmillan, 1966), 100–152. Also see "Leonardo da Vinci," http://www.loadstar.prometeus.net/leonardo/mona.html; and Celebriducks, "Mona Lisa," http://www.celebriducks.com/mona_lisa/.

### CHAPTER 6: THE DEVIL'S OFFER

1.  Edward J. Gracely, "Playing Games with Eternity: The Devil's Offer," *Analysis* 48 (June 1988): 113. See also Glenn W. Erickson and John A. Fossa, *Dictionary of Paradox* (Lanham, Maryland: University Press of America, 1998), 48.

2.  Glenn W. Erickson and John A. Fossa, *Dictionary of Paradox*, 48.

3.  Ibid.

4.  Clifford Pickover, *Keys to Infinity* (New York: Wiley, 1995). Also see Clifford Pickover, "Slides in Hell," *Skeptical Inquirer* 19 (July/August 1995): 36–39.

5.  J. Theodore Schuerzinger, personal communication.
6.  Sid Litke, "Survey of Bible Doctrine: Angels, Satan, Demons," http://www.bible. org/docs/theology/satan/angelout.htm.

## CHAPTER 7: THE REVELATION GAMBIT

1.  Genesis 14:18, Hebrews 7:11–28. Jim Bell and Stan Campbell, *The Complete Idiot's Guide to the Bible* (New York: Macmillan, 1999), 38.
2.  Bertrand Russell, *A History of Western Philosophy* (New York: Simon & Schuster, 1975).
3.  Steven J. Brams, *Superior Beings: If They Exist, How Would We Know?* (New York: Springer-Verlag, 1983), 15.
4.  Didymus Jude Thomas (ca. A.D. 75–100), *The Gospel of (According to) Thomas: The Hidden Sayings of Jesus*, trans. Marvin Meyer (San Francisco: Harper, 1992), verse 77.
5.  Steven J. Brams, *Superior Beings*, 15.
6.  Ibid., 19.
7.  This stable outcome is called a "Nash equilibrium"; see Steven J. Brams, *Superior Beings*, 20.
8.  Steven J. Brams, "Belief in God: A Game-Theoretic Paradox," *International Journal of Philosophy and Religion*, 13 (1982): 121–129.
9.  Paul Tillich, *Theology of Culture* (New York: Oxford University Press, 1959), 4–5.
10. Paul Tillich, "Theism Rewritten for an Age of Science," http://www.crosscur-rents.org/Tillich.htm.
11. Clifford Pickover, *The Stars of Heaven* (New York: Oxford University Press, 2001).
12. John Brooke, "Science and Religion: Lessons from History?" *Science*, 282(5396) Dec 11, 1985–1986, 1988.
13. Ibid.
14. C. S. Lewis, *Mere Christianity* (New York: Macmillan, 1943).
15. Kenneth C. Davis, *Don't Know Much About the Bible* (New York: William Morrow, 1998), 101.
16. Jim Bell and Stan Campbell, *The Complete Idiot's Guide to the Bible*, 70.
17. J. R. Porter, *The Illustrated Guide to the Bible* (New York: Oxford University Press, 1995).
18. Stephen Spignesi, *The Odd Index* (New York: Penguin, 1994). See also Dennis McKinsey, "Biblical Errancy," http://members.aol.com/ckbloomfld/.
19. Madalyn Murry O'Hair, "Kersey Graves—American Atheist," http://www.athe-ists.org/Atheism/roots/graves/. See also, Kersey Graves, *The World's Sixteen Crucified Saviors* (New York: The Truth Seeker Company, 1875).
20. Marcus J. Borg, *Reading the Bible Again for the First Time* (New York, Harper-Collins 2001).
21. Robert M. Martin, *There are Two Errors in the the Title of this Book* (Ontario, Canada: Broadview Press, 1992), 18.
22. J. R. Porter, *The Illustrated Guide to the Bible*, 99.
23. Thomas Nagel, *The Last Word* (New York: Oxford University Press, 1997).
24. Paul Tillich, *Systematic Theology*, vol. 1 (Chicago: University of Chicago Press, 1951).
25. Bahaullah, *Gleanings from the Writings of Bahá'u'lláh* (*Kitáb-i-Íqán*) (Wilmette, Illinois: Baha'i Publishing Trust, 1983), 50–55.

26. Ibid., 80.
27. Ibid.

#### CHAPTER 8: THE PARADOX OF EDEN

1. Richard La Croix, "The Paradox of Eden," *International Journal for the Philosophy of Religion* 15 (1984): 171. See also Glenn W. Erickson and John A. Fossa, *Dictionary of Paradox* (Lanham, Maryland: University Press of America, 1998), 54. Kenneth Lucey, *What Is God?* (selected essays of Richard La Croix) (Amherst, New York: Prometheus, 1993).
2. Allen Podet, "La Croix's Paradox: An Analysis" *International Journal for the Philosophy of Religion* 18 (1985): 69–72.
3. Glenn W. Erickson and John A. Fossa, *Dictionary of Paradox* (Lanham, Maryland: University Press of America, 1998), 54.
4. Ibid., 67–68.
5. Arthur Lovejoy, "Milton and the Paradox of the Fortunate Fall," *Essays in the History of Ideas*, ed. Arthur Lovejoy (New York: George Braziller, 1955), 277–295; Herbert Weisinger, *Tragedy and the Paradox of the Fortunate Fall* (East Lansing: Michigan State University Press, 1953). Donella Eberle, "Selected Critics on the Paradox of the Fortunate Fall in *Paradise Lost*," http://www.mc.maricopa.edu/users/eberle/ENH221Lectures/FortunateFall.html.
6. Marjorie Hope Nicolson, *John Milton: A Reader's Guide to His Poetry* (Syracuse, New York: Syracuse University Press, 1998).
7. Arthur Lovejoy, "Milton and the Paradox of the Fortunate Fall," 162–163.
8. Diane McColley, "Eve's Dream," *Milton Studies* 12 (1978): 25–45.
9. Virginia Mollenkott, "Milton's Rejection of the Fortunate Fall," *Milton Quarterly* 6 (March 1972): 1–4.
10. Alan Dershowitz, *The Genesis of Justice* (New York: Warner Books, 2000), 231, 235.
11. Marcus J. Borg, *Reading the Bible Again for the First Time* (New York: HarperCollins, 2001), 12.

#### CHAPTER 9: THE BRAIN AND GOD: WHO'S IN CHARGE?

1. "Postdiluvian" refers to the period of time after Noah's flood—in contrast to antediluvian, the period of time before the flood. A "patriarch" is one of the scriptural fathers of the human race or of the Hebrew people—such as Abraham, Isaac, Jacob, and Joseph.
2. I discuss these and other experiments with the brain and time distortion in my book, *Time: A Traveler's Guide* (New York, Oxford University Press, 2000).
3. Daniel Dennett and Marcel Kinsbourne, "Time and the Observer: The Where and When of Consciousness in the Brain," *Behavioral and Brain Sciences* 15 (1992): 183–247. Also see Rainer Wolf, "Believing What We See, Hear, and Touch: The Delights and Dangers of Sensory Illusions," *Skeptical Inquirer* 20, no. 3 (May/June 1996): 23–30.
4. Ibid.

#### CHAPTER 10: THE BODHISATTVA PARADOX

1. Jasmine Hamlett, "Living Large: The World's Largest Seated Buddha Statue! July 1, 2000," http://www.worldtrek.org/odyssey/asia/070100/070100jaslarge-buddha.html.

2. Arthur Danto, *Analytic Philosophy of Action* (Cambridge: Cambridge University Press, 1973); Arthur Danto, *Mysticism and Morality: Oriental Thought and Moral Philosophy* (Harmondsworth, England: Penguin, 1976); Glenn W. Erickson and John A. Fossa, *Dictionary of Paradox* (Lanham, Maryland: University Press of America, 1998), 24–25.

3. Edward Ch'ien, "The Conception of Language and the Use of Paradox in Buddhism and Taoism," *Journal of Chinese Philosophy* 11 (1984): 375–399.

4. John Cage, *Indeterminacy* (audio CD), Smithsonian Folkways #40804 / September 22, 1992.

5. Buddhist Information Service of New York, "A Collection of Koans," http://www.bodhiline.org/Directory/Koans.html.

6. Glenn W. Erickson and John A. Fossa, *Dictionary of Paradox* (Lanham, Maryland: University Press of America, 1998), 140.

7. Clifford Pickover, *The Stars of Heaven.*

8. Robert Lawrence, *Closer to Truth* (New York: McGraw-Hill, 2000).

9. Timothy Ferris, *The Whole Shebang* (New York: Simon & Schuster, 1997), 312; also see Clifford Pickover, *The Stars of Heaven.*

10. John Fowles, *The Magus* (New York: Dell Publishing, 1985).

11. Hendrik Willem Van Loon, *The Arts* (London: Harrap, 1937).

### CHAPTER 11: THE PARADOX OF PASCAL'S WAGER

1. W. W. Rouse Ball, *A Short Account of the History of Mathematics*, 4th ed. (New York: Dover, 1961).

2. Michio Kaku, *Hyperspace* (New York: Anchor, 1994), 330–331.

3. This is from a personal correspondence I had with Dr. Gracely. Similar notions have been discussed by Antony Duff in "Pascal's Wager and Infinite Utilities," *Analysis* 46 (1980): 107–109. Duff actually argues that even "trying" to believe in God has logical problems. Any action one takes to make oneself believe has some finite probability of failing, and any action at all (even pursuing unbelief) has some finite probability of leading to belief. Therefore, it doesn't matter what one tries to do—all actions have a probability of one's coming to belief in God, so all have infinite utility.

4. Ed Gracely, personal communication.

5. Jan Narveson, "Future People and Us," *Obligations to Future Generations*, ed. B. Barry and R. I. Sikora (New York: White Horse Press, 1978).

6. Barry McGuire, "Pascal in Peoria," *Skeptic* 8, no. 4 (2001): 31.

### CHAPTER 12: TWO UNIVERSES

1. For further reading on this topic, see Clifford Pickover, *The Alien IQ Test* (New York: Dover, 2002).

2. James W. Deardorff, "The Meier Case and Its Spirituality," http://www.spiritweb.org/Spirit/billy-meier.html.

### CHAPTER 13: GÖDEL'S PROOF OF GOD

1. Hao Wang, *Reflections on Kurt Gödel* (Cambridge, Massachusetts: MIT Press, 1987). See also Hao Wang, *A Logical Journey: From Gödel to Philosophy (Representation and Mind)* (Cambridge, Massachusetts: MIT Press, 1996).

2.  For further reading on this topic, see Clifford Pickover, *The Loom of God* (New York: Plenum, 1999) and Clifford Pickover, *Wonders of Numbers* (New York: Oxford University Press, 2001).
3.  The Whole Shebang: The Starlab Magazine, "Kurt Gödel," http://www.shebangmagazine.com/Shebang4/godel.htm.
4.  Hao Wang, *A Logical Journey*, 101.

**CHAPTER 14: THE PARADOX OF UZZAH**

1.  Jashan A'al (Valeska Scholl), "Jehovah: Thoughts on the Old Testament God," http://www.jashan.net/corporate/sites/ascendancy/darkness/writings/jehovah.html.
2.  Ibid.
3.  Ibid.
4.  Ibid.
5.  Craig Becker, personal communication.
6.  Physicist Andrei Linde's theory of self-reproducing universes implies that new universes are being created all the time through a budding process. In this theory, tiny balls of spacetime called "baby universes" are created in universes like our own and evolve into universes resembling ours. This theory does not mean we can find these other universes by traveling in a rocket ship. These universes that bud off from our own might pinch off from our spacetime and then disappear. (For a very brief moment, a thin strand of spacetime called a wormhole might connect the baby and parent universes. The wormholes would have diameters $10^{20}$ smaller than the dimension of an atomic nucleus, and the wormhole might remain in existence for only $10^{-43}$ seconds.) The baby universes would also have offspring, and all the countless universes could be very different. Some might collapse into nothingness quickly after their creation. Stephen Hawking has suggested that subatomic particles are constantly traveling through wormholes from one universe to another.

    Other researchers have also postulated that baby universes are spawned from parent universes, and the babies also have babies. According to one theory, the children inherit similar physical laws from their parents, and "successful" universes have a tendency to produce successful offspring. Successful universes are long-lived and have many children and stars, all of which encourages the formation of biological life. See Clifford Pickover, *The Stars of Heaven* (New York: Oxford University Press, 2001).
7.  Hugh Everett, "'Relative State' Formulation of Quantum Mechanics," *Reviews of Modern Physics* 29 (1957): 454–462.
8.  Michio Kaku, *Hyperspace* (New York: Anchor, 1994), 307.
9.  Timothy Ferris, *The Whole Shebang* (New York: Simon & Schuster, 1997), 308.
10. Robert Sawyer, *Calculating God* (New York: TOR, 2000). See also Clifford Pickover, *The Stars of Heaven* (New York: Oxford University Press, 2001).
11. In Karen Armstrong, *A History of God* (New York: Ballantine, 1994), 237.
12. Jane Roberts, *Seth Speaks* (San Rafael, California: Amber-Allen, 1994).

**CHAPTER 15: THE PARADOX OF DR. ECK**

1.  Richard R. La Croix, "The Incompatibility of Omnipotence and Omniscience" and "Omnipotence, Omniscience, and Necessity," in *What Is God?*, ed. Kenneth

Lucey (Amherst, New York: Prometheus, 1993), 26–30. Also see Richard R. La Croix "The Incompatibility of Omnipotence and Omniscience," *Analysis* 33 (April 1973): 176. Richard La Croix, "Omnipotence, Omniscience, and Necessity," *Analysis* 34 (December 1973): 63–64.

2. Karen Armstrong, *A History of God* (New York: Ballantine, 1994), 191.
3. Ibid., 193.
4. Ibid., 166.
5. Ibid., 319.
6. Ibid., 242.
7. Ibid., 150.
8. Ibid., 233.
9. Ibid., 303.
10. Isaac Newton, *Philosophiae Naturalis Principia Mathematica*. See also: Sir Isaac Newton, *The Mathematical Principles of Natural Philosophy*, Book III, trans. Andrew Motte (London: H. D. Symonds, 1803), Book II, 160–162 and 310–314. Reprinted in Marvin Perry, Joseph Peden, and Theodore H. Von Laue, eds., *Sources of the Western Tradition*, vol. II: From the Renaissance to the Present, 3rd ed. (Boston: Houghton Mifflin, 1995), 50–52. Also see Sir Isaac Newton's *Philosophiae Naturalis Principia Mathematica*, ed. Florian Cajavi, trans. Andrew Motte (Berkeley: University of California Press, 1934) and Karen Armstrong, *A History of God*, 304.
11. Karen Armstrong, *A History of God*, 304–305.

### CHAPTER 16: THE PARADOX OF LED ZEPPELIN

1. For an in-depth discussion, see Richard R. La Croix, "Divine omniprescience: Are Literary Works Eternal Entities?" in *What Is God?*, ed. Kenneth Lucey (Amherst, New York: Prometheus, 1993), 134–141. Also see Richard R. La Croix "Divine Omniprescience," *Religious Studies* 15 (1979): 28–87.
2. Eric Kaplan, personal communication.
3. Ibid.
4. Leszek Kolakowski, *The Keys to Heaven* (New York: Grove Press, 1972), 3–4.
5. Karen Karbo, "Stairway to Heaven: Is This the Greatest Song of All Time?" *Esquire*, November 1991, http://www.geocities.com/SunsetStrip/8678/stairway.html.
6. Robert Walser, *Running with the Devil: Power, Gender, and Madness in Heavy Metal Music* (Hanover, New Hampshire: University Press of New England, 1993).

### CHAPTER 17: A FEW QUICK PUZZLES AND SURVEYS

1. Jacques Boivin, *The Single Heart Field Theory* (Self-published, printed in Hull, Quebec, Canada, 1978).
2. Stephen W. Hawking, *A Brief History of Time* (New York: Bantam Books, 1988), 123.
3. Michael Murphy, *The Future of the Body: Explorations into the Further Evolution of Human Nature* (New York: Tarcher, 1993).
4. Karen Armstrong, *A History of God* (New York: Ballantine, 1994), 115.
5. Freeman Dyson, "Time without End: Physics and Biology in an Open Universe," *Reviews of Modern Physics* 51 (1979): 447–460.

6. Ibid.
7. Stephen R. Donaldson, *Lord Foul's Bane* (New York: Del Rey, 1984).
8. Shirley Jackson, *The Haunting of Hill House* (New York: Viking, 1984).
9. Fred Alan Wolf, *Parallel Universes: The Search for Other Worlds* (New York: Touchstone, 1984).
10. John Fowles, *The Magus* (New York: Dell Publishing, 1985).
11. Karen Armstrong, *A History of God*, 98.
12. J. B. S. Haldane's apocryphal quotation can be found in many sources, such as Arthur V. Evans, *An Inordinate Fondness for Beetles* (New York: Henry Holt & Company, 1996) and B. D. Farrell, "'Inordinate Fondness' Explained: Why Are There So Many Beetles?" *Science* 281 (1998): 555–559.
13. Ilkka A. Hanski and Yves Cambefort (Illustrator), *Dung Beetle Ecology* (New Jersey: Princeton University Press, 1991).
14. *The Urantia Book* (Chicago: Urantia Foundation, 1999).

### SOME FINAL THOUGHTS

1. Paul Kurtz, "The New Paranatural Paradigm: Claims of Communicating with the Dead," *Skeptical Inquirer* 24 (Nov/Dec 2000): 27–31.
2. Ibid.
3. Timothy Ferris, *The Whole Shebang* (New York: Simon & Schuster, 1997), 304. See also Clifford Pickover, *The Stars of Heaven*.
4. Ibid., 305. There is some controversy regarding just how "finely tuned" these nuclear resonances really are. Steven Weinberg suggests that we should be thinking about 3 energy levels:

   - 7.7MeV (maximum energy of carbon's excited state, beyond which no carbon forms) 0.05 difference from lower level
   - 7.65MeV (energy of carbon's actual excited state) 0.25 difference from lower level
   - 7.4MeV (total energy of beryllium 8 nucleus and helium nucleus at rest)

   Researchers have suggested that if the carbon resonance energy was higher than 7.7 MeV, no carbon would be formed because the collisions of a helium nucleus and a beryllium 8 nucleus would need a boost of at least 0.3 MeV, a collision energy unlikely to be provided at the temperatures found in stars. So we have several factors to consider. By one criteria, the energy misses being too high by a fractional amount of 0.05 MeV/0.25 MeV, or 20 percent. Weinberg does not find the 20 percent factor a "close call" indicative of "fine tuning." For more information, see Steven Weinberg, "A Designer Universe?" *The New York Review of Books* (October 21, 1999, p. 46). This article was originally given as a speech at the April 1999 Conference on Cosmic Design of the American Association for the Advancement of Science in Washington, D.C. Also see, M. Livio, D. Holwell, A. Weiss, and J. Truran, "On the Anthropic Significance of the Energy of the O+ Excited State of 12C at 7.644 MeV," *Nature* (July 27, 1989): 281. See also, Clifford Pickover, *The Stars of Heaven*.
5. Ibid. Also see, Fred Hoyle "The Universe: Past and Present Reflections," *Engineering & Science* (November 1981): 12.

6. Robert Jastrow, "The Astronomer and God," in *The Intellectuals Speak Out about God*, ed. Roy Abraham Varghese (Chicago: Regnery Gateway, 1984), 22.

7. The anthropic cosmological principle asserts, in part, that the laws of the universe are not arbitrary. Instead the laws are constrained by the requirement that they must permit intelligent observers to evolve. Proponents of the anthropic principle say that human existence is only possible because the constants of physics lie within certain highly restricted ranges. Physicist John Wheeler and others interpret these amazing "coincidences" as proof that human existence somehow determines the design of the universe. There are alternative explanations of why the universe appears to be fine-tuned for life, and these explanations do not require a God or designer. For example, our universe may be one among a huge number of universes. If these universes have random values for their fundamental physical constants, then, just by chance, some of them will permit life to emerge. Using this reasoning, we would be living in one of those special universes, but no designer is needed to set the parameters.

   This area of speculation is controversial. Victor J. Stenger, former professor of physics at the University of Hawaii, has published numerous books and articles that suggest that the conditions for the appearance of a universe with life (and heavy element nucleosynthesis) are not quite as improbable as other physicists have suggested. For more information, see his web site http://spot.colorado.edu/~vstenger/. Also see his various books listed at Amazon.com, *The Unconscious Quantum: Metaphysics in Modern Physics and Cosmology* (Amherst, New York: Prometheus, 1995), and "Cosmythology: Is the Universe Fine-Tuned to Produce Us?" *Skeptic* 4 (1996). Also see Craig-Pigliucci, "Does God Exist?" http://www.leaderu.com/offices/billcraig/docs/craig-pigliucci1.html.

8. Stephen W. Hawking, *A Brief History of Time* (New York: Bantam Books, 1988), 123.

9. Fred Adams and Greg Laughlin, *The Five Ages of the Universe* (New York: Free Press, 1999), 198.

10. Ibid., 199. Note also that the sun powers our solar system by fusing four hydrogen nuclei (protons) into one helium nucleus (2 protons and 2 neutrons). Because helium is lighter than the four hydrogen nuclei, the mass lost is converted to energy by Einstein's $E=mc^2$. Cosmologist Martin Rees, author of *Just Six Numbers*, points out that the nucleus of a helium atom weighs 99.3 percent as much as the two protons and two neutrons that go to make it. This means that the remaining 0.7 percent is released as heat. It follows that the sun converts 0.007 of the hydrogen mass into energy when it fuses into helium, and the stellar lifetime relies on this number $\varepsilon$ ($\varepsilon = 0.007$). Subsequent conversion of helium all the way to iron releases only a further 0.001. The strong nuclear force binds the protons in helium and heavier nuclei together so that fusion is a powerful energy source that prevents the sun from compressing to a graveyard state in 10 million years. If $\varepsilon$ were smaller than 0.007, hydrogen would be a less efficient stellar fuel. If the "glue" holding together nuclei were weaker so that $\varepsilon = 0.006$ instead of $\varepsilon = 0.007$, a proton will not bond to a neutron, and deuterium (heavy hydrogen, an intermediate molecule in hydrogen fusion) would not be stable. Helium would never be produced if $\varepsilon = 0.006$. Without fusion, bright stars would not form in such a universe. On the other hand, if we set $\varepsilon = 0.008$, no hydrogen would have survived from the Big Bang. In our universe, two protons repel each other so strongly that the nuclear strong force does not bind them together without the

aid of one or two neutrons that help glue the nucleus together. However, if $\varepsilon$ = 0.008, then two protons can bind together directly, and no hydrogen remains in the infant universe. Without hydrogen, there are no stars or even water. We are lucky that $\varepsilon$ = 0.007 because we wouldn't be here if $\varepsilon$ were 0.008 or 0.006. Martin J. Rees, *Just Six Numbers: The Deep Forces That Shape the Universe* (New York: Basic Books, 2001). See also Clifford Pickover, *The Stars of Heaven.*

11. Paul Davies, *Other Worlds* (London: Dent, 1980), 160–161, 168–169.

12. John Barrow and Frank Tipler, *The Anthropic Cosmological Principle* (New York: Oxford University Press, 1986).

13. Paul Davies, *The Mind of God* (New York: Simon & Schuster, 1992), 16.

14. Fred Adams and Greg Laughlin, *The Five Ages of the Universe*, 202–203; Lee Smolin, 1997, *Life of the Cosmos* (New York: Oxford University Press: 1997). Roger Penrose and Stephen Hawking have suggested that the expanding universe is described by the same equations as a collapsing black hole, but with the opposite direction of time. Black holes may be the seeds for other universes. According to John Gribbin, in *Stardust*, the number of baby universes may be proportional to the volume of the parent universe.

　　Let's talk about the multiverse, God, and the *physics of polytheism*. In 1998, Max Tegmark, a physicist formerly at the Institute for Advanced Study at Princeton, New Jersey, used a mathematical argument to bolster his own theory of the existence of multiple universes that "dance to the tune of entirely different sets of equations of physics." The idea that there is a vast "ensemble" of universes (a multiverse) is not new—the idea occurs in the many-worlds interpretation of quantum mechanics and the branch of inflation theory suggesting that our universe is just a tiny bubble in a tremendously bigger universe. In Marcus Chown's "Anything Goes," appearing in the June 1998 issue of *New Scientist*, Tegmark suggests that there is actually greater simplicity (e.g., less information) in the notion of a multiverse than in an individual universe. To illustrate this argument, Tegmark gives the example of the numbers between 0 and 1. A useful definition of something's complexity is the length of a computer program needed to generate it. Consider how difficult it could be to generate an arbitrarily chosen number between 0 and 1, the arbitrary number specified by an infinite number of digits. Expressing the number would require an infinitely long computer program. On the other hand, if you were told to write a program that produced all the rational numbers between 0 and 1, the instructions would be easy. Start at 0, step through 0.1, 0.2, 0.3, and so on, then 0.01, 0.11, 0.21, 0.31. . . . This program would be easy to write, which means that creating all possibilities may, in some cases, be much simpler than creating one very specific one. In fact, in the REXX programming language, a simple, finite program to produce the infinite number of rational numbers might resemble: *say '1st 1/1 = 1'; do i = 2 to 10; jend = i–1; do j = 1 to jend; k = k + 1; say '#' k ':' j '/' i '=' j/i; end; end.* Tegmark extrapolates this idea to suggest that the existence of infinitely many universes $\gamma_1, \gamma_2, \gamma_3, \ldots \gamma_\infty$ is simpler, less wasteful, and more likely than just a single universe $\gamma$. Could one extend Tegmark's reasoning to God and argue that the existence of infinitely many gods $\gamma_1, \gamma_2, \gamma_3, \ldots \gamma_\infty$ is more likely than just a single God $\gamma$? Obviously, this is a controversial application of Tegmark's theories and a wild stretch of the imagination, but the Old Testament gives numerous examples that may suggest the existence of multiple Gods $\gamma_n$, $n>1$; for example, "Among the gods there is none like you, O Lord; no deeds can compare with yours" (Psalm 86:8); "I will bring judgment on all the gods of Egypt" (Exodus 12:12); or, "You shall have no other gods before me" (Exodus 20:3).

Physicist Dan Platt points out that the notion of a "multiverse" can be traced back to mathematician Gottfried Wilhelm Leibnitz (1646–1716) who explored one aspect of theodicy—why is there evil in the world if God is all-powerful and good? Leibnitz suggested that our universe $\gamma$ was the best of all possible universes $\gamma_1, \gamma_2, \gamma_3, \ldots \gamma_\infty$, and the evil in it was unfortunate—but at least our universe exhibited the smallest amount of evil one could hope for.

In 1893, several ancient letters on papyrus and clay were discovered on a small island in the Nile River about 550 miles south of Cairo. Apparently a small Jewish settlement thrived there in the fifth century B.C. These letters attest to the existence of a Jewish temple and that the Jews worshiped many gods. (For more information on these "Elephantine Letters" see David Howard, *Fascinating Bible Facts* (Lincolnwood, Illinois: Publications International, Ltd., 1998), 88.

15.  Charles Seife, "Big Bang's New Rival Debuts with a Splash," *Science* 292 (April 13, 2001): 189–191.

16.  Rudy Rucker, *Seek!* (New York: Four Walls Eight Windows, 1999), 150–151. See the chapter "Goodbye Big Bang," which discusses Andre Linde's baby universes.

17.  Michael Shermer, *How We Believe: The Search for God in an Age of Science* (New York: Freeman, 1999). See also Massimo Pigliucci, "Why Everybody Believes in Fairy Tales," *Skeptical Inquirer* 24 (May/June 2000): 50–51. Clifford A. Pickover, *Dreaming the Future* (Amherst, New York: Prometheus, 2001).

18.  Benjamin Radford, "Nostradamus 1999 predictions miss (again)," *Skeptical Inquirer* 24 (May/June 2000): 6. See also Clifford A. Pickover, *Dreaming the Future*.

19.  James Alcock, "The Belief Engine," *Skeptical Inquirer* 19 (May/June 1995): 14–18.

20.  Anton Thorn, "God and Omniscience," http://www.geocities.com/Athens/Sparta/1019/Omniscience.htm.

21.  Acme Inc., "Why Fear God," http://www.feargod.com/why_fear_god.htm.

22.  Clifford Pickover, *Strange Brains and Genius* (New York: Quill, 1999).

23.  Ibid.

24.  Eve LaPlante, *Seized: Temporal Lobe Epilepsy as a Medical, Historical, and Artistic Phenomenon* (New York: Harper, 1993).

25.  Ibid.

26.  William Grey, "Philosophy and the Paranormal," *Skeptical Inquirer* 18 (winter 1994): 148.

27.  Stephen Hawking, *A Brief History of Time* (New York: Bantam, 1988).

28.  Lewis Browne, *This Believing World: A Simple Account of the Great Religions of Mankind* (New York: Macmillan, 1927). Also Eric Kaplan, personal communication.

29.  Richard Hooker (Washington State University), "The Hebrews: A Learning Module: National Monolatry and Monotheism (~1300–1000 BC)," http://www.us-israel.org/jsource/Judaism/Monolatry.html.

30.  Richard Hooker (Washington State University), "The Birth and Evolution of Judaism: The Prophetic Revolution (~800–600 BC)," http://www.us-israel.org/jsource/Judaism/Prophetic.html.

31.  William L. Rowe, "The Problem of Evil & Some Varieties of Atheism," *The Evidential Argument from Evil*, ed. Daniel Howard-Snyder (Indianapolis: Indiana University Press, 1996), 5.

32. Karen Armstrong, *A History of God*, 181, 182.

33. Hans Jonas: "The Concept of God after Auschwitz: A Jewish Voice," http://www.furman.edu/~ateipen/jonas-auschwitz.html. Peter Sewitz, "Hans Jonas: The Philosopher of Life," http://www.germanembassy-india.org/news/may97/05gn05.htm.

34. Hans Jonas, *The Phenomenon of Life* (New York: Dell, 1966), 275–277. Also see Hans Jonas: "The Concept of God after Auschwitz: A Jewish Voice," http://www.furman.edu/~ateipen/jonas-auschwitz.html.

35. Ibid.

36. Ibid.

37. Karen Armstrong, *A History of God*, 267.

38. Ibid., 268.

39. Ibid., 270.

40. Anton van Harskamp, "Thinking towards God and the Evil of Auschwitz," http://www.vu.nl/Bezinningscentrum/godevil.htm.

    Author Scott Adams in *God's Debris* takes this general direction of thought to an ultimate conclusion. An omnipotent God is generally thought of as having no challenges. However, it is possible that God's only challenge would be to destroy Himself. Adams wonders if God's omnipotence or omniscience would include knowing what happens after He loses His omnipotence by self-annihilation. Adams writes, "A God who had one nagging question—what happens if I cease to exist?—*might* be motivated to find the answer in order to complete his knowledge." After much thought, Adams concludes that God has in fact taken the challenge and self-destructed—and that we are God's debris. Humankind's fate is clear. We are evolving—like a colony, hive, or cells in a body—to reform God's shattered self. In the twenty-first century, we are in the early stages of reassembling. We do not realize we are reforming God in the same way that one of the cells in our body is not aware it is part of a thinking human being. (Scott Adams's *God's Debris* is a DigitalOwl E-book, and it may be downloaded from www.dilbert.com or http://icommerce.digitalowl.com/ScottAdams/display-book.asp?Product_ID=1375.)

41. Marc Fonda, "Fonda's Notes on Jung's Answer to Job," http://www.clas.ufl.edu/users/gthursby/fonda/jung04.html. Also see Joseph Campbell, *The Portable Jung* (Middlesex: Penguin Books, 1976), 519–650.

42. Joseph S. Fulda, "Partially Resolving the Tension between Omniscience and Free Will: A Mathematical Argument," http://cogprints.soton.ac.uk/documents/disk0/00/00/03/64/cog00000364–00/god.html. Also see Joseph S. Fulda, "The Mathematical Pull of Temptation," *Mind* 101(April 1992): 305–307.

43. Ibid.

44. Ibid. See also Jack Katz, *Seductions of Crime: Moral and Sensual Attractions in Doing Evil* (New York: Basic Books, 1988); Joseph S Fulda, "Partially Resolving the Tension between Omniscience and Free Will: A Mathematical Argument," *Sorites* 9 (1998): 53–55. My colleague Dennis Gordon reminds us that $0.99^{9000}$ is so small we can barely comprehend the number's smallness. Because variable $a$ is not very important when compared to $b$, Gordon writes, "Maybe humans are arithmetic and God is geometric. God geometrizes. Einstein said something like 'the greatest failure of humans is to understand the exponential function.'"

45. Norbert Wiener, *The Human Use of Human Beings* (New York: DaCapo Press, 1988).

46. Joseph Francis Alward, "Is God Omniscient," http://members.aol.com/JAlw/ omniscience.html. Alward is a physics professor at the University of the Pacific, Stockton, CA. He received his Ph.D. in theoretical solid state physics. His home page is http://members.aol.com/jalw/joseph_alward.html.

47. Anton Thorn, "God and Omniscience," http://www.geocities.com/Athens/ Sparta/1019/Omniscience.htm.

48. David King, *Guide to Objectivism*, also titled *A Guide to the Philosophy of Objectivism*. The entire text can be found on various web sites, including http://www.vix.com/objectivism/Writing/DavidKing/GuideToObjectivism/CHAPTR 09.HTM.

49. Xyla Bone, *I Am My Husband's Hippocampus*. Xyla Bone is a pseudonym for Cliff Pickover. This endnote is merely a check to see if readers actually read endnotes. If *I Am My Husband's Hippocampus* were an alternate title for the *Paradox of God*, this endnote would have been the ultimate example of a self-referential paradox. It will be fascinating to see if the publisher of this book allows me to keep this endnote.

50. Elie Wiesel, *Night* (New York: Bantam, 1982).

## APPENDICES

### Appendix C: Thirty Examples of God Entering the Time Stream and Aiding Mass Killing

1. Shelby Sherman, "Mass Killings and Cruelties Ordered, Committed, Approved by God," http://members.aye.net/~abrupt/house/godkill.html. Also see Curt van den Heuvel, "Old Testament Problems," http://www.primenet.com/~heuvelc/ bible/otprob.htm; Jashan A'al (Valeska Scholl), "Jehovah: thoughts on the Old Testament God," http://www.jashan.net/corporate/sites/ascendancy/darkness/ writings/jehovah.html; Jim Merritt, "A List of Biblical Contradictions," http:/ /www.infidels.org/library/modern/jim_meritt/bible-contradictions.html; Dennis McKinsey, "Biblical Errancy," http://members.aol.com/ckbloomfld/; C. Dennis McKinsey, *The Encyclopedia of Biblical Errancy* (Ithaca, New York: Promethean Press, 1995).

### Appendix D: Can a Just God Support Cannibalism and Child Sacrifice?

1. Curt van den Heuvel, "Old Testament Problems," http://www.primenet.com/ ~heuvelc/bible/otprob.htm; Jim Merritt, "A List of Biblical Contradictions," http://www.infidels.org/library/modern/jim_meritt/bible-contradictions.html; Dennis McKinsey, "Biblical Errancy," http://members.aol.com/ckbloomfld/; C. Dennis McKinsey, *The Encyclopedia of Biblical Errancy* (Ithaca, New York: Promethean Press, 1995).

### Appendix E: Aquinas's God and Maxwell's Demon

1. *Manifold*—the only journal ever published entirely on the subject of mathematical theology—began as a publication created by half a dozen graduate students at the University of Warwick (UK). The journal started in 1968 and ran for 20

issues, until 1980. Tim Poston, a researcher at the Institute of Systems Science at the National University of Singapore, led me to several interesting articles regarding God and mathematics that appeared in *Manifold*. Tim's article "Aquinas's God versus Maxwell's Demon" appeared in *Manifold* 11 (1971): 71–72. See also Clifford Pickover, *The Loom of God*.

### Appendix G: The Paradox of the Flood

1. John Paulos, *Innumeracy* (New York: Vintage, 1990).

### Appendix H: Saint Augustine and The City of God

1. Saint Augustine, *The City of God*, trans. Marcus Dods (New York: Modern Library, 1994), Book XII, Chapter 19.

### Appendix I: Does God Make Mistakes and Learn?

1. Micah B. Harper, "God Learns," http://studentweb.tulane.edu/~mharper/prose5.html. Although this web page is now defunct, the essay may be requested from Micah at micah@webbeginnings.com.

### Appendix J: God Wants Fear

1. Acme Inc., "Why Fear God," http://www.feargod.com/why_fear_god.htm.

### Appendix K: Two Proofs that God Is Not All-Knowing?

1. Peter Kirby, "Omniscience vs Free Will," http://home.earthlink.net/~kirby/xtianity/freewill.html.
2. Quoted in Edward Wierenga, "Omniscience, Foreknowledge, and Free Will," http://www.courses.rochester.edu/wierenga/REL111/omnis.html.
3. Ibid.
4. C. S. Lewis, *Mere Christianity* (New York: Macmillan, 1943).

There is a fundamental difference between the Old Testament, and the New Testament and Koran. . . . If you pattern your behavior after Jesus and Mohammed, you will be a just person. In sharp contrast, the characters in the Jewish Bible—even its heroes—are all flawed human beings. . . . Even the God of Genesis can be seen as an imperfect God, neither omniscient, omnipotent, nor even always good.

—Alan Dershowitz, *The Genesis of Justice*

# Further Reading

*God has deliberately made the hereafter invisible, in order to see whether we are willing to accept it on faith.*

— *Alan Dershowitz*, The Genesis of Justice

*Let's say you dug up all the dirt and rocks and vegetation of a holy place and moved it someplace else, leaving nothing but hole that is one-mile deep in the original location. Would the holy land now be the new location where you put the dirt and rocks and vegetation, or the old location with the hole?*

— *Scott Adams*, God's Debris

## BOOKS AND ARTICLES

Karen Armstrong, *A History of God* (New York: Ballantine, 1994).

Jim Bell and Stan Campbell, *The Complete Idiot's Guide to the Bible* (New York: MacMillan, 1999).

Marcus J. Borg, *Reading the Bible Again for the First Time* (New York: HarperCollins, 2001).

Steven J. Brams, "Belief in God: A Game-Theoretic Paradox," *International Journal of Philosophy and Religion*, 13 (1982): 121–129.

———, *Superior Beings: If They Exist, How Would We Know?* (New York: Springer-Verlag, 1983).

Richmond Campbell and Lanning Sowden, *Paradoxes of Rationality and Cooperation: Prisoners' Dilemma and Newcomb's Problem* (Vancouver: University of British Columbia Press, 1985).

Claude-Bernard Costecalde and Peter Dennis (illustrator), *The Illustrated Family Bible* (New York: DK Publishing, 1997).

William Lane Craig, "Divine foreknowledge and Newcomb's paradox," *Philosophia* 17 (1987): 331–350; see reprint of paper at: http://www.leaderu.com/offices/billcraig/docs/newcomb.html.

Kenneth C. Davis, *Don't Know Much About the Bible* (New York: William Morrow, 1998).

Glenn W. Erickson and John A. Fossa, *Dictionary of Paradox* (Lanham, Maryland: University Press of America, 1998).

Nicholas Falletta, *The Paradoxicon* (New York: Doubleday, 1983).

Martin Gardner, *Knotted Doughnuts and Other Mathematical Entertainments* (New York: Freeman, 1986).

———, *The Night Is Large* (New York: St. Martin's Griffin, 1996).

Edward J. Gracely, "Playing Games with Eternity: The Devil's Offer." *Analysis* 488 (1988): 113.

Norwood Russell Hanson, "The agnostic's dilemma, and what I don't believe," in *What I Do Not Believe, and Other Essays*, ed. Stephen Toulmin and Harry Woolf (Dordrecht, Holland: D. Reidel, 1971), 303–331.

Dallas M. High, *New Essays on Religious Language* (New York: Oxford University Press, 1969).

Isaac Levi, "A Note on Newcombmania," *Journal of Philosophy* 79 (1982): 337–342.

Kenneth Lucey, *What Is God?* (Selected essays of Richard La Croix.) (Amherst, New York: Prometheus, 1993).

Robert M. Martin, *There Are Two Errors in the the Title of This Book* (Ontario, Canada: Broadview Press, 1992).

George I. Mavrodes, "Rationality and religious belief—a perverse question," in *Rationality and Religious Belief*, ed. C. F. Delaney (Notre Dame, Indiana: University of Notre Dame Press, 1979), 31.

C. Dennis McKinsey, *The Encyclopedia of Biblical Errancy* (Ithaca, New York: Promethean Press, 1995).

Jack Miles, *God: A Biography* (New York: Vintage, 1996).

Robert Nozick, "Newcomb's Problem and Two Principles of Choice," in *Essays in Honor of Carl G. Hempl*, ed. Nicholas Rescher, Synthese Library (Dordrecht, Holland: D. Reidel, 1969), 115–116. Robert Nozick, cited in Martin Gardner, "Mathematical Games," *Scientific American* (March 1974): 102.

J. R. Porter, *The Illustrated Guide to the Bible* (New York: Oxford University Press, 1995).

William Poundstone, *Labyrinths of Reason* (New York: Anchor, 1990).

———, *The Prisoner's Dilemma* (New York: Anchor, 1992).

Rudy Rucker, *Seek!* (New York: Four Walls Eight Windows, 1999), 150–151. See the chapter "Goodbye Big Bang," which discusses Andre Linde's baby universes.

Donald P. Ryan, *The Complete Idiot's Guide to Biblical Mysteries* (New York: Alpha Books, 2000).

Gerald Schroeder, *The Science of God* (New York: Broadway, 1997).

Yahweh, *Holy Bible* (New International Version.) (Colorado Springs, Colorado: International Bible Society, 1984).

## WEB SITES

As many readers are aware, Internet web sites come and go. Sometimes they change addresses or completely disappear. The web site addresses listed here provided valuable background information when this book was written. You can, of course, find numerous other web sites relating to the god paradoxes and omniscience by using web search tools such as the ones provided at www.google.com.

Jashan A'al (Valeska Scholl), "Jehovah: Thoughts on the Old Testament God," http://www.jashan.net/corporate/sites/ascendancy/darkness/writings/jehovah.html.

Acme Inc., "Why Fear God," http://www.feargod.com/why_fear_god.htm.

Scott Adams, *God's Debris*, DigitalOwl E-book, www.dilbert.com or http://icommerce.digitalowl.com/ScottAdams/displaybook.asp?Product_ID=1375.

Joseph Francis Alward, "Is God Omniscient," http://members.aol.com/JAlw/omniscience.html.

Jonathan Blumen, "The Prisoner's Dilemma," *The Ethical Spectacle*, http://www.spectacle. org/995/.

Barry Bryant and Michael Mattei (editor), Wesley Center for Applied Theology, Northwest Nazarene University, "Molina, Arminius, Plaifere, God, and Wesley on Human Free Will, Divine Omniscience, and Middle Knowledge," http://wesley. nnu.edu/theojrnl/26–30/27.4.html.

Austin Cline, "Omniscience," http://www.atheism.about.com/religion/atheism/library/weekly/aa063099.htm.

Janet Chen, Su-I Lu, and Dan Vekhter, "The Flood-Dresher Experiment," http://www. stanford.edu/~jjchen/game/flood.html.

William Lane Craig, "Divine Foreknowledge and Newcomb's Paradox," http://www. leaderu.com/offices/billcraig/docs/newcomb.html.

Ariel Dolan, "Prisoner's Dilemma," http://www.aridolan.com/ad/adb/PD.html.

Donella Eberle, Mesa Community College, "Selected Critics on the Paradox of the Fortunate Fall in *Paradise Lost*," http://www.mc.maricopa.edu/users/eberle/ ENH221Lectures/FortunateFall.html.

*Encyclopedia Britannica*, http://www.britannica.com.

Marc Fonda, "Fonda's Notes on Jung's Answer to Job," http://www.clas.ufl.edu/users/ gthursby/fonda/jung04.html.

Joseph S. Fulda, "Partially Resolving the Tension between Omniscience and Free Will: A Mathematical Argument," http://cogprints.soton.ac.uk/documents/disk0/00/00/ 03/64/cog00000364–00/god.html.

Richard Hooker (Washington State University), "The Birth and Evolution of Judaism: The Prophetic Revolution (~800–600 BC)," http://www.us-israel.org/jsource/Judaism/Prophetic.html.

———, "The Hebrews: A Learning Module: National Monolatry and Monotheism (~1300–1000 BC)," http://www.us-israel.org/jsource/Judaism/Monolatry.html.

Hans Jonas: "The Concept of God after Auschwitz: A Jewish Voice," http://www.furman.edu/~ateipen/jonas-auschwitz.html.

Peter Kirby, "Omniscience vs Free Will," http://home.earthlink.net/~kirby/xtianity/ freewill.html.

Steven T. Kuhn, "Stanford Encyclopedia of Philosophy: Prisoner's Dilemma," http:// plato.stanford.edu/archives/spr1999/entries/prisoner-dilemma/.

Sid Litke, "Survey of Bible Doctrine: Angels, Satan, Demons," http://www.bible.org/ docs/theology/satan/angelout.htm.

Dennis McKinsey, "God's Shortcomings," http://members.aol.com/chas1222/bepart56. html.

———, "Biblical Errancy," http://members.aol.com/ckbloomfld/index.html.

Jim Merritt, "A List of Biblical Contradictions," http://www.infidels.org/library/modern/jim_meritt/bible-contradictions.html.

"Negotiation and Game Theory," http://math.holycross.edu/~dbd/games/assignments/discussion14/discussion14.html.

Peter Sewitz, "Hans Jonas—The Philosopher of Life," http://www.germanembassy-india.org/news/may97/05gn05.htm.

Shelby Sherman, "Mass Killings and Cruelties Ordered, Committed, Approved by God," http://members.aye.net/~abrupt/house/godkill.html.

Bill and Kriss Tenny-Brittian, "If God Is Omniscient, Do We Really Have Free Will?" http://www.thewaters.org/columns/reasonable.html.

Anton Thorn, "God and Omniscience," http://www.geocities.com/Athens/Sparta/1019/ Omniscience.htm.

Paul Tillich, "Theism Rewritten for an Age of Science," http://www.crosscurrents.org/ Tillich.htm.

Curt van den Heuvel, "Old Testament Problems," http://www.primenet.com/~heuvelc/ bible/otprob.htm.

Anton van Harskamp, "Thinking towards God and the Evil of Auschwitz," http:// www.vu.nl/Bezinningscentrum/godevil.htm.

Edward Wierenga, "Omniscience, Foreknowledge, and Free Will," http://www.courses. rochester.edu/wierenga/REL111/omnis.html.

---

Maimonides believed that Torah study is so demanding that husbands engaged in this exhausting work should be obliged to have sex with their wives only "once a week, because the study of Torah weakens their strength."

—Alan Dershowitz, *The Genesis of Justice*

---

There is more information in one thimble of reality than can be understood by a galaxy of human brains. It is beyond the human brain to understand the world and its environment, so the brain compensates by creating simplified illusions that act as a replacement for understanding. When the illusions work well and the human who subscribes to the illusion survives, those illusions are passed to new generations.

—Scott Adams, *God's Debris*

---

There do not seem to be any exceptions to this natural order, any miracles. I have the impression that these days most theologians are embarrassed by talk of miracles, but the great monotheistic faiths are founded on miracle stories—the burning bush, the empty tomb, an angel dictating the Koran to Mohammed—and some of these faiths teach that miracles continue at the present day.

The evidence for all these miracles seems to me to be considerably weaker than the evidence for cold fusion, and I don't believe in cold fusion.

—Steven Weinberg, *Skeptical Inquirer*

---

Religion without mystery ceases to be religion.

—Bishop William Thomas Manning

# About the Author

CLIFFORD A. PICKOVER RECEIVED HIS PH.D. FROM YALE UNIVERSITY'S Department of Molecular Biophysics and Biochemistry. He graduated first in his class from Franklin and Marshall College, after completing the four-year undergraduate program in three years. His many books have been translated into Italian, German, Japanese, Chinese, Korean, Portuguese, French, Greek, and Polish. He is author of the popular books *The Zen of Magic Squares, Circles, and Stars* (Princeton University Press, 2002), *The Stars of Heaven* (Oxford University Press, 2001), *Dreaming the Future* (Prometheus, 2001), *Wonders of Numbers* (Oxford University Press, 2000), *Surfing through Hyperspace* (Oxford University Press, 1999), *The Science of Aliens* (Basic Books, 1998), *Time: A Traveler's Guide* (Oxford University Press, 1998), *Strange Brains and Genius: The Secret Lives of Eccentric Scientists and Madmen* (Plenum, 1998), *The Alien IQ Test* (Basic Books, 1997), *The Loom of God* (Plenum, 1997), *Black Holes: A Traveler's Guide* (Wiley, 1996), and *Keys to Infinity* (Wiley, 1995). He is also author of numerous other highly acclaimed books, including *Chaos in Wonderland: Visual Adventures in a Fractal World* (1994), *Mazes for the Mind: Computers and the Unexpected* (1992), *Computers and the Imagination* (1991), and *Computers, Pattern, Chaos, and Beauty* (1990), all published by St. Martin's Press—as well as author of more than 200 articles concerning topics in science, art, and mathematics. He is also coauthor, with Piers Anthony, of *Spider Legs*, a science-fiction novel once listed as Barnes and Noble's second-best-selling science-fiction title.

Pickover is currently an associate editor for the scientific journals *Computers and Graphics* and *Theta Mathematics Journal*, and is an editorial board member for *Odyssey, Idealistic Studies, Leonardo,* and *YLEM*. He has been a guest editor for several scientific journals.

Editor of the books *Chaos and Fractals: A Computer Graphical Journey* (Elsevier, 1998), *The Pattern Book: Fractals, Art, and Nature* (World Scientific, 1995), *Visions of the Future: Art, Technology, and Computing in the Next Century* (St. Martin's Press, 1993), *Future Health* (St. Martin's Press, 1995), *Fractal Horizons* (St. Martin's

Press, 1996), and *Visualizing Biological Information* (World Scientific, 1995), and coeditor of the books *Spiral Symmetry* (World Scientific, 1992) and *Frontiers in Scientific Visualization* (Wiley, 1994), Dr. Pickover's primary interest is finding new ways to continually expand creativity by melding art, science, mathematics, and other seemingly disparate areas of human endeavor.

The *Los Angeles Times* recently proclaimed, "Pickover has published nearly a book a year in which he stretches the limits of computers, art and thought." Pickover received first prize in the Institute of Physics's "Beauty of Physics Photographic Competition." His computer graphics have been featured on the covers of many popular magazines, and his research has recently received considerable attention by the press—including CNN's "Science and Technology Week," The Discovery Channel, *Science News*, *The Washington Post*, *Wired*, and *The Christian Science Monitor*—and also in international exhibitions and museums. *OMNI* magazine recently described him as "Van Leeuwenhoek's twentieth-century equivalent." *Scientific American* several times featured his graphic work, calling it "strange and beautiful, stunningly realistic." *Wired* magazine wrote, "Bucky Fuller thought big, Arthur C. Clarke thinks big, but Cliff Pickover outdoes them both." Among his many patents, Pickover has received U.S. Patent 5,095,302 for a 3-D computer mouse, 5,564,004 for strange computer icons, and 5,682,486 for black-hole transporter interfaces to computers.

Dr. Pickover is currently a research staff member at the IBM T. J. Watson Research Center, where he has received thirty invention achievement awards, three research division awards, and numerous external honor awards. For many years, Dr. Pickover was the Brain Boggler columnist for *Discover* magazine. He currently is the Brain Strain columnist for *Odyssey*, and he also publishes popular puzzle calendars.

Dr. Pickover's hobbies include the practice of Ch'ang-Shih Tai-Chi Ch'uan and Shaolin Kung Fu, raising golden and green severums (large Amazonian fish), and piano playing (mostly jazz). He is also a member of The SETI League, a group of signal processing enthusiasts who systematically search the sky for intelligent extraterrestrial life. Visit his web site, www.pickover.com, which has received over 500,000 visits. He can be reached at P.O. Box 549, Millwood, New York 10546–0549 USA.

# Index

Aaron, 150, 215
Abdu'l-bahá
  on happiness, 95
Abel, 2, 15
  Cain and Abel's dilemma, 27–38
  Doré illustration, 3
abortion, 168
Abraham, 15, 77, 196
  marriage of, 37
Adam, 15, 16, 36, 221
  cherubim and, 63
  and the Fortunate Fall, 99–100
  and the paradox of Eden, 98–99
  punishment of, 214, 215
"Adam lay ibounden" (medieval hymn), 99–100
Adams, Douglas, 18, 22
Adeodatus, 220
Adler, Felix
  on unique personality and real life, 66
afterlife, 190
  theologians accepting idea of, 102–3
Age of Reason, The (Paine), 213
Ahab, King, 214
Ahern, Dennis, 53
al-Balkhi, Hiwi, 7–8
Alcock, James, 184
algae, parable of, 39–44
Allen, Woody
  on death, 165
  on God, 44
Alward, Joseph Francis, 200, 210
American Pastoral (Roth), 103, 123
Analysis journal, 69–70, 71
Ananias, 212–13
angels
  the bible and, 64
  ranks of, 62
  See also cherubim; seraphim
Anselm, Saint, 155
anthropopatheia, 15
apocalypse, 169–70
Aquinas, Saint Thomas, 23, 56, 58, 155, 218
"Aquinas's God versus Maxwell's Demon" (Poston), 217–18

Ark of the Covenant, 92–93
  and the paradox of Uzzah, 141–44, 144–45
  treatment of, 150
arks, deciding between, 46–52
Armstrong, Karen, 2, 154, 191, 194
  on Milton's God, 58
  on the relevance of religion, 10
  on science and God, 204–5
Arts, The (Van Loon), 121–22
ash-Shaytan, 75
Ashari, Abu al-Hasan ibn Ismail al-, 155
Asimov, Isaac, 52–53
Athanasius, Saint, 154
atheism, 180
  definition of, 2
Augustine, Saint, 56, 122, 220–21

Bacchus
  Christ's similarities with, 90
Baha'i faith, 223
  and God, 2, 7
  and the Prophets of God, 94–95
Bahaullah, 7, 94, 156, 223
Balaam, 213
Balak, King, 213
Ball, W. W. Rouse, 129
Bar-Hillel, Maya, 52, 53
Bar-Jesus of Paphos, 91
Barrow, John, 180
Basil, Saint (Bishop of Caesarea), 154, 171
Bear, David, 188
Becker, Craig, 147
Beelzebub, 74
Begley, Sharon, 203
Belial, 74
"Belief in God: A Game-Theoretic Paradox" (Brams), 85
Bell, Jim, 88
Berkeley, George, 135, 230
  on existence, 66
Bertrand Russell on God and Religion (Seckel), 42–43
Beza, Theodorus, 57

Bible, 202–3
   ethnic cleansing and genocide in, 37–38,
      184–85, 207–13
   and God's omniscience, 206–7
   incest in, 196–97
   literal interpretation of, 102, 150, 171–73
   printed as a single unit, 38
   and stories of negotiation
      as the word of God, 10, 15
Bible (New Testament)
   Acts, 90–91, 207, 212, 213, 222
   Colossians, 64
   II Corinthians, 74
   Ecclesiastes, 223
   Hebrews, 36, 186, 200, 206, 206, 207,
      223
   I John, *vi*, 36, 186, 206, 207
   Jude, 64
   Luke, 35, 200, 223
   Mark, 35, 64
   Matthew, 64, 74, 186, 223
   I Peter, 207
   Philippians, 223
   Revelations, 169
   Romans, 43, 185, 201, 207, 215
Bible (Old Testament)
   I Chronicles, 206
   II Chronicles, 208
   Daniel, 215
   Deuteronomy, 38, 209, 214, 216, 222
   Ecclesiastes, 185–86
   Esther, 121
   Exodus, 88–89, 95, 121, 185, 189, 195,
      196, 206, 209, 214, 215, 216, 223
   Ezekiel, 63, 206, 209, 214, 215, 217, 219
   Genesis, 15, 16, 17, 36, 96, 97, 102, 103,
      172, 181, 185, 196, 205, 209, 214, 215,
      216, 219, 221–22, 222, 230
   Isaiah, 62–63, 140, 186, 207, 217, 219
   Jeremiah, 91, 189, 204, 206, 217, 222
   Job, 15, 64, 121, 216
   I John, 206
   Jonah, 205
   Joshua, 37
   Judges, 57, 216, 218, 219
   I Kings, 214
   II Kings, 93, 205, 212, 214, 218
   Leviticus, 215, 216, 217
   Malachi, 54, 64
   Nahum, 219
   Numbers, 17, 57, 150, 210, 212, 214, 217
   Proverbs, 206
   Psalms, 64, 186, 200, 207, 218, 222,
      222–23
   I Samuel, 92–93, 142–43, 197, 204, 205
   II Samuel, 185, 214, 215, 215, 219
"Biblical Errancy" (McKinsey), 217
Bierce, Ambrose
   on Heaven, 75
Bjostad, Lou, 173

Black Death
   God and, 129–30
Blumen, Jonathan
   on Jewish resistance against the Nazis,
      34–35
Boethius, 225
Boivin, Jacques, 167
Bone, Xyla, 202
Borg, Marcus J., 10, 38, 85, 91, 103
Brams, Steven J., 5, 77, 80, 84, 85–86
Brethren of the Free Spirit, 155
"Bridegroom of Blood," 88–89, 213
*British Journal for the Philosophy of Science*, 52
*Broca's Brain* (Sagan), 159
bronze snake (Nehushtan), 212
Brooke, John, 87
*Brothers Karamazov, The* (Dostoyevsky), 177
Browne, Lewis, 189
Buddha, 7, 167
   Bodhisattva paradox, 116–23
   Po Lin Monastery statue, 11–18
   *See also* Buddhism
Buddhism, 2
   Nirvana, 117–18, 118–19, 120
   and the omniscience of God, 7
   Zen, 119–20
Byron, Lord, 58–59

Cabrini, Mother Francis Xavier, 230
Cage, John, 119
Cain, 2, 15
   Cain and Abel's dilemma, 27–38
   Doré illustration, 3
   family of, 36–37
*Cain: A Mystery* (Byron), 58–59
*Calculating God* (Sawyer), 151
Campbell, Stan, 88
cannibalism
   the Bible and, 216, 217
   cannibals and resurrection, 27
carbon as essential element of life, 179–80
Cathedral of Saint John the Divine (NYC),
      77, 228
Central American gods
   omniscience of, 8
Chemosh (national god of Moab), 93
cherubim, 28
   appearance of, 63
   and the ranks of angels, 62
   *See also* seraphim
children
   ghost children, 168–69
   God's punishment of, 102, 213–16
   as human sacrifice, 216
Christianity
   and the afterlife, 102–3
   and God, 2
   and God as a male deity, 2, 5
*City of God, The* (Augustine), 220–21
Clarke, Arthur C., 24

Clement of Alexandria, 154, 171
*Closer to Truth* (Lawrence), 121
*Confessions* (Augustine), 220
*Contact* (Sagan), 24
Copenhagen interpretation of quantum
    mechanics, 143–44, 150
cosmic omniscience and the relativity theory,
    131
Craig, William Lane, 53–54
crucified saviors, other examples of, 89
Cuban Missile crisis
    and the paradox of omniscience, 13, 17

da Vinci, Leonardo, 49–50, 64–65
dancing butterflies, schematic diagram of,
    59–61
Daniel, 215–16
Dante, 122
Danto, Arthur, 118
Darius, King of Persia, 215
Darwin, Charles, 87
David, King, 142–43, 214, 215
Davies, Paul, 180
Davis, Kenneth, 17, 88
Dawkins, Richard, 22
*De consolatione philosophiae* (Boethius), 225
De Vries, Peter, *vi*
Deardorff, James W., 133
Dennett, Daniel, 113, 114
Dershowitz, Alan
    on God's creations, 165
    on God and perfection, 26, 66, 75
    on God's punishment of children, 102
    on justice, 203
    on knowledge, 123
devil
    God's reliance on, 8
    names for, 74–75
    *See also* Satan
"Devil's Dictionary, The" (Bierce), 75
Devil's Offer, 67–69
    Edward J. Gracely and, 69–70, 71
    infinite sequences and, 70–71
*Dirk Gently's Holistic Detective Agency* (Adams),
    18
*Divine Comedy* (Dante), 122
    Doré illustration, 123
Doctrine of the Trinity, 35
*Don't Know Much About the Bible* (Davis), 17
Donaldson, S. R., 170, 231
doomsday predictions, 184
Doré, Gustave, 1–2
    illustrations, 3, 4, 79, 103, 123
Dorfman, Ariel, 104
Dostoyevsky, Fyodor, 177, 187
"Dr. Eck," 11–14
    paradox of, 152–54, 158, 162
dreams, God and, 170
Dresher, Melvin, 32–33, 34
Dubos, Rene, 9–10

*Dung Beetle Ecology* (Haldane), 171
Dunn, Luke, 18
Dyson, Freeman, 169, 170

ear-diver myths, 8
Einstein, Albert, 19–20, 131, 135, 140
    on the subject of time, 61
*Einstein and Religion* (Jammer), 135
ekpyrotic model (of the universe), 181
Eleazar, 217
Elkin, Stanley
    on omniscience and omnipotence, 27
En-Sof (hidden God), 194
*Encyclopedia of Hell* (Olson), 66, 115
*Enlightened Mind, The* (Mitchell), 166
Enoch, 36
epilepsy and religious leaders and prophets,
    186–88
Erigena, Scotus, 155
Estes, Clarissa Pinkola, 228
Estling, Ralph
    on design in the universe, 145–46
    eternity, Greek philosophy and, 61
"Ethical Philosophy of Life, The" (Adler),
    66
*Ethical Spectacle* journal, 34
ethnic cleansing and genocide in the Bible,
    37–38
Euler, Leonhard, 44
Eve, 2, 15, 16, 36, 221
    cherubim and, 63
    and the paradox of Eden, 97–98, 98–99
    punishment of, 214
Everett, Hugh, III, 148, 149
Ezekiel, 208–9

faith
    absolute, 94
    Americans and, 179
    fear and, 183–88
    paradox of, 93
Farabi, Abu Nasr al-, 102
fear and religion, 183–88
Feibleman, James, 98
Ferris, Timothy, 121, 150–51
Fielding, Andy
    on a self-contradictory God, 151
Finno-Ugric gods, omniscience of, 8
Flaubert, Gustave, 187
Flood, Merrill M., 32–33, 34
flood, paradox of, 219
forbidden fruit, premise of, 98–99
Fortunate Fall, Paradox of the, 99–100
Fowles, John, 121, 171
    on human knowledge, 39
free will
    definition of, 56–58
    God's, 149
Freud, Sigmund, 155
Frost, Robert, 169

Fulda, Joseph, 197
*Future of the Body, The* (Murphy), 167

Galileo, 61
Garden of Eden, 15, 28–39
    cherubim and, 63
    expulsion from, 36
    paradox of, 96–103
    tree of knowledge, 96, 98–99
Gardner, Martin, 22, 52, 54–55, 183
Gates, Bill
    on the efficiency of religion, 26
Gehennah, 74
*Genesis of Justice, The* (Dershowitz), 26, 66, 75,
    102, 103, 123, 165, 203
genocide and ethnic cleansing
    in the Bible, 37–38
ghost children, 168–69
Gibeonites, 215
Giocondo, Francesco del, 65
*Glasgow Herald*, 220
God
    Americans and, 2, 17, 179
    and angels, 64
    anger and cruelty of, 57, 184–85, 218–19,
        222–23
    atrocities committed or encouraged by,
        37–38, 184–85, 207–13
    belief in, 85–88
    changeable mind of, 205–6
    children, punishment of, 102, 213–16
    definitions and attributes of, 2–6, 154–57
    evidence of, 42–44
    and evil, 19–26
    evolution of, 76–95
    and genocide, 37–38
    and hypertime, 58–62
    as an imperfect teacher, 26
    Internet opinions and, 22–25, 138–40
    as limited, 175–76, 191–97
    as a male deity, 2, 5
    mathematical proof of, 136–38, 138–40,
        140
    nonomniscience and fallibility of, 15–16,
        221–22
    revelation gambit and, 77–85
    *See also* omnipotence; omniscience
*God & Golem, Inc.* (Wiener), 14
*God Within, A* (Dubos), 9–10
God's existence, paradox of, 93
God's formula, 44
Gödel, Kurt, 137–38, 140
    mathematical proof of God, 136–38,
        138–40, 140
Gödel's Theorem, 24
Gordon, Dennis, 147–48
    on faith, 95
Gould, Stephen J., 22
Gracely, Edward J., 69–70
    on infinite sequences, 70–71

on Pascal's Wager, 130–31
    on the solution of the Devil's Offer, 71
*Grand Dictionnaire Universel* (Larousse),
    177
Graves, Kersey, 90
Greek gods
    omniscience of, 8
green light/red light experiment, 113–15
"Green Man, The" (Fowles), 39
Gregory I (the Great), Pope, 155
Gregory XI, Pope, 175
Gregory of Nyssa, 154, 167
*Grooks* (Hein), 1
*Guide for the Perplexed* (Maimonides), 143
*Guide to Objectivism* (King), 201–2

Hades, 74
Haldane, J. B. S., 171
Halevi, Judah, 154
Hamidal-Ghazzali, 5
Hananiah, 91
Harper, Micah B, 221
Hasidism, 156
Hawking, Stephen, 167, 180, 188
Heaven, 75
Hein, Piet, 1
Heinlein, Robert, 148
hell, names for, 74
henotheism, 189
*Henry VI* (Shakespeare), 69
Hercules
    Christ's similarities with, 90
Hermes
    Christ's similarities with, 90
Hezekiah, King, 205
Hinduism
    and the nature of God, 7
*History of God, A* (Armstrong), 2, 10, 154, 191,
    194, 204–5
*History of Mathematics in America Before 1900,
    A* (Smith), 44
*History of Western Philosophy, A* (Russell), 77
*Hitchhiker's Guide to the Galaxy* (Adams), 22
holocaust, God and, 191–93, 203
*How We Believe* (Shermer), 184
Hoyle, Sir Fred
    on atheism, 180
*Human Use of Human Beings, The* (Wiener),
    199–200
hyperspace, as final refuge, 149–50
*Hyperspace* (Kaku), 129, 149
hypertime
    God and, 58–62

*I Am My Husband's Hippocampus* (Bone), 202
Iblis, 75
"IBM's Deep Stew" and prediction, 55–56
incest in the Bible, 196–97
*Indeterminacy* (Cage CD), 119
*Innumeracy* (Paulos), 219

*International Journal for the Philosophy of Religion*, 98
Internet
    and belief in God, 22–25
Isaiah, 62–63
Islam
    and Allah, 5
    Allah as a male deity, 2, 5
    Allah, names of, 7
    and the afterlife, 102–3
    *See also* Muslim religion
Islamic Hadith, 152
Ismailis, 121

Jackson, Shirley, 170
James, William, 187–88
Jammer, Max, 135
Jastrow, Robert, 180
Jehovah's Witnesses, 184
Jennings, Peter, 232
Jeremiah, 189
Jesus
    on the existence of angels, 64
    on the Light of the Father, 85
    omniscience and, 35–35
    similarities with pagan gods, 90
Jews
    God's continual punishment of, 57
    and resistance against the Nazis, 34–35
Job, 15, 81, 195
    Doré illustration, 82
Jonas, Hans, 191–93
    on God, 192–93
Joshu (Zen master), 119, 120
Joshua, 2
    and the conquest of Canaan, 37
Judaism, 189
    and the afterlife, 102–3
    and God, 2
    and God as a male deity, 2, 5
Judas, 90
Jung, Carl, 195

Kabbalah, Lurianic, 8, 193–94
Kaku, Michio, 129, 149
Kalinda and the cubical grid of stars, 25–26
Kant, Immanuel, 155
Kaplan, Eric, 163–64
Kasner, Edward, 44
Kennedy, John F., 13
*Keys to Heaven, The* (Kolakowski), 11, 164
Khrushchev, Nikita, 13
King, David, 201–2
Kinsbourne, Marcel, 113, 114
Kirby, Peter, 224
"Knots" (Laing), 122
koans, 119–20
Kolakowski, Leszek, 11, 164
Kolers, Paul, 113
Kotzk, Menaham Mendelof, 166

Krauthammer, Charles, *vi*

La Croix, Richard, 98, 162
"La Croix's Paradox: An Analysis" (Podet), 98
"La Gioconda." *See* Mola Lisa
*Labyrinths of Reason* (Poundstone), 56
Laing, R. D., 122
Lao-Kung, 122
LaPlante, Eve, 188
Larousse, Pierre
    on truth, 177
*Last Word, The* (Nagel), 93
Lawrence, Robert, 121
Led Zeppelin, paradox of, 160–61, 164, 164–65
Lewis, C. S., 87–88, 226
Libet, Benjamin, 113
Linde, Andrei, 183
*Living End, The* (Elkin), 27
*Logical Journey, A* (Wang), 138, 140
Lord-Wolff, Peter, *ix*, 45
Lot, 196
Lovejoy, Arthur O., 99, 101
Lucifer, 74
Luria, Isaac ben Solomon, 155, 193–94

McColley, Diane, 101
McGuire, Berry, 131
*Mackerel Plaza, The* (De Vries), *vi*
McKinsey, Dennis, 217
*Magus, The* (Fowles), 121, 171
Maimonides (Moses ben Maimon), 56
    on knowing God, 141
*Manifold* journal, 217
Marcion, 154
Margalit, Avishai, 52, 53
Martin, Robert, 43, 91
*Mascara* (Dorfman), 104
Masson, David, 60
"Mathematical Games" column (Gardner), 52
"Mathematical Pull of Temptation, The," (Fulda), 197
*Mathematics and the Imagination* (Kasner/Newman), 44
"Meier Case and Its Spirituality, The" (Deardorff), 133
Melchizedek, 77
*Memnoch the Devil* (Rice), *vi*, 59
*Mere Christianity* (Lewis), 226
Mesha, King of Moab, 93
"Metatheism" (La Croix), 162
Milton, John, 57–58, 100–102, 155
mind
    green light/red light experiment, 113–15
    playing tricks on time, 104–13, 113–15
Miriam, 57
"Miss Muxdröözol"
    and the Ark of Covenant, 141–44, 144–45
    and Belief vs. Unbelief, 128
    and the brain collection, 104–13

and the fish tank, 40–42
and the Garden of Eden, 28–29
and God's desire for goodness, 20–21
and Pascal, 125–28
Mitchell, Stephen, 166
Mithras
 Christ's similarities with, 90
Moab, kingdom of, 93
Molech, 74
Mollenkott, Virginia, 101–2
Mona Lisa (da Vinci)
 and deciding between arks, 46–52
 history of, 64–65
 various versions of, 65
Monica, 220
monotheism, 91–92, 189–90
Moses, 2, 57, 77, 78, 81, 83, 92, 150, 187,
 189, 195–96, 209, 210, 215, 217
 and the "Bridegroom of Blood," 88–89, 213
 and the "bronze snake," 212
 Doré illustration, 3, 79
 myth echoing life of, 89
*Mote in God's Eye, The* (Niven/Pournelle), 76
Muhammad, 187
Murphy, Michael, 167
Muslim religion, 2, 5, 154
 and the afterlife, 102–3
 Iblis and ash-Shaytan, 75
 Ismailis, 121
 *See also* Islam
*Mysterious Stranger, The* (Twain), 1

Naboth, 214
Nagel, Thomas, 93
Napoleon, 64
Narveson, Jan, 131
Nazism, 203
 Jewish resistance against, 34–35
Neanderthals, 17–18
 funeral practices of, 9
Nehushtan (bronze snake), 212
Nephilim
 as a term, 17
"Nephilim" (paradox of omniscience), 11–14
Newcomb, William A., 52
Newcomb's paradox, 52–54
 and divine foreknowledge, 46–66
 superpredictors, 54–55
Newman, James, 44
*Newsweek* magazine, 17, 203
Newton, Isaac, 61, 156–57
Nienhuys, Jan Willem
 on God as a concept, 177
*Night* (Wiesel), 203
Nirvana, 117–18, 118–19, 120
Niven, Larry, 76
Noah, 2, 209, 223, 231
Noah's ark, 171–73
North American Indian gods
 omniscience of, 8

Nostradamus, 184
Nozick, Robert, 52, 53
*Number of the Beast, The* (Heinlein), 148
numbers, religious significance of, 174–75

*Obligations to Future Generations* (Narveson),
 131
*Odd Index, The* (Spignesi), 90
Olson, Martin, 115
 on cosmic omniscience and the relativity
 theory, 131
 on the Cosmos and loneliness, 66
omnipotence, *vi*, 1, 2, 6, 7–8
 Stanley Elkin on, 27
 suffering and, 190–91
 *See also* God
omniscience, 7–8, 54–55, 115, 200–203,
 224–27
 conditional,176–77
 Doctrine of the Trinity and, 35–36
 Stanley Elkin on, 27
 John Fowles on, 39
 and free will, 56–58
 limited, 175–76, 191–97
 paradox of, 11–18
 science of, 8–10
 suffering and, 190–91
 *See also* God
Onan, 185
Ormazd (Ahura Mazda), 7
Osiris
 Christ's similarities with, 90
*Out of My Later Years* (Einstein), 19–20

pagan gods, Christ's similarities with, 90
Page, Jimmy, 161
Paine, Thomas, 213
Pakudah, Bahya ibn, 5
*Paradise Lost* (Milton), 57–58
 and the Fortunate Fall, 100–102
"Paradox of Eden, The" (La Croix), 98–99
parallel worlds, 148–50, 181
Pascal, Blaise, 11, 124, 125, 128
Pascal's Wager, 124–28, 128–30, 130–131
Patricius, 220
Paul, Saint, 91, 187
Paulos, John, 219
Penfield, Wilder, 113
*Pensées* (Pascal), 11, 124, 125, 128
Perseus
 Christ's similarities with, 90
Persinger, Michael, 188
Perugia, Vincenzo
 and the theft of the Mona Lisa, 64–65
Peter, 212
*Phenomenon of Life, The* (Jonas), 192–93
*Physics of Immortality, The* (Tipler), 27, 136
Pierce, Benjamin, 44
Pirsig, Robert, 116
Plane, Robert, 161

Plato, 221
Platt, Dan, 202–3
"Playing Games with Eternity: The Devil's
    Offer" (Gracely), 69–70
Plotinus, 122
Podet, Allen, 98
poisoner's dilemma, 32–34
    RAND Corporation and, 34
*Poisoner's Dilemma, The* (Poundstone), 32
polytheism, 91–92
Porter, J. R., 88
Poston, Tim, 217–18
Poundstone, William, 32
    on the poisoner's dilemma, 32, 34
    on predetermination, 56
Pournelle, Jerry, 76
predetermination, 56–58
*Principia Mathematica* (Newton), 157
*Principles of Human Knowledge, The* (Berkeley),
    66
"Problem of Evil & Some Varieties of
    Atheism, The," (Rowe), 190
Prometheus
    Christ's similarities with, 90
pseudo-Dionysius, 62

Randi, James
    on the Bible, 232
Ranters (Christian sect), 155–56
rape, the Bible and, 216, 217
*Reading the Bible Again for the First Time*
    (Borg), 10, 85, 91
"red" trial/"black" trial, 197–98
*Reflection on Kurt Gödel* (Wang), 138
Rehad and the King of Jericho, 35
Reimarus, Samuel, 155
"Relative State Formulation of Quantum
    Mechanics" (Everett), 148
relativity theory, cosmic omniscience and, 131
religion
    Americans and, 179
    the efficiency of, 26
    fear and, 183–88
religion and science, 178–83, 204–5
    mathematical proof of God, 136–38,
        138–40, 140
    separation of, 136
resurrection, cannibals and, 27
revelation gambit, 77–85
    belief in God, 85–88
*Reviews of Modern Physics*, 148
Rice, Anne, *vi*, 59, 122, 178
Richardson, W. Mark, 132–33
Riemann, Georg Bernhard, 148
Roberts, Jane, 151
Roelofs, C., 113
Roman gods, omniscience of, 8
Roth, Philip, 103, 123
Rowe, William L.
    on suffering, 190

Rucker, Rudy, 183
Rumi (Persian poet), 231
*Running with the Devil: Power, Gender, and
    Madness in Heavy Metal Music*
    (Walser), 165
Russell, Bertrand, 42–43, 77

Saddiq, Joseph ibn, 154
Sagan, Carl, 24, 159
Sakyamuni, 7
    *See also* Buddha
Samuel, 197
Sapphira, 212–13
Sarah, 215
Sargon of Akkad, 89
Satan
    and God, 15
    *See also* Devil
Saul, 197, 215
Sawyer, Robert, 151
Scandinavian gods, omniscience of, 8
Schlesinger, George, 53
Scholl, Valeska, 146
Schroeder, Gerald
    on energy and matter, 151
Schuerzinger, J. Theodore, 73
Schwartz, Lillian, 65
science and religion, 178–83, 204–5
    Gödel's proof of God, 136–38, 138–40, 140
    separation of, 136
"Science Finds God" (*Newsweek* article), 203
*Science of God, The* (Schroeder), 151
*Scientific American* magazine, 52
*Search for Signs of Intelligent Life in the
    Universe, The* (Wagner), 98
Sebastian, John, 165
Seckel, Al, 42–43
Seife, Charles, 181
seraphim
    mystery of, 62–64
    and the ranks of angels, 62
    *See also* cherubim
Sermon on the Mount, 186
Seth, 37
Shakespeare, William, 69
Sheol, 74, 190
Shermer, Michael, 7, 184
*Short Account of the History of Mathematics, A*
    (Ball), 129
silence, 121
    as a poem, 121, 171
    and truth, 121
*Silence in Heaven, The* (Lord-Wolff), *ix*, 45
Silesius, Angelus, 61
Simon Peter on women, 65
*Single Heart Field Theory, The* (Boivin), 167
*Skeptic*, 177, 232
*Skeptic's Sense of Wonder, A* (Richardson),
    132–33
*Skeptical Inquirer, The* (Estling), 145–46

slavery and the Bible, 216
Slavic gods
    omniscience of, 8
slide with ten holes, 71–74
Smith, David Eugene, 44
Sodom and Gomorrah, 196, 209
Solomon, the judgement of, 35
South American gods
    omniscience of, 8
Spignesi, Stephen, 90
Spinoza, Baruch, 155
Spinrad, Norman, 60
spirituality, questions to ponder, 227–32
"Stairway to Heaven" (Led Zeppelin), 160,
    161–62, 164, 164–65
    playing lyrics backward, 164
*Stars of Heaven, The* (Pickover), 87
Stephan, Ralf, 172–73
*Strange Brains and Genius* (Pickover), 187
*Summa Contra Gentilla* (Aquinas), 218
*Summa Theologica* (Aquinas), 23
*Superior Beings* (Brams), 77, 85
Suzuki, D. T., 119
Symons, Donald, 5

*Tale of the Body Thief* (Rice), 122, 178
Ten Commandments, 102
*Theology of Culture* (Tillich), 86–87
*There Are Two Errors in the the Title of This
    Book* (Martin), 43
Theudas, 90
*This Believing World: A Simple Account of the
    Great Religions of Mankind* (Browne),
    189
Thomas, Gospel of, 77–78
    Jesus on the Light of the Father, 85
    on Simon Peter and women, 65, 76
Thorn, Anton, 185
    on human reason, 201
Tillich, Paul, 86–87, 93–94
time
    Albert Einstein and, 61
    green light/red light experiment, 113–15
    legends of time-distortion, 61–62
    mind playing tricks on, 104–13, 113–15
    scientific study of, 61
*Time: A Traveler's Guide* (Pickover), 113
"Time and the Observer: The Where and
    When of Consciousness in the Brain"
    (Dennett/Kinsbourne), 114
*TIME* magazine, *vi*, 26
Tipler, Frank, 180
    on cannibals and resurrection, 27
    on separation of science and religion, 136

Tophet, 74
Tower of Babel, 221–22
"Traveler's Rest" (Masson), 60
*Treatise Concerning the Principles of Human
    Knowledge* (Berkeley), 135
Tucker, Albert W. 32
Twain, Mark, 1
"'Twas Brillig . . ." (Randi), 232
two universes, 132–35
Tzu, Chuang, 119

*Understanding Philosophy* (Feibleman), 98
universe
    as a computer program, 147
    design in the, 145–46
    parallel worlds, 148–50
*Urantia Book, The*, 174
Urantia religion, 174
Uzzah, 141–44, 144–45, 150, 185

van der Waals, H., 113
van Harskamp, Anton, 195
Van Loon, Hendrik Willem, 121–22
Vernon Collection, 65
Voltaire, 203
von Grünau, Michael, 113

Wagner, Jane, 98
Walser, Robert, 165
Wang, Hao, 138, 140
"Weed of Time, The" (Spinrad), 60
Weisinger, Herbert, 99
*Whole Shebang, The* (Ferris), 121, 150–51
*Why We Believe* (Shermer), 7
Wiener, Norbert, 14, 199–200
Wierenga, Edward, 225–26
Wiesel, Elie, 203
*Without Feathers* (Allen), 44, 165
Wolf, Fred Alan, 170
Wolf, Rainer, 113
women
    rape and the Bible, 216, 217
    Simon Peter on, 65
*World's Sixteen Crucified Saviors, or
    Christianity Before Christ, The*
    (Graves), 90

Zen, 119
    koans, 119–20
*Zen and the Art of Motorcycle Maintenance*
    (Pirsig), 116
Zipporah, 88–89
Zoroastrianism
    and the omniscience of God, 7